ONEONTA IN OLDEN TIME & BITS OF ONEONTA HISTORY.

ONEONTA IN OLDEN TIME & BITS OF ONEONTA HISTORY.

AN INTERESTING SERIES OF ARTICLES
BY HARVEY BAKER.

Published in the Oneonta Herald

During the Years 1892 -1893.

Compiled by the
Greater Oneonta Historical Society
Oneonta, NY.

SQUARE CIRCLE PRESS
VOORHEESVILLE, NEW YORK

Oneonta in Olden Time and Bits of Oneonta History

Published by
Square Circle Press LLC
137 Ketcham Road
Voorheesville, NY 12186
www.squarecirclepress.com

Copyright © 2010 by Greater Oneonta Historical Society.
The text of the newspaper articles in this publication is in the public domain; all other content is covered by U.S. and international copyright laws and cannot be reproduced in any format without written permission of the publisher. All rights reserved.

First paperback edition 2010.
Printed and bound in the United States of America on acid-free, durable paper.

ISBN 13: 978-0-9789066-7-2
ISBN 10: 0-9789066-7-5
Library of Congress Control Number: 2010934131

Publisher's Acknowledgments
The cover design is by Richard Vang, Square Circle Press, using the Corel suite of graphics software. The text of this book was created and formatted by Square Circle Press using OpenOffice.org, a free suite of office software. The book title and chapter subtitles are set in Latin Extra Condensed type, the book subtitle and chapter titles in Engravers, the compiler's name in PTBarnum, and the text in Garamond.

Please refer to the Preface for personal and professional acknowledgments related to the publication of this work.

CONTENTS

The newspaper articles reproduced in this book are presented in chronological order by the date of their publication. Many readers might find that reading through the articles in this order is preferable, especially since Baker frequently mentions or refersto a previous article along the way. Certainly the reader is encouraged to read them in this way to obtain the full flavor and scope of Baker's history. However, the table below groups the articles under general subject matter headings, with the hope that this might be easier for those who wish to explore only specific topics of Baker's writings. One word of caution is that Baker sometimes covers multiple subjects in a single article. This being the case, some articles are listed under multiple subject headings. Ultimately, the reader should consult the detailed index at the back of the book for a more in-depth search of a particular topic.

Harvey Baker portrait, *frontispiece*
Preface, *ix*
Acknowledgments, *xi*
A Brief Biography of Harvey Baker, *xii*

Pre-Oneonta History
  January 21, 1892: Which Treats of Oneonta in the Eighteenth Century, *3*
  January 28, 1892: Which Carries the History Down to Revolutionary Days, *7*
  February 4, 1892: Which Tells of Indian Settlements and Clinton's Expedition, *10*
  February 11, 1892: Hidden Mines and Indian Recollections, *14*
  February 18, 1892: The "Dreamlands" of Sir William Johnson, *17*
  February 25, 1892: First Settlements After the Revolution, *21*
  May 11, 1893: The Scramling Family and Early Indian Reminiscences, *192*
  June 15, 1893: The Wolf Family and Some General Historical Notes, *205*
  June 22, 1893: More About the Early Appearance of the Village of Oneonta (Part 1), *208*
  July 6, 1893: More About the Early Appearance of the Village of Oneonta (Part 2), *211*
  July 13, 1893: Last Words About the Early Appearance of the Village of Oneonta (Part 3), *213*

Oneonta's Settlement, Development & Incorporation
  February 25, 1892: First Settlements After the Revolution, *21*
  March 17, 1892: The Early History of Town and County, *31*
  April 7, 1892: Turnpikes, Canals, and Early Efforts for a Railway, *39*
  September 29, 1892: The Town Officials of Oneonta (Part 1), *111*
  October 6, 1892: The Town Officials of Oneonta (Part 2), *114*
  October 27,1892: Oneonta Village Incorporation (Part 1), *121*
  November 3, 1892: Oneonta Village Incorporation (Part 2), *124*
  June 15, 1893: The Wolf Family and Some General Historical Notes, *205*
  June 22, 1893: More About the Early Appearance of the Village of Oneonta (Part 1), *208*

Contents: Oneonta's Settlement, Development & Incorporation (continued)

July 6, 1893: More About the Early Appearance of the Village of Oneonta (Part 2), *211*
July 13, 1893: Last Words About the Early Appearance of the Village of Oneonta (Part 3), *213*

Oneonta's Schools & Churches

January 12, 1893: The Early School History of Town and Village (Part 1), *146*
January 19, 1893: The Early School History of Town and Village (Part 2), *148*
February 9, 1893: The Oneonta Normal School, *151*
February 23, 1893: The History of the Presbyterian Church and Society from Its Organization, *164*
March 2, 1893: The History of the Methodist Episcopal and the First Baptist Societies, *166*
March 9, 1893: The History of the Episcopal, Free Baptist and Universalist Societies, *169*
March 16, 1893: The Roman Catholic and United Presbyterian Churches, *172*

Oneonta's Newspapers

November 17, 1892: Oneonta's First Newspapers (Part 1), *127*
November 24, 1892: Oneonta's First Newspapers (Part 2), *131*
December 29, 1892: More about Various Newspaper Ventures in the Valley City (Part 1), *142*
January 5, 1893: More about Various Newspaper Ventures in the Valley City (Part 2), *144*

Residents, Families & Folklore

March 3, 1892: Manners and Customs of Long Ago (Part 1), *24*
March 10, 1892: Manners and Customs of Long Ago (Part 2), *28*
March 24, 1892: Witchcraft and Other Superstitions, *35*
June 30, 1892: C. P. Huntington and the Central Pacific (Part 1), *75*
July 7, 1892: C. P. Huntington and the Central Pacific (Part 2), *78*
August 4, 1892: Biographical Sketches of its Oldest Inhabitants (Part 1), *87*
August 11, 1892: Biographical Sketches of its Oldest Inhabitants (Part 2), *90*
August 18, 1892: Biographical Sketches of its Oldest Inhabitants (Part 3), *93*
August 25,1892: Biographical Sketches of its Oldest Inhabitants (Part 4), *96*
September 1, 1892: Biographical Sketches of its Oldest Inhabitants (Part 5), *100*
September 8, 1892: Biographical Sketches of its Oldest Inhabitants (Part 6), *102*
September 15,1892: Biographical Sketches of its Oldest Inhabitants (Part 7), *105*
September 22, 1892: Brief Biographical Sketches of its Oldest Inhabitants (Part 8), *108*
September 29, 1892: The Town Officials of Oneonta (Part 1), *111*
October 6, 1892: The Town Officials of Oneonta (Part 2), *114*
March 30, 1893: An Historical Sketch of the Old Emmons Family, *174*
April 6, 1893: An Historical Sketch of the McDonald Family, *178*
April 13, 1893: A Brief Historical Sketch of the Well-Known Brown Family, *182*
April 20, 1893: A Brief Historical Sketch of the Well-Known Parish Family, *184*
April 27, 1893: A Tribute to Eliakim R. Ford, Long Oneonta's Most Distinguished Citizen (Part 1), *186*
May 4, 1893: A Tribute to Eliakim R. Ford, Long Oneonta's Most Distinguished Citizen (Part 2), *189*
May 11, 1893: The Scramling Family and Early Indian Reminiscences, *192*

Contents: Residents, Families & Folklore (continued)

May 18, 1893: Jacob Dietz and His Early Interest in the Susquehanna Railroad, *195*
May 25, 1893: Brief Sketches of the Houghtaling and Alger Families (Part 1), *199*
June 1, 1893: Brief Sketches of the Houghtaling and Alger Families—Concluded (Part 2), *202*
June 15, 1893: The Wolf Family and Some General Historical Notes, *205*

Military Interests

October 13, 1892: Military Organizations of Oneonta, *117*
December 1, 1892: A Visit to McClellan's Army (Part 1), *134*
December 8, 1892: A Visit to McClellan's Army (Part 2), *138*
April 27, 1893: A Tribute to Eliakim R. Ford, Long Oneonta's Most Distinguished Citizen (Part 1), *186*
May 4, 1893: A Tribute to Eliakim R. Ford, Long Oneonta's Most Distinguished Citizen (Part 2), *189*

Railroading History

April 7, 1892: Turnpikes, Canals, and Early Efforts for a Railway, *39*
April 14, 1892: The Organization of the Albany and Susquehanna Railroad Company, *43*
April 21, 1892: The Struggle for the Railroad (Part 1), *47*
April 28, 1892: The Struggle for the Railroad (Part 2), *51*
May 5, 1892: The Struggle for the Railroad (Part 3), *54*
May 12, 1892: The Struggle for the Railroad (Part 4), *57*
May 26, 1892: The Struggle for the Railroad (Part 5), *61*
June 2, 1892: The Struggle for the Railroad (Part 6), *64*
June 16, 1892: The Struggle for the Railroad (Part 7), *67*
June 23, 1892: The Struggle for the Railroad (Part 8), *71*
June 30, 1892: C. P. Huntington and the Central Pacific (Part 1), *75*
July 7, 1892: C. P. Huntington and the Central Pacific (Part 2), *78*
July 14, 1892: The Location of the Railroad Shops, *82*
April 27, 1893: A Tribute to Eliakim R. Ford, Long Oneonta's Most Distinguished Citizen (Part 1), *186*
May 4, 1893: A Tribute to Eliakim R. Ford, Long Oneonta's Most Distinguished Citizen (Part 2), *189*
May 18, 1893: Jacob Dietz and His Early Interest in the Susquehanna Railroad, *195*

Index, *217*

Illustrations, *following page 154*

PREFACE

His name is not as widely known today as other famous Oneontans, but Harvey Baker was arguably the most important presence in Oneonta's history. Baker was a prolific writer who contributed to several of the Otsego County papers throughout his life, including many opinion pieces for the *Oneonta Herald*. However, in 1892 and 1893, late in his life and more than fifty years after he first moved to Oneonta, Baker wrote regular columns for the *Oneonta Herald*. Based on his research of the area's history dating back to before the Revolutionary War, his account of how Oneonta developed during his lifetime was published in a series of sixty-three articles.

These particular articles were clearly intended to be a large body of work, since the first article carries the sub-heading of "chapter one." The numbering of the articles continues through "thirty-nine," which was erroneously repeated twice by the type-setter, after which the chapter numbering is dropped. Another interesting aspect is that the series was originally entitled, "Oneonta In Olden Time." This seemed to work well as long as Baker continued with a fairly straightforward chronological history, however, as he wandered off on to singular subjects, the series title was changed to "Bits Of Oneonta History."

The idea to reproduce these columns came from a typewritten transcription of them held in the collections of the Greater Oneonta Historical Society (GOHS). This anonymous document was apparently created to give greater access to Baker's columns at a time when photocopying, microfilming, and or other technologies were not readily available. Whatever its intent, the document was not a faithful transcription. The anonymous typist took some liberties with the content, sometimes updating information, adding comments, or at times deleting entire paragraphs. Why (or even when) this was done, is unknown. Perhaps it was to make the articles more relevant to contemporary readers, perhaps the editor wanted to portray Baker in a particular light, or perhaps the person was simply eliminating redundant information. Regardless, considering the amount of typing it required, it was certainly a noble effort. This current publication of Baker's history makes it widely accessible for the first time since its initial publication more than one hundred years ago.

Over the course of a few years, a committee of interested members of GOHS worked to collect all the original articles and ensure their accurate transcription. The articles are here reproduced as they were printed in the *Herald*. **It was decided that it would be best to retain the original text as set by the newspaper, with typos, spelling variations and all. Typographical errors have been kept for several reasons.** While the handwritten pages of some of Baker's columns have only recently surfaced, it is impossible to know if Baker misspelled certain words and the typesetter was completely accurate in translating the errors, or if Baker was a meticulous speller and the typesetter the one who made mistakes. Variations in spellings of surnames, places, and organizations were common for the time, and so rather than try to make editorial decisions that might misrepresent Baker's original intent, it was thought to be more important to preserve the "character" of an early publication and to provide a primary source document for researchers.

Due to the discrepancy mentioned above, the original chapter numbering system has been dropped in favor of using the publication dates to identify individual articles. In the case where more than one article bears the same title for Baker's ongoing narrative, the series is identified by "(Part #)" at the end of the article title.

Bob Brzozowski, Director
Greater Oneonta Historical Society

Richard Vang, Publisher
Square Circle Press

ACKNOWLEDGMENTS

The Greater Oneonta Historical Society wishes to express its gratitude to the following for their support of this project:

To the Baker book committee: Bob Brzozowski; John Carney, PhD; David Hayes; Len Pudelka, PhD; and Art Torrey. Len contributed his academic background in US history, John his knowledge of book selling, and David his experience with book publishing. Art was our task master, reminding us of the importance of the project and our need to complete it. Bob directed the project and compiled the biography.

To Richard Vang of Square Circle Press. He gave us the jump start we needed! Richard also compiled the index.

To David Anthony, Deb Bruce, Janice Downie, Janet Potter, Mark Simonson, and Cynthia Squires for their help at various stages along the way.

To John Carney, for permission to reproduce images from postcards in his private collection, which were chosen by Art Torrey and Bob Brzozowski.

To Kermit and Margaret Baker Witherbee, for permission to reproduce images of Harvey Baker artifacts in their family collection.

To the staffs of the New York Room of the Huntington Memorial Library in the City of Oneonta and Milne Library at the State University College at Oneonta.

A very special thanks goes to the following for their financial commitment to this publication:

Jane Bachman & Bob Brzozowski
In memory of Raymond Charles Baker
Dory Brown & David Anthony
John & Peg Carney
Andrew Raymond Clark
Jason Alexander Clark
Suzanne Baker Clark
Heather Emily Gallien
Justin Shelby Gallien
Timothy Baker Gallien

Tom Heitz
Irene Baker Konstanty
Kevin Kurkowski/Gordon B. Roberts Agency, Inc.
Janet Potter
Leonard & Virginia Pudelka
Helen & Dave Rees
Holly Suzanne Schaffer
Art & Barbara Torrey
Kermit & Margaret Baker Witherbee

A BRIEF BIOGRAPHY OF HARVEY BAKER

According to Baker family genealogical records, Harvey Baker's ancestor, Alexander Baker, arrived in the New England colonies from England in 1635. Baker's father, Thomas, was born in Lebanon, New Hampshire in 1788 and moved with his parents to Lisle, Broome County, New York, in 1804. Thomas married Lois Munson of Munson's Mills, now Upper Lisle, in 1810. In the next year, they moved to Rochester, where, according to Harvey, they built the first frame house and barn in the "dense swamp" that would become Rochester. Thomas and Lois had three sons in Rochester before moving back to Lisle, where Harvey Munson Baker was born on October 16, 1818. Several years later their first daughter and fifth son were born.

According to his entry in the 1893 *Biographical Review*, Harvey loved both reading and physical labor, and by the age of 14 had decided to become a mechanic, and later, a millwright. He practiced both trades until 1838, when he was offered a teaching position in Genesee for $2 a day. But Baker apparently remained more interested in mechanics; he began rebuilding water wheels in saw, grist, and other mills and factories, utilizing newly patented technology. In February 1841 he made what seems to be his first visit to Oneonta, sleighing from Unadilla to Oneonta, then taking a horse to Colliersville, where he "made his first contract to put in his wheels in the upper mill of Collier & Goodyear." This initial job led to others, and by 1841 he purchased a lot at the corner of River and Main streets in Oneonta. He sent for his parents and his younger brother Enos, and by May 1842 his newly-built house at 39 Main Street was occupied. At the same time he became a partner in Collier & Goodyear's mill operations in Oneonta.

In March 1846 Harvey married Betsey Rose (b. 1825), the daughter of Nathan and Deborah (Morehouse) Rose of the nearby town of Maryland. They had two children: Helen (1849 – 1926), who never married; and Charles (1853 – 1925), who married Emma Birdsall, the daughter of Harvey and Jane Birdsall of Oneonta. Charles operated a dairy farm on the South Side of Oneonta and developed what was long known as Baker Row, now named Bevins Road. Charles and Emma had five children, all sons: Harry (b. 1873); Fred (b. 1876); Merton (b. 1880); Louis (b. 1885); and Clarence (b.1888). All except the youngest stayed in Oneonta, where many Baker descendants remain.

Harvey Baker worked for decades to bring the railroad to Oneonta. He was an original stockholder of the Albany & Susquehanna Railroad. He purchased four tracts of land near the settlement and developed them, later selling the land to the Delaware & Hudson Canal Company, upon which the D&H located their machine shops. In addition to being a gifted public speaker and lobbyist for the cause, he also contracted to build the rail beds, bridges, and trestles, often being the "go to" man when schedules were behind.

Apart from railroading, Baker was very much involved in other aspects of community life. He served in several positions, including village trustee, town supervisor, trustee of the school board, railroad commissioner, and street commissioner. He owned two farms and, in addition to the articles included in this book, wrote extensively on farming in the *Otsego Farmer*. Baker also owned Howe's Cave Lime and Cement Company, and he was a charter trustee of the Oneonta Savings Bank—both of which were surely advantageous to a railroad stockholder, mechanical engineer, and real estate developer.

Betsey Baker died in January 1903, and Harvey died in the family home on February 8, 1904. His obituary in the *Oneonta Daily Star* called him "one of the pioneers who paved the way for Oneonta's growth and prosperity." The newspaper described the following columns presented here as "a series of historical articles which form, beyond doubt, the most complete history of Oneonta yet."

Sources:

Milener, Eugene D. *Oneonta: The Development of a Railroad Town*. Plainview: EPI, 1983.

Biographical Review, Biographical Sketches of the Leading Citizens, Otsego County, New York. Boston: Biographical Review Publishing Co., 1893.

Oneonta Daily Star, February 9, 1904; March 20, 1925.

ONEONTA IN OLDEN TIME.

HARVEY BAKER BEGINS HIS INTERESTING SERIES OF ARTICLES.

JANUARY 21, 1892
WHICH TREATS OF ONEONTA IN THE EIGHTEENTH CENTURY

All history is a record of past events. It is composed of a register of them at the time of their occurrence; or it is preserved in memory by those familiar with the facts; or traditions hand it down from generation to generation. Of this latter class is much of our ancient history, both sacred and profane.

The value of history depends upon its reliability and correctness. History formed from traditions, to give it value, must be substantiated and established by collateral facts and confirming circumstances.

In the following pages I shall be compelled to use each of these sources of information, for my personal knowledge will extend over but a small portion of what I shall relate. In all cases of doubt I shall give such confirmatory facts as I can, and leave the reader to judge of its truth.

Of the occupants of this valley we know nothing except by tradition, previous to 1600. Nor do we of any portion of our state. Tradition tells that before the European races entered this locality, it was occupied by a numerous and powerful tribe of Indians called "Tuscaroras," and that their control extended over a vast territory.

History informs us that in 1608, when Samuel Champlain first sailed up the St. Lawrence river, he found at a place called Three Rivers a bloody war raging between an Indian tribe called the Adirondacks, whose possessions were in that vicinity, and an Indian confederacy called the Five Nations, then residing north and east of that place. All the country occupied by these contending Indian warriors was north of the river St. Lawrence, in the province of what is now known as Lower Canada.

Champlain having with him quite a force of men at once espoused the side of the Adirondacks, and by use of firearms, a weapon wholly unknown to the aborigines, soon scared and drove the confederate tribes over and across Lake Ontario and the river St. Lawrence into the province now embraced within the state of New York. The tribes composing the Five Nations were the Mohawks, the Onondagas, the Oneidas, the Senecas and the Cayugas. The tradition is that the formation of their confederation was many years previous, and that their friendship was long-tried and lasting. No one claims to know the length of time of its existence.

The Mohawks located upon what is now known as the Mohawk valley and river, the other tribes in the localities which still bear their respective names. History and tradition are alike silent as to the terms made with the Tuscaroras, the original possessors of our soil, but that they jointly occupied it for quite a season is evident from the fact that they came to use the same dialect and intermarry with each other. At a later date these Tuscaroras separated from the Iroquois, as the Five Nations were called, and going first west and then south, they finally settled with the Cherokee nation in the Carolinas and formed an alliance with them. These Cherokees were called the most civilized of all Indian tribes, having at that early day a written language and a form of civil government.

At the time the Dutch first settled where Albany now is, these Five Nations had the lands of the state westerly of the Helderburgs divided among themselves, each tribe having its chief, its totem or mark of distinction and its castle. At this early date these Iroquois exercised complete dominion over all the lands west of the Hudson to the Atlantic coast, to the middle of the Carolinas, to the Ohio and down the Ohio to the Mississippi, up the Mississippi to the lakes, and south of the lakes to the river Sorel and the Hudson.

The English, early in 1600, made a treaty with these confederated tribes, recognizing all their rights and virtually taking them under the protection of that government. It was under and by virtue of such treaty that the English nation, during the French War, laid claim and possession to all this vast domain. In the meantime these confederate tribes had opened trade with their Dutch neighbors, purchased of them firearms and learned their use. They now declared war against their old enemy, the Adirondacks, and not only conquered but utterly annihilated the entire tribe. These Five Nations continued to occupy their possessions, making the other or minor tribes within their domain tributary to them; but they exercised entire control of the Susquehanna Valley far into the state of Pennsylvania.

About 1735 Sir William Johnson made their acquaintance, obtained their confidence and friendship, and was by them received into their confederacy and made a chief. For his aid in the French and Indian war he was by his government made an agent and promoted as a baronet, and remained as agent for the English government during the rest of his life.

Early in 1700 the Tuscarora and Cherokee nations decided that they would expel the whites, who were then fast settling in the Carolinas, entirely from their domain. They at once made a raid upon the more advanced white settlements with great slaughter. Emboldened and animated by their success, they planned a second raid. In the meantime the Europeans had become aroused and they fell in force upon the Indians and severely punished them, and drove them from the states of Carolinas.

The remnants of the defeated Tuscaroras and some Cherokees came north and allied themselves to the Iroquois, and were thereafter known as the "Six Nations." By the terms of this union they were to have no share in the lands, no chiefs of the confederacy, and were to have and hold only a minor position in the compact. They were settled upon the lands of the Senecas, in what is now mostly Chenango and Cortland counties, westerly of the Unadilla river. In the division of the lands of our state among themselves the Mohawks seem to have the full control of all the lands east and south of the Unadilla and Mohawk rivers, so that the entire valley of the Susquehanna was under their control. Earlier I find that other tribes claimed the Susquehanna Valley below the Unadilla as belonging in part to them all; but evidently before 1768 the Mohawks had virtually sold all the entire region of the Susquehanna, and probably all of Otsego County. Friendly relations seem to have existed between these different tribes, all hunting and fishing wherever they chose, fish and game being free to all.

There were several small or minor tribes scattered among these principal ones, which were of course under control of the tribe owning the lands upon which they were located. As our "scraps of history" confine us mainly to this vicinity, I shall confine my papers wholly to the tribes that were located upon the lands of the Mohawks.

As before named, all the lands in the Schoharie Valley and in the Schenevus and Susquehanna valleys were owned and, when sold, conveyed by the Mohawks. The largest of these minor tribes was that of the Schoharies. They were located upon the Schoharie creek, the possession of which was given them by a Mohawk chief. There was also a tribe in this town called the Oneontas. Their village was located westerly of the mouth of the Charlotte, on the lands owned by the Slades and upon the big island opposite, usually called Beam's island. Upon this island is a mound supposed to contain the remains of a noted chief of the tribe, named Alagatinga.

Oneonta by the Indians was called and spelled Onahrienton. Oneonta creek is spelled the same way in the Otsego land grant patent of 1770. This tribe had quite a large clearing and an orchard at an early date, and Sir William Johnson managed to obtain not only the Indian title, but also a grant known under the name of the Charlotte patent, which was intended to cover the site of this Indian village and clearing. The more recent discoveries have fixed its site beyond a doubt. How late in the last century this village was occupied by the tribe, I have not been able to ascertain. Its name, under the changed, shorter and far more musical one of Oneonta, is destined to maintain and perpetuate itself in our town, our village and our future city for generations yet unborn.

Another Indian village called Wauteghe was located near the Otego creek on its easterly side. The old Indian orchard and clearing extended up the north bank of the Susquehanna River, up to and across the farm of the Van Woerts, the farm now owned by Mr. Calkins and also that of Ephraim Parish, formerly known as the Stoughten Alger farm. As better and more satisfactory proof of the existence of this village, I will quote a few passages from the diary of the Rev. Gideon Hawley of Stockbridge, Mass., of June, 1753.

"June 1st, 1753, is with me a memorable day." (It was of his leaving the Indian village then located at Colliers, of which he wrote). "We got off as silently as we could, with ourselves and our effects. Some went by water and others by land with the horses. I was with the land party. ... Neither party met until we arrived at Wauteghe, at which place had been an Indian village, where were fruit trees and considerable cleared land, but no inhabitants. Here, being unmolested and secure, we all refreshed ourselves." I would gladly quote his whole diary, but it can be found in the documentary history of our state. In that the Indian name of Oquaga is spelled Onuhhuhguaugeh. It is now Windsor, in Broome county.

The Indian name for Unadilla is Tianaderha and of Charlotte, Adaquitaneie. I am inclined to think that the Indian village of Oneonta and of Wauteghe were evacuated and deserted about 1751 or 1752, for the reason that the Mohawk Indians had in several conveyances sold to Sir William Johnson all the Susquehanna lands between the Charlotte and the Unadilla rivers, previous to 1753. See volume 1, page 521, documentary history of New York.

JANUARY 28, 1892
WHICH CARRIES THE HISTORY DOWN TO REVOLUTIONARY DAYS

Timothy Woodbridge and the Mr. Hawley quoted in our article last week came from Massachusetts as missionaries among the Oquaga in 1735. They came from Albany up the Mohawk to Sir William Johnson's, for information and advice. From, there up the Schoharie creek to Schoharie, by the aid of Indian guides. At Schoharie they obtained a white woman by the name of Ashley and her Indian husband to accompany them, the woman as interpreter.

Mrs. Ashley was captured at Deerfield, Mass., and carried as prisoner to Canada when a girl. Her maiden name was Briggs. In Canada she grew to womanhood among the Indians, married an Indian named Ashley, and moved with him to Schoharie among the Schoharie Indians. She had remembered her native English language and was thus a competent interpreter, and was now engaged by Messrs. Hawley and Stockbridge for such purpose. She died at Oquaga in 1756.

Having obtained Mr. and Mrs. Ashley and horses and provisions, they set out with Indian guides by way of the Cobleskill and Schenevus creeks for the Susquehanna river at Colliers. At that time there was a small Indian village on the easterly side of the river, which Mr. Hawley describes and where they made a stop of a day or two. At this place they decided that part of their party must go by water, and sent some of the men to look for suitable material to construct a boat. Just at this time a Mr. George Windecker came down from Otsego lake with a batteau, on his way to Oquaga to trade with the Indians. An examination of Mr. Woodbridge's papers revealed the fact that Sir William Johnson was personally interested in this Susquehanna Indian trade, and that quite a portion of its sales was rum.

Whether the Indian village at the mouth of the Otego was peopled with Oneonta Indians I am unable to learn. But this much I learn, and that is that all the Indians, located as tribes or parts of tribes in Otsego county and in Schoharie county, were directly under the control of the Mohawks, and that they made all the conveyances I have been able to find, making sale of lands either in Otsego or Schoharie counties. There was also a tribe by the name of Unadillas located at the mouth of the Unadilla river, nearly opposite where Sidney, (formerly called Albout) now is.

Unadilla village (formerly called Wattles' Ferry) was a village of considerable note years before the revolution, and while the Indian tribe above named were still occupying their village at the mouth of the Unadilla river some five or six miles below. There was also a tribe of Indians and a large clearing at the junction of the Chenango and Susquehanna rivers at Binghamton upon the flat lands between the two rivers. I think they were

Chenangoes, but the largest of any in this valley was the tribe at Oquaga, and for some reason the ones who seem to have enlisted the most efforts in the eastern states for their christianization. This tribe together with all others all the way to Wyoming seem to have been under the especial influence and control of the Mohawks and of Sir William Johnson; who, in fact, obtained of them a title to the Susquehanna valley all the way to Wyoming.

It is not strange that all these Mohawk Indians during the revolution should have been loyal to the British; Sir William Johnson would naturally carry them with him in that direction. Nor is it to be counted at all strange that they should under such influence as that of Sir William or his son, Sir John, vent their savage natures against the advocates of the American cause. In fact it is almost a miracle that any but Tories should have existed at all under such influences in all this valley. No doubt a large number of the settlers previous to 1870 were of that class. From what has come to us of the savage atrocity of these Mohawks, it seemed to make but little difference whether the settlers were Whigs or Tories, if they failed or refused to join them in their works of devastation and plunder.

So great had become these outrages and so disastrous to the American cause, that in 1779 Congress assembled an army of 4,000 men, gave the command of it to General Sullivan and directed him to conduct it into the country inhabited by the savages and inflict upon them punishment in sort. Of this army one division marched from the Mohawk, the other from Easton by way of Wyoming and joining at Tioga on the Susquehanna proceeded on the 22nd of August towards the Seneca lake. On an advantageous position the Indians in conjunction with 200 Tories had erected fortifications to oppose their progress, these were assaulted. The enemy, after a slight resistance gave way and disappeared in the woods. The army advanced into the western part of the state of New York. The Indians deserted their towns, the appearance of which denoted a higher state of civilization than had ever before been witnessed in the North American wilderness. The houses were commodious; the apple and peach trees were numerous; and the crops of corn then growing abundantly. All was destroyed, not a vestige of human industry was permitted to exist.

I have quoted this lengthy passage from pages 195-6 of the premium history of the United States, published in 1825. The quotation is made for the purpose of showing the civilized state of these six nations and that they relied but little on fish and game for a livelihood. I will now make a quotation from Leavitt and Allen's history of America, book 7, chapter 20, page 14 of the North American portion of such work: (An old work.)

"The Indians who formed the confederacy of the six nations as commonly called; the Mohawks were the objects of this expedition. They had been advised by congress, and they had promised to observe a neutrality in the war, but they soon departed from this line of conduct. The Oneidas and some others were friends to the Americans. Overcome by the presents and promises of Sir John Johnson and other British agents, and their own native appetite for depredation, they invaded the frontiers, carrying slaughter and devastation wherever they went. When General Sullivan was on his way to the Indian country (he went by way of Wyoming) he was joined by the American General Clinton with upwards of 1,000 men. The latter made his way down the Susquehanna by a singular contrivance. The stream of water in that river was too low to float his batteaus. To remedy this inconvenience, he raised with great industry a dam across the mouth of the lake Otsego, which is one of the sources of the river Susquehanna. The lake being supplied by springs soon rose to the height of the dam. General Clinton got his batteau ready, opened a passage through the dam for the water to flow; this raised the river so high that he was enabled to embark his troops and float them down to Tioga. To the surprise of the Americans, they found that lands about the Indian towns well cultivated, and their houses large and commodious. The quantity of corn destroyed was immense. Orchards in which were several hundred fruit trees were cut down; and of them many appeared to have been planted for a long series of years. The gardens replenished with a variety of useful vegetables were laid waste. The ears of corn were so large that many of them measured twenty inches in length."

General Washington in general orders October 17th, 1779, thus speaks of General Sullivan's expedition and its results: "The commander-in-chief has now the pleasure of congratulating the army on the complete and full success of Major General Sullivan and his troops against the Seneca and other tribes of the six nations as a just and necessary punishment for their wanton depredations, their unparalleled and innumerable cruelties, their deafness to all remonstrance and entreaty, and the perseverance in the most horrible acts of barbarity. Forty of their towns have been reduced to ashes, some of them large and commodious, that of Genesee containing 128 houses. Their crops of corn have been entirely destroyed—by estimation 160,000 bushels, besides large quantities of vegetables of various kinds."

Such is the historical and official report of the raid made by General Sullivan and his forces against the six nations. I look upon it as a misfortune that this vengeance could not have fallen upon the Mohawks instead of upon the tribes who had as far as they could remained neutral. Our government however at a later date compensated them as far as possible for such loss—and still continues it to their posterity.

These savage and unparalleled acts of cruelty were mostly in the valley of the Susquehanna and its vicinity. Few of the former citizens who were here before the revolution were ever seen here again and I think I may safely add anywhere else. The bounty of eight dollars in gold per scalp said to have been paid by British agents to the Indians for them, was an inducement to make them as numerous as possible. That such bounty was ever paid by British authority is denied, and for humanity's sake I hope the denial to be true; but I have so many times heard it affirmed by old revolutionary soldiers, as well as stated in history, that with me the positive far outweighs the negative testimony.

FEBRUARY 4, 1892
WHICH TELLS OF INDIAN SETTLEMENTS AND CLINTON'S EXPEDITION

At Fort Stanwix (Rome) a council or treaty was held in September and October, 1768, which was called for the purpose of fixing the bounds as they then existed between the English and the Iriquois nation. The governors of New York, Pennsylvania and New Jersey were present, and also a deputation from Virginia. More than 3,000 Indians were present. At this council the south boundary of the lands of the Six Nations was described as "up the Unadilla river to the head of the same." The Mohawks, previous to that date, had actually sold all, or nearly all, the lands of Otsego county, most if not all of Schoharie and a large portion of Herkimer. Had it not been for the Johnsons and their influence, no doubt the acts of Indian cruelty would have been far less numerous than they were in this region of the country.

Immediately after the close of the war the Mohawks fled to Canada, and there located on a grant of land given them by the British nation; and their descendants there remain to this day. In their flight they claimed to carry with them right and title to all unsold parts of their possessions. In 1797 they sent a delegation composed of their chief, Captain Brant, and another to Albany to meet our officials, and then they "sold to the state of New York, all the right and title of said nation to lands within the said state."

After the close of the revolutionary war many Indians still remained in the Susquehanna valley. They were friendly, and seldom if ever committed any depredations upon the property of the whites. There was in this valley, as I have before stated, many settlers before the Revolution. It will be noticed by what I have written before that the Susquehanna river, as early as 1750, had become quite a noted thoroughfare. I wish here to copy a portion of the diary kept by Lieutenant Erkuries Betty, who was an officer in General Clinton's army and accompanied it on his entire expedition from its start to its return. I will copy only the portion relating particularly to this locality, commencing at the foot of Otsego lake:

"Tuesday, Aug. 3d, 1779. I had like to have forgotten to remember that there was a command of 150 men under Major Parr, on Sunday morning went to Oaks Creek, about three miles from here, with the cattle to pasture. I am informed there is a house there, and about 50 acres of cleared land on which is excellent grass. . . .

"Monday, Aug, 9th. Agreeable to yesterday's order the general beat at six o'clock and the troops marched about eight, excepting three men who were to remain in each boat and take them down the river."

I would here state that there were 250 of these boats, and to man them would require a force of 750 men. Probably there were nearly as many more who marched on foot, as General Clinton's army is variously stated as from 1,200 to 1,500 men.

"Marched 16 miles, within five miles of Yorkams, where we encamped on a small improvement called Burrows' farm, where were many rattlesnakes. One killed had 15 rattles."

This farm was the Collier farm, Major Colliers father, Isaac Collier, purchasing it a year or two after the date of the above event. Isaac Collier was of German descent, and came with his family to the place before the close of the war. He came from the Mohawk by way of Otsego lake, and down the river. I have often heard Major Peter Collier say that at the time his father settled there the nearest mill was at Mohawk, and no road but the army trail and Indians paths. The portion of Clinton's army who came on the boats landed on the farm on the opposite side of the river, called the Van Valkenburgh farm. It was a part of the old John Dietz farm, now owned by Miss Ella Lyman. I learn this from the diary of Lieutenant Van Hovenburgh, an officer on the boats:

"Tuesday, the 10th. Rained a little last night, and this day till 1 o'clock. Marched off the ground at 3 o'clock and went five miles to Yorkams, where we encamped. The men on the boats encamped on the farm which lies on the east side of the river, and the remainder on the side opposite."

Lieutenant Van Hovenburgh says that the men on the boats encamped on the farm of Joachim Van Valkenburgh. That farm was the old Hackett farm, now owned by Mr. Williams, lying east of and adjoining the farm of John Youngman. The Yorkams (or Yokams Van Derwerker) farm was then what is now the Ford or Morrell farm, lying south of the depot. The foot portion of the army bivouacked on both the Ford and Morrell island farms in Oneonta village. A bayonet was plowed up on that part known as the Brown farm, some sixty years ago, which doubtless was lost by General Clinton's army. Mrs. Yokam Van Derwerker lived in a log house which formerly stood on the John Amsden farm, some eighty years ago. Mr. Huntington Parish remembers her well.

"Wednesday, the 11th. Marched this morning at sunrise and proceeded fourteen miles down the river, where we encamped on a small farm. Passed several small farms today, with very poor houses. . . . Encamped on the Ogden farm—a very poor camping ground."

Van Hovenburgh says that his party went about two miles below the mouth of the Otego creek and encamped; and the following night at Unadilla Beatty continues:

"Thursday, the 12th. Marched this morning at seven o'clock. Proceeded down the east side of the river as usual, 12 miles; came to a small Scotch settlement called Albout (Sidney) on the other side of the river, five miles from Unadilla, which we burned; but the people had gone to the enemy last spring. Went on to the Unadilla river and crossed to the east side, where we encamped. The river was about middle deep where we waded it. This settlement was destroyed last fall except one house, which belonged to one Glasford, who went to the enemy last spring. His house was immediately burned."

During the advance of this army down to Tioga they encamped but a single time in the forest. It will be noticed that many of these first settlers were Tories in the Revolution. Unadilla was a village of note previous to the war. Colonel William Butler made a raid against the Indians and Tories down the Susquehanna river in the spring of 1779, and reports the "burning of the town of Unadilla, which was on both sides the river, and a gristmill and sawmill—the only ones in the Susquehanna valley."

In the summer and fall of 1840 I built a gristmill in Cincinatus, Cortland county for Dr. McWhorter. He was then an octogenarian. He studied and commenced its practice in Unadilla, while it was in Albany county, and he lived in Cortland county previous to the revolution. There were no roads nor bridges, and all travel in that locality was by forest paths, or by fording or swimming the streams. The farms of many of these old settlers in the Susquehanna valley never were again occupied by the same families after the war. They were mostly squatters, as very little of the land in this valley could possibly have been purchased previous to 1770—in fact I know of no English patent here previous to that date.

Scattering families of Indians were numerous in this valley after the close of the revolution. They were mostly of those who claimed to have maintained a neutrality during that eventful struggle. They were not, however, of the Mohawks. Their acts were too well known and remembered to have them allowed to remain, even if they so desired.

These Indians were friendly, and were not feared by the whites. In fact, their presence was often counted as a safeguard, particularly against beasts of prey, which had vastly increased in numbers during the continuance of the war. But our state and nation took early measures to settle with them and purchase of all the remaining tribes their titles to any lands in our state, except such as were reserved as permanent Indian reservations. Such reservations in our state, even at this late day, number about 87,677 acres of land, and our Indian wards who occupy these various reservations now number about 5,000. See pages 4 and 5 of Report of Indian Commissions, 1889.

These Indians have degenerated in every respect—physically, morally and intellectually, since the commencement of their contact with the European or white race. They seem to have imbibed and absorbed all the vices of civilized life, and rejected as a race its virtues. All our outlays and efforts for the civilization and christianization of these American aborigines have been an utter failure. There may be many noble exceptions, but not enough to change the general rule. I verily believe that one single active trader, with plenty of intoxicating liquors, can and will in a decade of years, do more evil to the Indian races than can be counterbalanced by a hundred missionaries and another hundred teachers, and both aided and backed in their efforts by all the force of our government beside.

It is an incontrovertible truth that the Indians, as found by the whites at the settlement of our state, were far in advance, physically, morally and socially, of any of the remnants of these same tribes to-day. Two hundred years of continued contact has not improved them. Nor will the future do it on any line of policy yet tried.

Some of these original tribes, like the Cherokees, were said to have had a written language, a code of laws and form of government before 1700. We have some of their descendants now in our state. How much have they improved? Sullivan's campaign demonstrates officially the condition of the Six Nations in 1779. How are their descendants today in comparison? When the German Palantines settled in the Schoharie valley about 1714 they found the Schoharie flats most of the way from Esperance to Middleburgh in a high state of cultivation. Numerous as they were, these Schoharie Indians furnished them with corn and beans for their winter's food, and also for seed the next year; and besides they taught them their way of cultivating them.

FEBRUARY 11, 1892
HIDDEN MINES AND INDIAN RECOLLECTIONS

This vicinity was ever famous for its Indian traditions of valuable mines. Gold, silver and lead were said to be known to the Indians in abundance, and the two latter were of remarkable purity. Lead ore was said to be melted and cast directly into bullets, and silver worked from the ore into various kinds of ornaments. These traditions were fully believed. So strong was their faith in such ores, that a number of excavations were made by the early settlers more than fifty years ago. Silver ore in very large quantities was believed to exist in the hill south of the river between Oneonta village and the mouth of the Otego creek, and in the range of hills between the Otego and Otsdawa creeks, and also in the range of hills north of Oneonta village.

In my opinion, tradition is about the only thing upon which such a belief can be based. Not that I claim to be a mineralogist, and capable of judging in the matter, but for my lack of faith in such traditions. Such lack of faith, however, was uncommon among the old settlers when I first came here to reside.

Still stronger belief also prevailed in salt springs of great saline strength. I have often heard Major Peter Collier state that when he was young the Indians used to keep his father's family supplied with salt for use. They used often to bring it while still warm in their camp kettles, to exchange for things they wanted. J. R. L. Walling of this village informs me that he has often heard the story told in his father's family of his grandfather and grandmother, Timothy and Sarah Walling, being at Collier's when four strong Indians brought there a large iron kettle nearly full of salt, which they had just made, having borrowed the kettle two or three days previous for such purpose.

The locality of such salt spring was never so satisfactorily established as to warrant a search. It was believed to be somewhere between the mouth of the Schenevus and Charlotte rivers. It was stated that an Indian, while under the influence of liquor, in part disclosed its locality and also described how it was protected. His story was that the spring was stoned up and covered with a large, flat stone; that a stone drain was laid from the spring to the deep water in the river, and the spring thus secured from discovery.

I have heard Major Collier say that his father would not let any one follow the Indians or in any way try to learn the locality of the salt spring, thinking it unsafe to do so. It is not impossible, in fact it is highly probable that the Onondaga salt belt may extend to this valley and even farther. I have heard related quite a number of stories during my lifetime, and will no doubt be pardoned if I relate one.

There lived in this valley soon after the Revolution an Indian called Pete. He was a famous hunter, and always kept his hut well supplied with good venison. His hut was not far from a farmer named John. In fact, Pete's hut was located in John's woods. Pete was a clever Indian and he and John were fast friends. There lived in the neighborhood a shiftless sort of fellow called Jake. Jake was lazy; he neither worked nor hunted, and seldom fished. He was often seen around the neighborhood with his fishing tackle, but was seldom seen using it. It was a wonder how he lived. Most people, to live in those times, had either to work, hunt or fish; but Jake seemed to live without either.

One day Pete killed a fine deer and dressed it, and hung its quarters up on the trees near his wigwam, as was his custom. On arising in the morning early, he found a hindquarter missing. He carefully examined, as only an Indian could, and then went over to farmer John for counsel. After bidding John good-morning and passing with him his accustomed friendly salutation, he inquired: "Have you seen a short old man with a short gun, smoking a clay pipe, accompanied by small dog with a bob tail and a short right ear, pass this morning with a hind-quarter of venison on his shoulder?"

"Why, Pete," says John, "how can you so well describe a man and his dog if you have not seen them?"

"Why," says Pete, "I know by his tracks. I know he was a short man, because he had to pile up a heap of stones to take down the venison, which I easily hung up. I know he was an old man by his short steps. I know he had a clay pipe for I saw where he emptied out its ashes to refill it. I know he had a short gun by the mark it made on a tree where he stood it when he took down the venison. I know he had a small dog by his short, small tracks. I know the dog had a bob tail by the mark where he sat while waiting for his master to get the meat, and I know he had a short right ear by the mark he made when he rolled over in the path."

"Well, Pete," says John, "a thief must stand a poor chance with such eyes as yours after him. I have seen just the man and dog you describe, and also with a quarter of venison on his shoulder. It was just daylight. I thought possibly he had been hunting with you, and was on his way home. It was Jake. You go on and you will find your meat. No man can hide from such an observing man as you are."

"Go with me, John. I don't care for meat, as I would have given it to him if he had asked for it. But we must learn him not to steal. No good man steal. We cure him, John, so he no more steal."

John and Pete visited Jake. What they did or said to him no one ever learned, except that they completely remade him. After their visit he was a changed man. He at once became industrious and honest, and so continued for many years. He was finally killed in a storm by a tree falling upon him. John used to say that was the last theft committed in his neighborhood, so long as Pete remained there. Pete, with his wife, removed to one of the reservations. John's name often appears in the official list of a certain town. And Pete's truthful saying, "No good man steals," is, and ever will remain a sacred fact.

After the Indians had all practically retired from this valley it was a common thing for a family of two or three of them to come and make rude pole and bark or brush wigwam and spend several months at a time, the squaws usually making moccasins and baskets while the men would apparently be prospecting. There were two such wigwams occupied in the town of Milford in 1841, which I saw several times. Indians and squaws, Indians in pairs or single Indians passing up and down this valley were very common for the first ten years of my residence in it. I have myself seen many, and heard of others whom I did not see. The old citizens used to think they were looking for mineral land marks. I noticed they more often passed on the south side of the river than on the north side—perhaps for the reason that there was usually less travel on that side.

Before leaving the Indian portion of my subject, I must note some of the things we have gained from them. The first and most important is that we have virtually adopted their form of government. The Iroquois confederacy existed for a long time as a sample of such union, for strength, prosperity and success. We have adopted many of their articles of production. Indian corn, our greatest of cereals, was first found among the American Indians; so too were potatoes and pumpkins; tobacco, a plant so universally used by all nations, was not known until discovered among the American Indians. So we might multiply the list until we would find that these aborigines, rude and uncivilized as we called them, have actually furnished us more of what has tended to make us a great and prosperous people by far, than has all that we have received from the eastern hemisphere.

While we grow, multiply, prosper and progress, they are fast moving toward the setting sun and final extinction. Civilize them we cannot. In savage cruelty alone do they succeed. The massacre of Custer's army, for its perfect success and barbarous cruelty, was not surpassed at Wyoming or Cherry Valley. The Indian problem is a hard one, and one I shall not attempt to recommend a way of solving.

FEBRUARY 18, 1892
THE "DREAMLANDS" OF SIR WILLIAM JOHNSON

We have still another tradition, which must not be omitted in my scraps of history. That is that the veritable "Dreamland" is located in this valley, and in the town of Oneonta. I suppose that almost all adult persons have heard the story of the dreams of the Mohawk chief and of Sir William Johnson. I have a number of times mentioned the name of Sir William Johnson in the preceding pages. I will now give a short biographical sketch of this notable person.

He was born in Ireland in 1715. He came to America in 1738 as an agent for his uncle, Admiral Sir Peter Warren. He soon made the acquaintance and obtained the friendship of the Mohawk Indians and through them of the Six Nations, and became so firm a friend of the confederacy that they made him one of their sachems. For his aid to the British during the French and Indian war the crown made him a baronet, and its trusted Indian agent. He died at Johnson hall, in the Mohawk valley, in 1774. His influence over these tribes, especially the Mohawks, was almost unbounded. It was this influence of his which carried so fully these Mohawk Indians to the British interests during the Revolution. Sir William Johnson's home was a famous resort for the Iroquois chiefs, and particularly so of those of the tribe by which he was surrounded. At one of these visits of the Mohawk chief, about 1750, he happened to see a new gold lace trimmed suit of clothes the baronet had obtained for his own use. On his appearance before Sir William the next morning the chief said: "Me dream last night." "What did my brother dream?" inquired the baronet. "Me dream that you gave me that fine suit of clothes," quoth the chief. "They shall be yours," said Sir William, and he at once ordered them brought and presented them to the chief.

Some months after Sir William Johnson accompanied the chief to the Susquehanna valley and they stopped over night at the Indian village of Wauteghe, situated as I have before named on the east side of the Otego creek near its mouth, on the north side of the Susquehanna river. Its location was on the farms formerly known as the Van Woert farms in this town.

On arising and meeting the chief in the morning Sir William thus addressed him: "I, too, had a dream last night." "Ah," replied the chief; "and what did my pale face brother dream?" "I dreamed you gave me a deed of all the lands I could see from yon eminence," answered Sir William, at the same time pointing to a hill on the opposite side of the river. After a moment's thought the chief replied, "You shall have it, but we will neither of us dream again."

This is the story of the Mohawk chief and Sir William Johnson's dreams, as related to me by Major Peter Collier more than fifty years ago. I have often heard the same story from other old men in this vicinity, and have had the lands on the plains below pointed out to me as their dreamlands. I have also at a later date had the story in part confirmed by J. R. L. Walling, and noticed them as located on a map of his of that part of our town. Thus the matter rested with me until I chanced to see a map of the Otego grant or patent, made in 1770 by order of the British crown to Charles Reed and others. I at once noticed marked off on that map a strip of land extending from a mile or so below the mouth of the Otego creek up the river about as far as Beams' hill, east of Oneonta village, as "lands of Sir William Johnson and others." I then procured and read a copy of the Otego grant, and found that the Johnson tract had been surveyed some time before the Otego patent, and the latter followed the marked trees of the former survey. This map and grant copy are the property of Counselor R. M. Townsend in this village, and the same may be found in his office. I have examined the original of the map and grant at the office of the secretary of state in Albany.

Sir William obtained a number of different Indian deeds, and also several royal land grants. This lot in question was never granted to him by patent, and probably he never had any other title of it except that obtained from the Mohawk chief. He obtained at different times from the Indians a title to nearly all the lands in the entire Susquehanna valley, far down into the state of Pennsylvania. The tract of land in the town of Oneonta, which we believe to be the true "Dreamland," is, I believe, mostly covered by a patent granted to Alexander Wallace and familiarly known as the Wallace patent.

The story of the dreams of Sir William and the Mohawk chief was well known to all the old inhabitants of the valley. That distinguished scholar, Loomis J. Campbell, informed me recently that he had often heard his grandfather, Dr. Joseph Lindsay, tell the story and point out the lands named as the veritable dreamlands. Mrs. Ephraim Parish recently informed me that she had often heard the story in her younger days, and that its relators believed it to be true.

In order to deal fairly with this matter and present no claim to which other localities might be entitled, I now copy a portion of the contents of vol. 1, pages 314 and 315, from J. R. Simm's late work called "Frontiersmen of New York." In Simm's history of Schoharie county, published in 1835, he relates the dream story, placing its location in Herkimer county and chief Hendrick as the Mohawk chief who had the memorable dream. But I now quote entirely from his later work as above named:

"The tract of land owned by Sir William Johnson, called the Royal grant, which contained nearly one hundred thousand acres of choice land situate in the county of Herkimer, was obtained from Hendrick in the following manner: Being at the baronet's house (Fort Johnson) the sachem observed a new coat, richly embroidered with gold lace, which the former intended for his own person. On entering his presence after a night's rest he said to him, 'Brother, me dream last night.' 'Indeed,' responded the royal agent; 'and what did my red brother dream?' 'Me dream,' was the chief's reply, 'that this coat be mine.' 'Then,' said the sagacious Irishman, 'it is yours, to which you are welcome.'

"Soon after this interview Sir William returned his guest's visit, and on meeting him in the morning said to him, 'Brother, I dreamed last night;' 'What did my pale face brother dream?' interrogated the sachem. 'I dreamed,' said his guest, 'that this tract of land'—describing a square bounded on the south by the Mohawk, on the east by Canada creek and on the north and west by objects familiar to them—'was all my own.'

"Old Hendrick assumed a thoughtful mood, but although he saw the enormity of the request, he would not be outdone in generosity, or forfeit the friendship of the British, and soon responded, 'the land is yours; but you must not dream again.' The title to this land was confirmed by the British government, on which account it was called the royal grant."

Mr. Stone says in his life of Sir William Johnson (vol. 1, page 551): "The famous story of Sir William dreaming with King Hendrick for the royal grant, or indeed for any other piece of land, is pure fabrication." Again Mr. Stone says, "The romantic story of his dreaming away from King Hendrick, the royal grant, which even Mr. Schoolcraft in his notes on the Iroquois gravely relates as a fact, is false." Hendrick had been in his grave five years before this tract was given. Indeed, the uprightness of Sir William's dealings with the Indians, which was the chief cause of his ascendancy over them sufficiently proves its falsity, even if we had not the above positive testimony. It is quite time that the numerous silly stories in regard to Sir William Johnson and resting solely on tradition, should be done away with."

Here we have the claims of Herkimer county to dream land; and also its denial by Mr. Stone, Sir William Johnson's able biographer. The latter's expression, "or indeed for any other piece of land" is presumptive evidence that other pieces of land were known to him as being claimed as dreamlands. Our claim to their location rests upon no such disputable grounds. The Indian deed under which we base our claim was made in 1751, and the lands were surveyed during the decade of 1750; and the Otego patent was surveyed by surveyor William Cockburn in 1768. A copy of the old Indian deed made to Sir William Johnson of lands in the Susquehanna valley, may be found in Liber 26, page 127, in the Indian records of titles, in the office of the secretary of state in the capitol in Albany.

Among writers who relate and fully believe the story of the dreams of the Mohawk chief and Sir William are Spafford, Simms and Schoolcraft, but none of them have the corroborative testimony for establishing its location as does this town. This dream story is said to have been current during Sir William Johnson's lifetime, and no one reports his ever denying its truth.

That an Indian title was given to Sir William Johnson, as a reward for a dream, and as payment for a suit of clothes obtained in a like way, hardly admits of a doubt. That the actual lands given for such dream are located in Oneonta, and the parcel shown on the Otego land grant as lands of "Sir William Johnson and others" is the tract so conveyed, is so well authenticated as to hardly admit of a doubt of its being the true dreamland. I am informed by reliable parties that some of the old deeds of portions of this land are named as being a part of the dreamland tract. I found no such recorded in the Otsego county clerk's office, but I found three which were in part bounded by and named as such adjoining lands the "Sir William Johnson lands." I am myself fully satisfied of the truth of the dream story, and as firmly believe the true "Dreamland" to be a part or the whole of the tract above named.

More about the Dreamlands appears at the end of the following chapter.

FEBRUARY 25, 1892
FIRST SETTLEMENTS AFTER THE REVOLUTION

The early settlers of Oneonta and vicinity, and particularly up and down the valley of the Susquehanna after the war of the Revolution, were mostly from east of the Hudson river. Some of them were soldiers who had served in General Sullivan's army, and who obtained their first knowledge of the valley by then passing through it. Others learned of it from the description given by those returning soldiers to their eastern homes.

Among the soldiers who came down the Susquehanna river with the army of General Clinton, as described in a previous chapter, was Simeon Walling, the grandfather of our respected townsman, J. R. L. Walling. Among the army of General Sullivan was also his grandfather Lee, who started with him at Easton and came by way of Wyoming to Tioga, where the union of the northern and southern wings of that army were perfected. Immediately after the close of the war Mr. Walling returned to this valley, and ever after made it his home. He first settled in 1784 on lands on the south side of the river, near the site of the Indian village I have before mentioned—the present Slade farm. In 1785 he purchased the two lots containing the former Bronson farm and the present J. R. L. Walling farm, and as was then the universal custom, erected a log house and barn. In 1800 he built the frame house which stood nearly in front of the present Walling brick residence. The latter was the first brick house erected in the limits of Oneonta. It was built in 1853.

Among those who are known to have resided in this town previous to the Revolution was Stoughton Alger, the father of Stoughton Alger jr., who was the father of our present townswoman, Mrs. Ephraim Parish. He first settled on the farm where old Mr. Bingham now resides. The farm then included the present Bingham and Pierce farms, and extended northerly to the original line on the hill northeasterly of the old turnpike road, and contained between two and three hundred acres of land.

Henry Scramling also came here before the Revolution, and purchased 1,000 acres of land near the mouth of the Otego creek. It was mostly off the old "Dreamland" tract. Eight hundred acres were on the north and two on the south side of the Susquehanna river. Both these families were compelled to return to their former Mohawk homes to escape massacre by the Indians in the employ and aid of the British during the war. After the war they returned again to their deserted homes. Henry Scramling was accompanied by his two brothers, David and George, and his brother-in-law, David Young, and John Young, the brother of David.

David Scramling, the father of George Scramling, who was the father of the present Scramling family in this town, settled on what is now known as the John Van Woert farm. He also owned the westerly hundred acres of the present Scramling farm, on the south side of the river. The title of that hundred acres has never passed from the David Scramling descendants, and is still in the ownership of Allen, Albert and others of the Scramling family.

Henry Scramling owned the lands westerly of the David Scramling farm, and also above them on the Otego creek. His westerly line was where Nelson Cole's western line now is.

George Scramling, the other brother, settled on what is known as the Peter Van Woert farm, now owned by Messrs. Tyler, Jenks and others. He also owned the other hundred acres on the south side of the river, known as the Kelsey R. Kelly farm. That is now owned by the Scramling family. George Scramling kept the first tavern known to have been kept in this town. It was kept where the old Peter Van Woert residence formerly stood.

The next farm east of George Scramling's—the present Peter Van Woert and Calkins farms, was settled immediately after the war by Adrian Quackenbush. John Van Woert, when a boy, lived with him until of age.

David Young settled on the farm now owned by Ephraim Parish, long known as the Stoughton Alger jr. farm, and upon which he resided until his death.

John Young, the brother of David, settled on the farm now owned by Mr. Gallup, and the old Averill farm lying east of and adjoining it. He married for his wife Molly, the daughter of Yokam Van Derwerker, and for a number of years kept tavern at that place.

Yokam Van Derwerker is the same "Yorkam" named in Chapter III as being the owner of the David Morrell farm, where the land force of General Clinton's army encamped when on their way to join General Sullivan at Tioga, in August, 1779. He was known further by his given name of Yokam than by his surname, Van Derwerker. This same Van Derwerker built the first grist-mill erected in this region. It stood on the Morrell flats, a little easterly of its west line, and water to propel it was taken from the river, near his easterly line. The line of the old ditch can still be seen. After Mr. Van Derwerker's death his widow for some years resided on the old Esq. Parish farm, now owned by John Amsden, on the south side of the river.

The Joachim Van Valkenburgh named in the same chapter as living on the Williams farm, on which the boatmen of General Clinton's army to the number of 750 men encamped in 1779, was the father of Garrett and Everett Van Valkenburgh, persons well known to the former residents of this town, where many of their descendants still reside. He and his wife spent the last years of their life with Gloud Wans of Barnesville, east of Cooperstown Junction, and their remains now rest in the old burying ground just west of the Junction. The old Van Valkenburgh farm named as being on the easterly side of the river at Colliers, is supposed to have been the farm of the father of Joachim.

Van Valkenburgh and Van Derwerker were the only two families known to have remained in this town, so far as I can learn, during the last years of the Revolutionary war. Others may have settled here before the war and again returned thereafter, but if so I am unable to learn the names of any except Alger and Scramling. Isaac Collier, the father of

Peter Collier, settled at Colliersville about 1780, same months after the passage of General Clinton's army down the Susquehanna.

The raid made in the country of the Six Nations by the armies of Generals Clinton and Sullivan rendered this valley comparatively safe from Indian depredations; but the destruction of so much of the property, and the evacuation of it by nearly all its former citizens rendered it for a time very undesirable indeed as a place of residence. The village of Unadilla had thus far been its most populous and prosperous settlement, with the near-by Scotch settlement where Sidney now is, as its neighbor. The junction of large streams, as it will everywhere be noticed, were points at all times chosen by the Indians and also by pioneer settlers, as proper places for locating their villages. But as we have before noted, both of these places and their mills had been burned during the war.

Mills with early settlers were of vast importance. Wherever mills were erected in our early history, they formed a nucleus around which trade, mechanical and manufacturing industries centered. The want of mills was one of the first needs of this, as well as all other newly-settled localities. I have often heard Major Peter Collier say that for some years after his father settled at the "Burrus farm," now Colliersville, the nearest mill was at Mohawk. There had been both a grist-mill and saw-mill at Unadilla at an earlier day, but both had been burnt by Butler's army in April, 1779.

More About " Dreamland."

Editor Herald: —Since my article in your last issue was in type, I have been able to obtain the last unsupplied link, and to positively establish the true locality of "Dreamland" in this town, as there stated.

On the 17th of February, while on my way to Cooperstown, Willard Jenks happened to be in the same car and seated near me. He said, "I notice The Herald of this week is to contain your article on "Dreamland." I have a package of old deeds, being former conveyances of the premises of which I am now part owner, in which I think each refers to the land as a part of 'Dreamland,' and I think the same is contained in my own deed."

Knowing his farm to occupy a part of the site of the old Indian village of Wauteghe, which I have before described and also being formerly known by the name of the "Indian orchards," I was extremely glad of such information from so reliable a source, and with thanks assured him I would avail myself of it and add such proof to my forthcoming number. The day following I called at the county clerk's office, where I soon found the deed, from which I made the following extract: "Being a parcel of the Sir William Johnson dreamland tract."

At my former examination we failed to find it, as I gave the wrong name as grantor to this conveyance. The clerk also informed me that he was confident he had seen other such deeds in his examination of the records in the office. But as numbers would not make the proof more positive, I drop "Dreamland" with its true locality, as I believe indisputably established as being in the town of Oneonta."   H. Baker

MARCH 3, 1892
MANNERS AND CUSTOMS OF LONG AGO (PART 1)

We at this day and age can hardly picture in our minds, much less realize, the hardships and privations of early pioneer life. Imagine a young man full of life and vigor leaving an eastern home where the comforts of civilized life had for some years been enjoyed, changing those advantages for such as could in those early days not be found in any of the central or western portions of our state, which was then mostly a dense forest, inhabited only by beasts of prey. The war of the Revolution had but just closed. The people were poor. Money was scarce. The price for labor low. But the spirit of enterprise was alive and undaunted.

Imagine a young man leaving his New England home and pushing his way westward into our state. Each day removing him farther from his birthplace and civilized life. It is spring. Hope and expectation for the future, picture to him in imagination a home of independence and happiness. He is on his way seeking its location and to commence its improvement. He has left behind him a fair maiden, who is to share its joys and sorrows as his life companion.

After a journey of weeks he selects a site in the dense, unbroken forest. He must go far from improvements that he may buy as cheaply as possible. He builds a rude cabin and commences his toil. Trees of vast size and height are all around him. He has brought from the nearest point, provisions for two or three weeks supply. He in high hope, and full of persevering faith in himself commences felling the giant trees. If they were out of the way how much would his task be lessened. Even then a year must pass before he could receive any reward for his toil.

But to start to build up a home in such a spot and amid such surroundings, requires a will of iron and muscles of steel. No associates or means of communication with home or friends, he has certainly assumed a task of vast magnitude. The trees fall before his sturdy strokes of the axe. By mid-summer a number of acres are fallen. During the time his fallow is drying, he seeks help, either by exchange of labor or hire and builds a log house. He splits logs for its floors and covers its roof with bark. Saw mills are not yet within reach.

In due time he burns his fallow and proceeds to cut, pile and burn off the logs. He finally succeeds in getting ten or a dozen acres so cleared and fenced, perhaps with logs, that he can sow it to wheat or rye. He has worked early and late. Day after day, week after week, he has toiled, slept upon a bed of hemlock boughs and under the blanket he brought from his former home. His fare has been of the simplest and cheapest kind, while hope has furnished him a large share of his strength.

If during this first year he has accomplished so much, what may he not look forth to in the future, are the encouraging thoughts which fill his mind. As the cold weather approaches, he leaves his new and starts for his old home, his friends, and above all, for her who has been his angel of inspiration ever since he bade her adieu in the early spring months so long ago.

During the winter he marries and they, himself and bride, make all possible arrangements to remove to their new wilderness home as early as possible the coming spring. With his loved one, their goods, meager and scanty though they be, with his ox team and canvas-covered wagon, they for weeks pursue their way to their new but distant home. As his young bride far from her former home and nearing her new, desolate and untried one in the forest, faints or repines not, you may know she is of true metal and fully fitted for the task she has undertaken.

They carry, if possible, sufficient food to supply them until the coming harvest. They have vegetable seeds and fruit tree seeds of various kinds, to plant for future use. The tasks of the former year are repeated but under far less hardships. If health and hope fail not, after years thus diligently spent, a home is made, a farm cleared, fruit, stock and home comforts begin to accumulate.

Year after year thus our fathers toiled, perhaps battled with sickness or accidents, menaced by wild beasts, making their clothing as well as supplying all other needs, self-reliant, full of hope, persevering and unyielding in their struggle to clear the land and make the homes we now enjoy. Such is but a faint sketch of pioneer life. By their own personal efforts they have won life's battle, and with their families can feel an independence ever attendant upon persevering industry and economy. The house becomes a manufactory and a workshop, and all wants are supplied by home industry. This dim, imperfect picture but faintly portrays a few of the toils of the most successful. If sickness, accident, poor crops or misfortune befall one, failure is sure to result. But at best, years of excessive, unceasing labor must be perseveringly followed, before even the common comforts of life can be hoped for, or enjoyed. Orchards from the seed must be planted, every convenience on the farm or in the house supplied by home industry, genius and skill.

The clothing worn, the food consumed, the improvements made and the protection secured, all alike depend upon home personal efforts and labor. In addition to these positive indispensable needs, they must build bridges, school houses, churches, form town and county, road and school organization, and inaugurate all the institutions incident to society, and actual civilized life.

This is no imaginary picture, but one which has wholly or in part been repeated in every farm home among the pioneers in our state and county. They, too, were done under conditions and circumstances not possible to be repeated at this time, in any portion of our domain. The perseverance and industry which has transformed all this vast wilderness into improved happy farm homes, ever will command the admiration of all who become acquainted with such pioneer history.

Hard as was the lot of our early pioneer settlers, their lives were far from being void of social enjoyment. Neighbors, friends and friendship then were something besides an empty name. A union of interest and a communion of feeling bound the people by the strongest possible ties of friendship; jealousy and avarice had not then begun their baleful work. To cheat and defraud each other was no part of their lives' employ. Law and lawyers had not then become a necessity, and men were from fear or force of law.

Social gatherings were common, but their amusements were almost invariably combined with utility. Neighbors were brought together to assist each other. The raising of buildings, the logging bees, the chopping bees, the wood hauling bees, brought the men and boys together very often, but the corn husking bees at which both sexes took part, were by far the most interesting and enjoyable. No one who has ever enjoyed one but still remembers it as a most pleasant pastime of pioneer life.

The young maiden who chanced to find a red ear of corn was privileged to choose her own escort home or partner in the dance. So too was the lucky swain who was the finder of a like token. Many a red ear has been smuggled in, no doubt, and done duty more than once on such festive occasions. But the pumpkin pie, which was a universal attendent upon all such gatherings, had to come in new and fresh every time.

An old time Thanksgiving was a gathering long to be remembered. It was a pure New England custom dating back to the first harvest of our Pilgrim fathers, and a true Yankee would feel that he had failed in an important duty, if he neglected to celebrate in due form Thanksgiving day. No modern cookery can excel that of grandmothers and great grandmothers on those memorable festive occasions. It was then that the roast turkey or spare-rib before the open wood fire was "done to a turn." And no modern oven or means of baking can surpass the bread, pudding, cake or pies, given forth from those old style brick ovens of a former generation. I speak from actual knowledge of the past Thanksgiving days.

Christmas, although perhaps as well and thoroughly observed, could not excel in its feast or joys, the Thanksgiving which had so recently preceded it. No doubt the long months of increasing toil had fitted its guests peculiarly for their Thanksgiving feast.

Early in our history military training occupied the attention of our people. The ever-practiced plan of nation warring against nation and settling all differences by an appeal to arms, has made all people take more or less pride in military preparations. Our old-time company and general trainings will long be remembered by those who recall their engrossing annual interest. The annual general training was a great event with the last generation.

Quilting parties were a pastime of no small moment to our mothers and grandmothers in bygone days. A quilting was often a source of gain as well as of merriment. Sometimes the material for the quilt would be distributed and the blocks, squares or other figures to form the quilt pieced up by the mothers and daughters in the vicinity and then brought together and prepared for the quilting, in advance of the real event; usually the day previous. On the following day the quilting would be held. This would close by an evening gathering at which the young men of the neighborhood took a prominent part. These quilting parties were very enjoyable occasions. Dances, plays, games or other pastimes and sources of pleasurable enjoyments rendered these old-time quilting seasons of peculiar interest.

Spinning parties, called "spinning bees" were a common pastime, but like the quiltings the fun came in at their close. Wool, flax, or tow and sometimes cotton carded ready to spin, would be distributed around with the instructions to spin about so many knots to the pound, so as to have the yarn of the required fineness. At a given day the yarn would be brought to the place designated and an evening gathering of young men, and fun ended these spinning parties.

The old-fashioned apple paring bees will long be remembered. They came later as an institution among our old settlers. For fruit must be raised before it could be cut or dried. Such gatherings were just in the height of their glory in my boyhood days. The young people of both sexes from all the neighborhood would gather in the early evening, and engage with a will in paring, quartering, coring and stringing apples. Usually from ten to fifteen bushels would be cut in an evening. The work done, the floor would be swept, the pumpkin pie passed around and then the fun would begin. Usually plays like blind man's buff, snap and catch 'em, hold fast what I give you, the Indian marriage, etc., would fill the space until the small hours warned the guests of time for departure.

The manner of riding out with one's best girl in the time of about the second generation after the revolution, must not be omitted. The first age of all new, heavily timbered countries may be appropriately styled the ox age, as oxen were a necessity for all work on newly cleared farms. This was followed by horses as well as oxen, and horseback riding was the common way of travel, of both men and women. Every well-to-do farmer's wife had her side saddle, and every like family one or more "pillions." A pillion was a sort of cushion made expressly for use where a lady rode on the same horse behind a gentleman. It was a common sight in my boyhood days for the man and wife to ride to church or other places on the same horse. But the climax of such rides was for the gentleman lover to take his lady love behind him thus on the same horse. It must be a cold-blooded beau who could ride for even a few miles with the right arm of his loved one closely clasped around his body without feeling a desire to pop the question, which often proves so embarrassing to the timid, bashful swain. For real genuine love-making such horseback rides on moonlight evening can have no superior. Even now I am confident the cosiest parlor dims by contrast with this old-time custom. No coach and four, with an attendant outside and footman can at all compare with this former custom of our grandparents. If I were a boy I would strive to revive this long lost art.

MARCH 10, 1892
MANNERS AND CUSTOMS OF LONG AGO (PART 2)

One custom of the olden times must not go unnoticed. The love of superior show is of modern invention. Years ago as now, some people were more fortunate than others in gaining wealth—but as now it did not convert so many of them into self-made fools. The sons and daughters of the wealthy could of course dress in more costly garb than did the average of their neighbors, but it was rarely done. The daughters of the rich seldom wore more showy dresses than did their average neighbors. They scorned the idea of superior display. I well remember a daughter of Judge Wheeler who waited three days one time before commencing a term of school because the cloth for her home-made woolen dress had not in time come home from the clothing mill where it had been sent to be pressed. She said she would not go to school until she could dress as did her school mates in a home-made dress. She actually cut and made with her own hands in a single day and evening the dress, and wore it the next day to school. This trying to outdo our neighbors in display was not chargeable to our grandparents to the average extent of to-day.

The lumber-wagon as a common means of transit followed horse-back riding and was common sixty years ago. The old-fashioned wagon chairs were used as seats for its occupants. Six or eight persons thus rode to meeting on Sunday, those having teams usually carrying their less-favored neighbors. A common friendly feeling then prevailed which has gradually with the passing years been dying out. Civilization has its drawbacks as well as its gains. Crime, vice, intemperance, suicide and insanity are on the increase notwithstanding all the efforts made to increase the comforts and lessen the cares of the people and give all an opportunity to obtain a good education free. A return to former customs and common honesty then prevailing, would certainly be an improvement in modern society.

With our old inhabitants in our early history, money for the payment of taxes was extremely hard to obtain. Even as late as the decade of 1820, I well remember my father and grandfather commenced saving the small sums they received months in advance to meet such a call. Although were a mere trifle compared with now, yet the small sum demanded was hard to obtain.

William McCrum relates a story told him by Andrew Parish esq., which occurred when he resided on what is known as the John Fritts farm on the south side of the Susquehanna. It was then in the town of Kortright, Delaware county. The collector called on him about 1812 for his tax which was but 25 cents. He had not the money and came over the river to borrow it, but could not even obtain that small sum. Some days later having obtained it, he walked all the way to Kortright, a distance of nearly twenty miles, to pay that 25 cents tax. Such an occurrence is truly worth a historic record.

These great changes for both the better and the worse of our people have taken place during my lifetime. The transition from our primitive life and customs to those of the present have been very rapid. The improvements in the means of shortening time and space in all our life's transactions have been wonderful past computation; but with those advancements have also developed other things which to some have proved injurious instead of beneficial.

I am confident that among mothers generally there has not been that close care for the good of their children in their training as was practiced by the mothers of the former generations. They trust them more to nurses, servants, and teachers. No substitute can fill with the son or daughter, the care of a good mother. Look where you will among the useful and distinguished men in our country and you will almost invariably find the wise training and counsel of their mothers have been their inspiring influence, and their guiding star to success, usefulness and fame.

No teacher's work can equal a good mother's. No other can implant such true moral principles. No other can guide to the formation of such correct habits. Nurses, teachers and schools all contribute their part in making and developing the young mind; but the part of a good mother is supremely above all others. I conceive that here starts our retrograde movements towards intemperance and insanity. It is high time for a halt in these increasing causes of physical and mental ruin. We must look for it, hope for it, and find it, if ever found, in the training of the rising generation.

The increase of suicides and insanity is truly alarming. Statistics will show that now, at this very hour, in Otsego county more insane may be found, more suicides committed and more criminals reported in a single town than could have been found in the entire county with a larger population than now, sixty years ago. Such facts speak badly for our modern civilization.

An examination will also demonstrate the fact that the increase to the taxpayers of the expense for the support of paupers, orphans, insane, drunkenness and crime has evidently increased more than fifteen times in its actual taxation cost within sixty years, and that, too, on an actual diminished population. In 1830 not $5,000 can be put to the account of those things in the tax roll of that year, while 1890 will show fully $100,000 of the taxes levied, directly so chargeable. Such statistical fact, coupled with the other, that we had over 500 more population in 1830 than in 1890, is a lesson for the consideration of every true citizen.

The school system of our grandfathers contrasts wonderfully with that of today. Then the small, rude log school house was the place where the rudiments of an English education were received. Reading, writing and arithmetic constituted the necessary qualifications of the teacher in those days. Perhaps I should have concluded the list of qualifications with the will and ability liberally to use the rod, as that was certainly no minor accomplishment. The time spent in these rude schools was limited to the ability of the parents to pay their rate bill, and the time the children could be spared from necessary toil to attend the school. Such schools seldom, if ever, extended over two terms of twelve weeks each. Poor as were the school houses, and limited as were the qualifications of the teachers, and as necessary as was the labor of the children at home, truant children were far less in comparison than now, with all our modern free school advantages.

In the town records of Otego, which was in part Oneonta, for 1821, I found that the town received $88.80 from the state school fund and raised a like sum by tax upon the town, making the public money for that year $177.60 for school uses. In 1822, I find there were eight whole and three parts of districts in the town, and that the number of children taught was 485, and that the whole number in town between the ages of five and fifteen years was 414. This was then the age of those entitled to the benefit of public moneys. In 1825 I find the number of children between the ages of five and fifteen to have been 460, and the number who attended school the same year to be 562. These are the only two reports I find in our old town records of the number of scholars of school age, and the number taught each year. I wish a like proportion of our present school age might be found annually in our schools. In 1825 the record shows that if every scholar who drew public money had attended school, still 102 older and above that age was added to the list.

An examination of past statistical history has raised in my mind this query: Are we not making our present school system too easy and too cheap, to have it appreciated and improved as our legislators evidently intended it should be? Do the people it was intended to benefit profit or lose by its easy, cheap free system? My observation for a lifetime has been, that people prize the highest those things which cost them the most personal efforts to obtain. Those which come free and without cost or effort, no matter how useful or valuable, are the least sought or prized.

I very much doubt whether the present age presents scholars more profound, statesmen more wise, writers more chaste and correct in language or more true in facts, orators more eloquent and convincing, divines more pure in mind, lawyers more thoroughly versed in law, or physicians more skillful in the healing art than those who filled these exalted positions in our country three fourths of a century ago. The query is, do we really improve, except in our capacity to develop, create and worship mammon?

MARCH 17, 1892
THE EARLY HISTORY OF TOWN AND COUNTY

Oneonta has a unique history. It would be hard to produce its parallel. Previous to 1683 it was an unnamed part of the great American wilderness in the province of New York. From that date until 1772 it was in Albany county, which then embraced all the lands in this state west of the Hudson river. In 1772 a new county was formed in honor of Governor Tryon, called Tryon county. It embraced within its boundary all that portion of the state lying west of the Helderburghs and the Delaware river, and northward to the Canada line. In 1784 the name of Tryon was dropped and that of Montgomery adopted in its stead. This was done in honor of General Richard Montgomery, a distinguished officer in the war of the Revolution. It continued to be in Montgomery county until 1791, when the county of Otsego was formed. Its southern boundary was then the Susquehanna river.

The town of Unadilla was formed in 1792, and Oneonta was then included in the town of Unadilla. The towns of Otego and Suffrage were formed from Unadilla in 1776. The town of Otego then also embraced what is now the town of Laurens, which was taken from Otego in 1810. In 1801 the name of Suffrage was changed to the town of Milford. In 1822 the town of Huntsville was formed from Unadilla, Otego, and a tier of lots from Delaware county, on the south side of the Susquehanna river. That change took one entire tier of lots from Delaware county south of the Susquehanna river, and added it to Otsego county.

It would seem from the records kept that Otego claimed most of the present town of Oneonta in her former bounds up to 1830, for Oneonta has in its clerk's office the records of the town of Otego from its formation from Unadilla, and the first ten years of the records of the town of Oneonta are kept in the same book.

It will be seen from the above history that Oneonta has been in part or whole in Albany, Tryon, Montgomery, Delaware and Otsego counties. It has also been in whole or in part in the towns of Otsego, Unadilla, Otego, Suffrage, Huntsville, Milford, Franklin, Kortright, Davenport and Oneonta, where it still remains. Its records if properly kept will be found in the counties of Albany, Tryon, Montgomery, Delaware and Otsego. The town records will be in Unadilla, Otego, Suffrage, Hilford, Huntsville, Franklin, Davenport and Oneonta. I think a like local history of a piece of land cannot be found in our entire country.

Many years passed before the true bounds of the town of Oneonta were found by its inhabitants, although a full record of its bounds is contained in the law making of the town; and the boundaries of the town were also correctly recorded in the town book of records of Oneonta, previous to the making of any other entries in the same.

I have some old deeds of land I own south of the river, which in 1835 were recorded in Delaware county and dated and acknowledged in the town of Davenport, although in fact they had for over five years actually been in the town of Oneonta. There were many other like transactions. Esq. Andrew Parish was for many years a justice of the peace in Delaware county, as was supposed, when in fact he resided in Oneonta. A special act was passed by the legislature to correct and make legal all such transactions.

In the old Otsego records are some things worthy of note. The first town meeting was held at the house of Truman Harrison, April 5, 1796. The following persons were elected as the first town officers: Butler Gilbert, supervisor; Jacob Butts, town clerk; Czar Benedict, Samuel Cook and Jonathan Tickner, assessors; Jonathan Johnson, Ezra Barton and George Scramling, commissioners of highways; Job Strait and Samuel Sleeper, town masters; Jacob Butts, Griffin Craft and Leroy Jenks, commissioners of schools; Aaron Harrington, Samuel Gregory and Nathaniel Spencer, constables; Willis Draper, collector; Charles Eldred, Samuel Cook, Stoughton Alger and Job Strait, collector's bondsmen. Twenty one pathmasters were elected. The town must at that early date have had quite a population, even if every other man was a town officer. In 1798 James McDonald was one of the assessors, and also school commissioner. At this town meeting it was voted that sheep and hogs should not be "free commoners;" and that five dollars should be paid for every full-grown wolf caught within the town of Otego.

In 1801 the wolf bounty was increased to seven dollars, and in 1802 it was made ten dollars. Wolves were very troublesome at that date. The ten-dollar bounty so reduced their number that in 1804 the bounty was decreased to four dollars. In 1805 it was voted that "barns and barnyards and such other conveniences as they may think proper to erect shall be considered as pounds." In 1806 Christopher Lovis Stark was apprenticed to Samuel Allen by the poor master and two justices to learn the house carpenter's trade. James McDonald was highway commissioner in 1807. This year a vote was taken upon the division of the town, with 138 votes for and 121 against division, showing that 259 voters voted. It was voted in 1814 that the commissioner of schools should receive 25 cents per day. In 1818 a vote was taken upon the division of the county, and the forming of the county of Unadilla. The vote was unanimously against its division. A committee was chosen to remonstrate to the legislature against it.

In 1822 it was voted to give the collector three per cent for collecting the taxes. In 1826 it was voted that "horned cattle and sheep be free commoners unless breachy." In 1830 the records under the name of Otego close, and then begins in the same book the records of the town of Oneonta. In Spafford's Gazetteer of New York, published in 1813, Otego is named as having 2,512 inhabitants and 216 electors. Electors or voters for state offices, to be eligible as office holders at that time, must be the owners of $250 worth of real estate free from debt. These figures were from the census of 1810. Milford at the same date had 2,025 inhabitants and 139 electors. Each town then had one post office.

Otego in 1820 had 1,416 inhabitants, and Laurens, which had been taken from Otego, had 2,074. Milford at that census had a population of 2,505, and the entire county of Otsego had a population of 44,856. Otego and Milford are credited with one post office each, and the one at Milfordsville. Oneonta's name at that date is not named in any way, nor is the village. Otego had in 1820 366 farmers, 47 mechanics, 1 slave, 10 schools, 286 electors, 9,409 acres of improved land, 1646 cattle, 276 horses, 4,454 sheep, 1 grist-mill, 9 saw-mills, 1 fulling-mill, 1 carding-machine, 1 iron works, and made that year 14,983 yards of home-made or domestic cloth. In 1830 Otego is credited in the census with 1,148 inhabitants, Oneonta with 1,759 and Hilford with 3,025. It had at that time 13,931 acres of improved land, Oneonta had 9,571 acres and Milford had 13,069 acres. The assessed valuation of the real estate of Milford was $191,353; of its personal estate, $26,130. The real estate of Oneonta was $100,522; of its personal, $19,707. The real of Otego was $128,085; and its personal $14,073.

As the area of these three towns is now the same as when the above figures were made, I will follow them with the census report of 1890, sixty years later, and the assessed value of each as it appears in the supervisor's report of 1891. Milford in 1890 had a population of 2,051. Oneonta of 8,018 and Otego of 1,840. The real estate of Milford as assessed by its town assessors in 1891 was $903,080; its personal estate $56,700. The real estate of Oneonta as assessed by its town assessors was $1,660,225; its personal estate $195,575; the real estate of Otego as assessed by its town assessors was $491,100; its personal, $35,750. No words I could give could convey so well the comparative prosperity of the three towns since 1830.

In 1830, April 17th, by a legislative act Oneonta was formed from Milford, Otego and Huntsville. The name of Oneonta was given it at that time. In 1817, May 9th, it was by Esq. McDonald named Milfordville, and he was at that date appointed its first postmaster. Its change to Oneonta was entered on the books of the post office department at Washington March 13th, 1832. It has everywhere been known by the name of Oneonta since that date.

The street now known as River street was the first post road up the river, and the first post office was established in 1817, with Esq. James McDonald the first postmaster. The post office during his term of office was kept in his tavern, the building still standing on the northerly corner of Main and River streets. February 1st, 1829, Eliakim R. Ford was appointed post master, and the post office was removed to his store on the opposite side of River street. February 1st, 1830, Jacob Deitz was appointed postmaster, and the office was removed to his store standing where Mrs. L. L. Bundy's brick store now stands. October 21, 1831, E. R. Ford was again appointed, and the office again removed to his store on the south corner of Main and River streets. In 1832 the name of Oneonta was substituted for Milfordville, its former name, by the general post-office department, and March 13th E. R. Ford was appointed as postmaster under its new name of Oneonta, which position he retained until September 9th, 1835, when D. A. A. Ensworth was appointed. He held the office until July 3d, 1838, when Timothy Sabin was appointed his successor.

March 3d, 1841, William Angel was appointed, but his successor, William S. Fritts, was appointed December 24th of the same year—1841. He held office for about the term of two administrations, and was succeeded by Samuel J. Cook. Andrew G. Shaw was Cook's successor for two terms. Then Silas Sullivan was appointed. His successor was G. W. Reynolds and Reynold's successor was John Cope. Cary B. Pepper was his successor. Judge H. D. Nelson was then appointed, and soon afterward was followed by Harlow E. Bundy. Mr. Bundy's successor was the present incumbent, Charles F. Shelland. These last names since that of W. S. Fritts, I have written from memory, but think them correct as holding office in the order named. Oneonta has certainly been favored with able and gentlemanly post office officials for the past fifty years to my certain knowledge, having for that time received my mail at this office.

In continuing this history I shall be guided by no arbitrary rule in presenting acts and events, but shall record them in the order in which they come to my mind or notice; but I shall endeavor to give sufficient dates so that the reader will always be able to locate all occurrences at their true time, as near as practicable.

Early in Oneonta as well as all our county history, all the frame buildings erected were framed by what is known as the "scribe" or "cut-and-try" rule. In that way of framing all the timbers were put together and marked before attempting to raise them into a frame —a slow and laborious process.

MARCH 24, 1892
WITCHCRAFT AND OTHER SUPERSTITIONS

Most people in those times were firm believers in witches and leagues with the devil. Such persons were not all confined to a residence in Salem, Mass. An occurrence which could not readily be accounted for was very apt to be ascribed to witchcraft or works of the devil, or more often to both. In the first decade of this century the incident following is said to have occurred within the present limits of the village of Oneonta. I will relate it for the purpose of illustrating the force of superstition and the belief in witches and devils.

A man wanted a barn built. He was a prosperous farmer, and had in advance saved the money to pay for its erection. Just at that time a young man by the name of Keech came along, making inquiry for work as a carpenter. He was directed by Simeon Walling, with whom he stopped, to this farmer who wanted a barn. A bargain was soon made with Keech to hew the timber and frame and raise the barn.

He at once went to the woods to hew the timber, which he had ready in a short time for hauling to the location of the barn. When the farmer commenced to haul the timber the first stick drawn was the ridgepole, as Keech had told him he did not care which he hauled first nor whether he drew it faster than he could frame it, only have it on hand as fast as he framed it, so as not to delay his work. This somewhat surprised the farmer, as he had always supposed that the timber must be all on hand and men enough to lift and try it together as framed, commencing with the sills and thus progressing. He was still more surprised that Keech was going to frame it all alone; but as he had his farming on hand and it was already crowding him, Keech's accommodating and pleasing ways were very satisfactory, as he could more easily haul the timber a few sticks at a time.

Keech at once commenced framing the ridgepole. I will here explain that in all old fashioned timber frames, framed in the old way, a top stick called the ridgepole, hewed angling the form of the roof on its top side was nearly always used, and the rafters were morticed and pinned into the top timber. The next timber handy happened to be the plates and rafters, Keech framing it as hauled, and piling it up together out of his way. The posts and beams came next and last the sills. That a man was framing a building alone by some new plan and not trying and marking it, was soon noticed around among the people who by this date were becoming quite numerous in this vicinity. When raising day came everybody was on hand to see the wonderful frame go up. Nearly all, particularly the wise ones, had often and loudly prophesized a failure. They believed it to be an impossibility for a man to frame a barn alone and by having his timber in any place it chanced to be, and have his frame go together so as to form a building.

Keech found willing hands in all the host of men present to assist in raising. He went directly to each stick as wanted and only directed the side to be placed up and the ends wanted at the different points of compass, as the barn was to correspond with these directions. Each stick as carried to its place came together in position perfectly. The sills were soon in place with the floor sleepers all in. The bents came together in the same manner, every brace, mortice and drawbone just as it should be. When the bents were raised and the girts put in place all was found to be right, and also the plates and roof, even to the ridgepole.

What in the roof most surprised them was that he had framed a post under each end of the ridgepole, with a long brace under the pole into the posts at each end, and also long braces into these posts on their sides and into the beams below, upon which the posts stood and were mortised and pinned in. All this, which was a new device to them, also came together perfectly and greatly lessened the labor of raising the ridgepole and rafters, as they were usually raised, and also greatly strengthened the roof.

The frame up without any apparent mark or effort on the part of the carpenter was more than they could understand. The people got together in knots to look at and discuss the matter. Keech having completed his job picked up his tools, put them in his box, lifted the box to an ox cart and leisurely followed it to the house of his employer. The wise men immediately got together in council after his departure, and decided that a man who could do what he had accomplished must be in league with the devil, and a very dangerous man to have in any community.

A committee of three was appointed to call on the farmer and Keech, and to inform them that he must leave the place immediately. The discussion of this momentous matter had kept the council until after dark before the final decision was reached, and the notifying committee selected. After the final conclusion the men went home, and the committee proceeded at once to the house of the farmer to fulfill their part of the mission.

On arriving at the farmer's house one of the men called him out to inform him of the action and decision of his neighbors, and solicit his aid to carry it into effect. He told them that Keech was to all appearances a very fine man, a wonderful mechanic, and that the whole matter had been a marvel to him from the beginning; adding that Keech had told him that he could even have framed the building with the timber all round, as it grew in the woods, and but for putting on the covering the frame would be as strong as now.

This statement was the clincher. The committee now felt that the devil was, if possible, nearer than before. The carpenter must leave at once. The farmer plead for them to let the man remain until morning and then he would carry him away, but all in vain. A man in league with the devil could not be allowed to remain even until morning. Everybody was in danger. Public safety demanded his immediate departure.

They repaired to the house; Keech had gone up stairs to his bed, and was sleeping soundly. His dreams were not that he was to be warned out of town as a dangerous citizen, but rather he was rejoicing, even in his sleep, at his success in so surprising all these people by his skill. The farmer awoke him and informed him of the action of the people and the presence and orders of the committee. After a little consultation with the farmer, who offered him immediate transport, it was decided that it would best for all parties that he obey the command. He dressed himself and was soon with the farmer's son and another man, journeying eastward on the way from whence he came. After his departure fear left the minds of the people, and any dread of an immediate visitation of the devil departed.

Such in substance but not in exact words is the story as told me by that superior carpenter, Munson R. Watkins, nearly fifty years ago. I once happened to mention it while in company with J. R. L. Walling and was surprised to hear that it was literally true, and that this very carpenter, Keech, some ten or fifteen years thereafter, built a wagon house for his grandfather, Simeon Walling; and that he had heard the story related many times in his early life. He also related to me where the farmer lived and the barn stood, and that it was torn down since his remembrance that he had often seen it while it was standing.

So much for the belief in witches and aid of devils. But in my boyhood days belief in witches was common, and also of leagues with the devil. I have for hours heard an old man, a neighbor, tell of the acts of witches, and he himself was often, as he believed, under their influence. After he had left my mother or father was very careful to eradicate from the minds of their children any evil influence neighbor Bently's witch and devil stories might have produced on us. I was early educated not to believe in any such supernatural influences, and I can safely say the worst spirits I have ever yet seen the evil effects of in any community have been alcoholic spirits; and I am not certain but that kind had something to do with the men at Keech's barn-raising in influencing their foolish decision.

I have in a former chapter spoken of the various traditions in relation to the existence of valuable mines in this vicinity. I trust I may be pardoned for again alluding to this subject. In a recent conversation with Mrs. Ephraim Parish she told me the following story, which had been handed down in the family for two generations. In a former chapter it will be remembered I named Stoughton Alger as one of the pioneer settlers on what in part is now the Bingham farm. He resided on it on what is now the old turnpike, a short distance this side of where Mr. Murdock now resides, and carried on the blacksmith business, he being the first blacksmith located in this town.

One day while Mr. Alger was absent from his home a stranger called and asked for something to eat. It was readily given him. While eating his lunch he was noticed to carefully look over the children of the family. At the close of his meal, turning to the mother, he said: "If you will let that boy go with me on yon hill I will make him independently rich. I know where there is upon it a rich mine of gold, silver and lead. I will show it to that boy and give it to him."

The boy pointed out as the one selected was young Stoughton Alger jr., the father of

Mrs. Parish. He was then less than ten years of age. His mother refused to allow a boy so young to go so far into the woods in company with a stranger, but consented that an older brother might be substituted in his place. To this the stranger would not consent, but assured them that what he told them of the mine was true, and that he would reveal it to young Stoughton but no other; and that he would return before night and show them specimens of the ore which he would bring from that hill. Before dark he came back with a quantity of what he displayed as the different kinds of ore, glistening in its richness, and he then departed and they never saw him again.

The hill pointed out was the one now known as "rock hill," just northwest of Oneonta village, and was then upon the farm owned by the elder Alger. During his entire life thereafter, after arriving at manhood, Stoughton Alger jr. lived at the Plains, and I personally knew him for many years. At that time and when I first came to town, he owned and resided upon the farm now owned by his son-in-law, Ephraim Parish, at the Plains.

During the latter years of his life, when quite old and in his second childhood, he used sometimes to imagine himself poor and mourn that it was so, when such vast mineral wealth was his, and so near, but not in his possession. At other times he would imagine himself as immensely rich from the returns made him from the near-by development of these imaginary rich and valuable mines. I have repeated this story to demonstrate the force of such traditions, even upon strong-minded men, when they are thought by them to be true.

APRIL 7, 1892
TURNPIKES, CANALS, AND EARLY EFFORTS FOR A RAILWAY

In 1830 the population of Oneonta was given as 1,759 and in 1835 at 1,762, its gain being only three persons in five years. As I have before mentioned, the county of Otsego had a larger population by over five hundred in 1830 than in 1890. In 1780 it was 52,372 and in 1890 it was 50,861—a great loss considering the gain of the state and the United States. The reason of this decrease in our county must be ascribed to a variety of causes. But the main one was the opening of the canal and railroads, and thus creating a great thoroughfare to the prairie lands of the west. So great had become the emigration thither, that our county, among others, was not able to retain at home even its natural birthrate increase. The opening of the railroad lines helped to keep up a continued westward flow, and no means have yet been found to arrest it and retain in our rural counties even a moiety of their own natural increase.

Previous to 1822 Otsego county had five members in our state legislature. At that time the number was reduced to four and so continued until 1837, when we were reduced to three legislative members. In 1857 we were reduced to two, where we have since remained. We will no doubt soon fall to a number which will admit of no reduction, if we send as we have thus far done, whole men to that law-making council.

From 1812 to 1842 Otsego county alone constituted a congressional district, and sent its chosen member to that national legislative council.

Here we have a positive demonstration of the importance of easy and convenient means of transit. For lack of such for so many years the world around has continually increased in its numbers and political importance, while we have not been able to even hold our own. In fact, in our state we have lost three-fifths of our political power since 1822, and about two-thirds of our congressional strength during the same time. Rather a humiliating outlook for our county in this world of gain.

The citizens of Oneonta were never lacking in enterprise. Had their financial ability been at all in proportion to their ambition and foresight, Otsego county of to-day would be far in advance of its present position. Many important enterprises were projected in Oneonta, some of which were early carried into execution. Turnpikes and stage coaches were the popular sources of travel in 1830, and our people early awoke to the importance of such means of transportation.

In 1830, April 15th, a charter was obtained for the Charlotte turnpike, in which Jacob Deitz, William Angel and others of our citizens were named as directors. That enterprise was pushed to completion as rapidly as practicable. As early as 1835 the daily stage coaches were thundering through the streets of Oneonta on that then great thoroughfare.

In March, 1830, a law was passed in our state legislature instructing the canal board to order a survey "from Otsego lake to Tioga Point or Chemung river, to ascertain the feasibility of establishing by means of dams and slack-water, navigation between these points." A survey was made and a report of the same presented to the legislature but no further action was ever taken in the matter.

April 22d, 1831, a charter was granted for the Oneonta & Franklin turnpike, with William Angel and Jacob Deitz named among its directors. It was soon built and still continues in existence for four-fifths its former length. The mile nearest the village was abandoned by legislative action some years ago. The Charlotte turnpike has also ceased to exist except as a public highway, the toll bridge alone remaining.

April 26, 1832, a railroad charter from Cooperstown to Colliers was granted by the legislature. George Clark, Peter Collier and others were named as its directors. Peter Collier was a member of the legislature about that time, and no doubt his influence had much to do with the legislation of those sessions. Many important public measures were inaugurated by these legislatures.

April 25, 1832, a charter was granted for the Otsego & Schoharie railroad. Peter Collier, Eliakim R. Ford, Jesse Rose, John Westover and Leonard Caryl were named as its directors. Peter Collier, Jesse Rose and Jared Goodyear were also made members of its subscription committee.

April 25th, 1832, a law was passed chartering the Utica & Susquehanna Valley railroad. This road was to connect Utica with Unadilla. The Otsego and Schoharie railroad was to extend to Unadilla. Had these three roads been constructed, with their other contemplated connections, our country would early have received the benefit of railroad developing influence, in both its population and wealth-producing power.

May 18th, 1836, the Cherry Valley & Susquehanna Valley railroad was chartered. This line was to pass down the Cherry Valley creek to Milford, and then down the Susquehanna until it intersected the Erie. The same year another charter was obtained from Schoharie to the Susquehanna valley. Had these chartered roads been transferred to the soil at that early day, all the advantages of these later times would have been secured by them to our valley, and their benefits would have been enjoyed in part, at least, by the separation projecting them.

I have thus given a record of the legislative action secured by our people during the first six years of the decade of 1830. It will be noticed that each measure contemplated especial benefits to the people of this valley, and had they been followed to completion no locality would have received greater benefits therefrom than would our then young village of Oneonta. In paper railroads thus early we were not lacking. Although public improvements usually appear first in public minds and then on paper, their benefits tell but little for the public good until actual work in their construction is energetically commenced.

My first acquaintance with Oneonta commenced in the early spring of 1841. I came here in February and in March went to Colliersville, where I made my home until September. Since then I have been a citizen of Oneonta. At that time this was a lively, active business town, more active, I then thought, than was Binghamton.

The Timothy Sabin house was being built, and his store was being rebuilt and enlarged. The Solon Huntington store was building, and the E. R. Ford mansion was being completed. The late Charles Reynolds' house was being constructed, besides others unnecessary to name. The town was lively and business thriving. The next year the store where Cornell Brothers are was built, the house which George B. Baird removed, where his yard now is, the Newton I. Ford house, the Anthony White house and several others. During the fall of 1841 and winter of '42 my own residence was built. I, with my father's family, moved into it in May, 1842, and have resided there since. Among those who were here when I came was the late Dr. S. H. Case, Jacob Brown, Mr. Cutshaw, Ephraim Parish, who resided where Mr. Brown does, across the river, Huntington Parish, who then lived where his son George now does. Esek Blend, then a young man, lived up the creek near his present home, and William McCrum was then an apprentice to R. W. Hopkins. Some who were then boys still remain. Among whom are D. W. Ford, D. J. Yager, J. R. L. Walling and Dr. Meig's Case, although he was only four or five years old as I remember him.

Oneonta has ever had among its citizens many men of great ability and good practical common sense. Many of them have left undying evidence of their energy and perseverance for the public good. Among the men of good practical common sense, Timothy Sabin will ever be remembered. I must be pardoned for mentioning one of his sage pieces of advice.

About the time of the presidential campaign of 1848 Stephen Parish and myself had been invited to give a political talk at the William Richardson school house, up the Oneonta creek. Towards night on the day appointed we started in an open buggy to fill our engagement. As we passed Mr. Sabin's place of business he happened to see us, and running out, bare headed, he hailed us. On nearing the wagon he said, "Boys, do you know how to successfully talk politics?" "Not so well but we would be glad of your advice," I at once answered.

"Brag up your own party, brag up your own men, but don't say one word about your opponents," was his reply, at which he turned and hastily entered his store. For more than forty years I have closely observed the soundness of his advice, and have yet failed to note a single instance in which it was not the true policy to pursue. I will leave all further reminiscences for later papers.

From what I have before said of railroad charters in this section, it will be observed that citizens of Oneonta and its vicinity have always been alive on that subject. Having during the decade of 1830 been on the Central near Syracuse, while that road was being constructed, and at Owego while the Erie was driving the piles for that road, although afterwards the pile system was discarded and the earth road bed substituted, I had witnessed the life and activity given to these towns even by the construction and anticipation of railroads. It was but natural that I should imbibe some of their life and liking.

In the month of November, 1845, a call was issued for a railroad meeting at the Van Tuyl tavern, in the north end of the village of Richmondville. Jared Goodyear and myself attended it. Demosthenes Lawyer and myself were chosen secretaries. It was well attended, its call being for the purpose of considering the construction of a railroad from Schenectady to Binghamton. A route to Albany was thought at that time to be impracticable. Speeches were made and a subscription committee appointed to visit Boston and secure subscriptions, of which I was one. Before the meeting of the legislature petitions were circulated throughout this valley, and on the 13th day of May, 1846, a charter was granted for the "Schenectady & Susquehanna railroad to the Erie at Binghamton." We of this vicinity paid Col. W. W. Snow to attend at Albany and secure its passage, he having been a member of the legislature in 1844.

APRIL 14, 1892

THE ORGANIZATION OF THE ALBANY AND SUSQUEHANNA RAILROAD COMPANY

Jared Goodyear, Seth Chase, Leonard Caryl, Eliakim R. Ford and George H. Noble were among the directors of this early railway. The city of Schenectady failing at once to awaken to the importance of the enterprise, early in 1849 a survey was made by the efforts of Jedediah Miller and others through the valleys of the Normanskill and Bosakill creeks, and a feasible route to the city of Albany discovered.

Immediately meetings were held along the line of the road to awaken interest in the new project. At the particular request of Jedediah Miller of Lawyersville, made through Jared Goodyear, I made a call and circulated it for a meeting to be held in Oneonta, at which Mr. Miller, in his peculiar happy way, made one of his best railroad speeches. This meeting was represented from Windsor, Broome county, by Gideon Hotchkiss, and from Afton, Chenango county, by Henry Johnson, both of them men of influence and wealth. They were acquaintances of mine, and attended from an especial written request from me. Other meetings were held and the following year, April 2d, 1851, the organization of the Albany & Susquehanna railroad was perfected. Many of the citizens of Oneonta and vicinity are among its charter members.

It was my privilege to be one of them; and the stock I then subscribed I have ever held and still own as commemorative of that event. Many persons for themselves or others for them, have claimed the honor of inaugurating the Albany & Susquehanna railroad, but it will at once be seen that its conception was the work of a generation; and the most anyone can claim toward its progress is their individual favorable aid towards its final organization and completion. Its later start may be said to have originated in the village of Richmondville, and the only change since made in its line from its first charter was from Quaker Street to Albany, instead of Schenectady, as in the one of 1846.

The new company was formed under the general railroad law passed April 24th, 1850, instead of by special legislative enactment. The articles of association contain 323 stockholders' names, and represent 1,411 shares of stock. George W. Chase of Maryland, Otsego county, Joel B. Nott of Albany county and Robert H. Pruyn of the city of Albany made the affidavits of proof, which were duly certified by A. G. Johnson, deputy secretary of state. Its date is April 19, 1851.

Edward C. Delevan was made its first president, and its first directors were William V. Many, Robert H. Pruyn, Franklin Townsend, Charles Van Benthuysen, Erastus Corning jr. of the city of Albany, Joel P. Nott of the town of Guilderland, Charles Courter of Cobleskill, George W. Chase of Maryland, Samuel B. Beach of Oneonta, Arnold B. Watson of Unadilla, Richard W. Juliand of Bainbridge and Gideon Hotchkiss of Windsor.

The company immediately organized and began making the arrangements to forward the work.

March 27th, 1852, a law was passed allowing the "President and trustees of the village of Binghamton to take stock in the Albany & Susquehanna railroad" to the amount of $50,000.

April 10th, 1852, an act was passed to authorize the city of Albany to make a loan to the Albany & Susquehanna railroad company to the amount of $1,000,000. The terms of this loan were that the bonds issued by the city were to bear six per cent interest, to be paid semi-annually and to run for thirty years; but the railroad company was to pay seven per cent interest, which one per cent of interest and the premium the bonds brought at their sale, was to form a sinking fund for the final redemption of the bonds. It was found hard work for the company to advance fast enough to comply with the terms demanded by the forty-seventh section of the general railroad act, and in the winter of 1853 they made application to the legislature and got an extension on time for one year. This act was passed March 23d, 1853.

In the early summer of 1853 the company let the contract to a firm known by the name of Morris, Miller, Baker & Co., who themselves subscribed $60,000 dollars of its stock and paid in their ten per cent, and commenced work on several points between the Worcester summit and Albany. About the time the work was fairly under way the notable Schuyler fraud in New York City came to light. Railroad stocks and bonds sunk in value, and the company was compelled to cease work and abandon its contracts.

The failure of these contractors had a demoralizing influence upon all the hasty element among the stock holders of the road and gave its opponents, who were no insignificant number, an opportunity to do their best for its defeat. There immediately arose to the surface a large number opposed to the construction of the road. At its start it mostly came from localities which had grown to prominence and extra prosperity by the very improvements in their various localities which they were opposing in ours. Law suits were commenced by its enemies or forced upon its friends, which in either case caused delay, loss and discouragement, particularly to the faint hearted and hasty.

The first suit decided was that of several stockholders who combined their interests and refused to pay the called for installments of stock, and hoped to thus destroy the company. These suits were commenced in September, 1853, and by agreement, were finally referred to Judge Willard as sole referee. Every conceivable wrong, even to that which would constitute deliberate fraud, was charged against the directors of the company, particularly against those who had been prominently officious in obtaining such stock subscriptions. Among them our townsman and able director, E. R. Ford, came in for his full share of such abuse. E. R. Ford had been elected director in place of Mr. Beach. The decision was published May 23d, 1854, and the company was triumphant, beating on every count in the complaints. Thus from these and other causes the prosecution of the work was delayed. Its friends continued their efforts with untiring industry, and among them all, none possessed more ardent zeal or labored more indefatigably in the work than did its numerous friends in the Susquehanna valley.

The efforts of the friends of the Albany and Susquehanna railroad did not all relax with fleeting time. Every passing month continued to demonstrate more fully its necessity to the people along its line. In an undertaking for accomplishing a compromise with its old contractors, so great was the confidence of Jared Goodyear in the justice of the case and the necessity for the road, that he voluntarily stepped to the aid of the company as its bondsman, qualifying to $70,000 in value in real estate, an act no other man upon its entire line could at that time have done.

In the meantime the friends of the road had conceived a plan for putting in force a system by which the towns along the line and contiguous to the road might take stock in to the amount of $1,000,000, pledging their corporate responsibility to secure the same. Petitions were numerously signed and presented to the legislature of 1856, asking for the passage of a law allowing the towns along the line of the road to issue their bonds for a specified amount, and to receive therefor certificates of stock for a like sum.

So strong was the pressure brought to bear by the friends of the road, that on the 31st of March such law was passed; but its terms demanded the written consent of two-thirds of the tax payers and two-thirds of the property to be thus consented to, as shown upon the last assessment roll of each town. The law and an address by the directors of the company was immediately published and scattered among the people of the towns, for their examination. In it the estimated cost of the road was made plain, and its benefits to the real estate along its line clearly and fairly set forth. This was soon followed by a delegation of the directors, accompanied by their president, E. P. Prentice, who visited the various towns and held public meetings, and by their arguments and figures demonstrated to the people the importance of such aid and its risk and cost to them if they never received a single dollar back for the money so paid, except in the benefits of the road.

The writer was invited to attend and take part in these discussions, which he did, and was almost invariably put forward to make the first speech. He always based his arguments upon the idea that the gain to the towns would far more than compensate them for their outlay if the road was built, even if the stock should prove of no value; but that he considered the road so important and so near a trunk line road east and west, he felt sure the stock would be of par value soon after the road was completed, and that if such should be the case, the towns risked nothing except the interest they would pay before the stock reached such value. Figures based on safe estimates were given to sustain such position. It has been a great source of satisfaction that he has lived to see all of his predictions prove even more true than he had dared to hope.

Upon a canvass it was found that in some towns it would be an impossibility to obtain a two thirds consent, as in some of them a few persons—and those our enemies—held more than one-third of the property on the rolls. Efforts were made in all the towns to obtain the consents, but as I recollect Oneonta was the only town in Otsego county in which two-thirds of the tax payers were found willing to sign such consent.

The following winter, 1857, an effort was made to amend the law so that a majority consent of the taxpayers representing a majority of property on the roll might decide the matter. This effort aroused anew and with increased vigor all the elements of opposition to the railroad. Cobleskill, in Schoharie county, had given its consent. A suit was brought by Richard J. Grant against Charles Courter, a commissioner of that town, to test the constitutionality of the law, the plaintiff claiming the law to be unconstitutional. It was tried before Presiding Judge Wm. B. Wright. Wm. J. Hadley was counsel for the plaintiff and John K. Porter for the defendant. In this, as in all previous suits, the railroad company was successful.

APRIL 21, 1892

THE STRUGGLE FOR THE RAILROAD (PART 1)

The same year a decision was made by Justice D. Wright, which equally affected the Albany & Susquehanna road as well and the one in which the suit was brought, as it virtually decided the legality of the Albany loan. In 1854 a law was passed allowing the city of Albany to aid by its bonds the Albany Northern railroad company, and in May, the same year, the city had issued to such company $3,000,000 of such city bonds. This action was brought by John Benson and others to restrain the city officials from paying the interest on these bonds. The decision of Justice Wright was lengthy and exhaustive, and in this case the defendants won and the legality of the loan was sustained.

At the session of the legislature of 1857 the friends and directors of the A. & S. railroad petitioned the legislature to amend the law of 1856, allowing the consent of the towns to take stock in the road, changing it to a majority instead of a two-thirds consent. Its opposition was determined and spirited, but it was passed and became a law April 14, 1857. At the election of officers of the company the fall previous, Richard Franchot had been chosen president of the company and C. W. Wentz its chief engineer. During the following summer the work of obtaining the vote of the towns was vigorously pushed and the consent of most of those in Otsego county obtained to subscribe to the stock of the company. The work on the road had now actually commenced to a very limited extent.

The engineers' corps had been in part organized, and energetic work was being vigorously prepared for. Joseph H. Ramsey had the past year been added to the corps of inspectors, and among the friends of the road the determination to persevere to its completion had never been stronger or more decisive. I had devoted most of my time during the entire season to obtaining the consent of the towns to the taking of the stock of the road.

The enemies had been equally active. At the opening of the session of 1858 the legislature was literally flooded with petitions for the repeal of the law, allowing the towns to take stock in the road. Should that law be allowed to remain, its enemies saw impending defeat. With it, and the Albany loan law repealed, they knew the Albany & Susquehanna railroad must die. They spared no efforts to obtain the repeal of the town law, hoping also to obtain a repeal of the Albany loan.

The senate had the matter in charge. The committee on railroads was composed of Messrs. Brandreth, Darling and Hubbell, with Dr. Brandreth as its chairman. The day for a public hearing was set for February 24, 1858. The Susquehanna directors sent me as their only representative from this valley. I went by stage from Oneonta. The day was very cold, but the stage ran all the way on wheels. The coach was crowded.

From Schoharie a majority of the passengers were men from that county who were bent on the repeal of the law, and were on their way to Albany for that pose. I rode all the way in silence, listening to the talk of these anti railroad cranks. It required quite an exercise of will power to say nothing in defense of our road, but I said nothing. It was late when we arrived in Albany, and I stopped at the American hotel, my usual stopping place in those days.

At precisely 10 a.m. the next morning the committee convened in the old senate committee room, directly off the senate chamber in the old capitol building. The citizens of Albany were many of them already lukewarm in the matter of the road, and many others were its enemies. Erastus Corning was then their representative in congress, and he had been summoned home to aid in the defense of the measure as it was by these anti-railroad men understood; but I had never heard of his expressing himself either for or against it.

Schoharie county was liberally represented among its enemies, Harmon Becker and others taking teams and loads down to attend the committee sessions. A man and team from Lawyersville carried Jedediah Miller and General Lawyer, and I think Mr. Ramsey, the three only friends of the road, as I now remember, who were present from that county. At Mr. Goodyear's special request, General S. S. Burnside of Worcester had also driven to Albany to attend the session. Mr. Martin, cashier of the National bank of Albany, was the chosen champion before the committee for these railroad opponents. His speech occupied the whole session of the committee, and lasted until nearly night.

Immediately after the adjournment of the committee the friends of the road held a meeting and for some reason I could never fathom, chose me as their representative to present their side to the committee at its session on the morrow. I had the evening and night to prepare for the contest. I at once repaired to the library and procured a railroad engineer's state map and figures of census statistics which I wanted for use. I transferred the figures to paper, and as my memory was good they were thus fastened in my mind.

At the appointed time in the morning I appeared in the committee room and found them already convened and in readiness. My old friend, Jedediah Miller, who had accompanied me from the hotel to the committee room, introduced me as a farmer living near the center of the line of the contemplated railroad, and as the man who was to answer the arguments made before them the day previous. At the start but a moderate number were present beside the committee and the open friends and enemies of the enterprise.

I commenced my talk by opening the railroad map and pointing out upon it my place of residence, the area of country without a railroad, the distance to Deposit and to Fort Plain, our nearest points to reach a railroad, and then commenced to answer the objections to our road made by Mr. Martin. By that time the members of the senate and house were fast coming to the capitol, and it was noised among them that a country farmer was making an argument before the senate railroad committee.

The interest in the matter was such that these members and others filled every available space, and when after a talk of two or three hours I came to look around, nothing but a sea of heads and faces was visible. The committee room and its adjoining room were crowded to their utmost. After I closed I turned and crowded my way to a rear window and seated myself therein. Immediately Dr. Brandeth pressed his way through the crowd, at the same time saying, "I must shake hands with that farmer and congratulate him, for I myself have been through his valley and know the truth of every word he uttered." He heartily shook my hand, and congratulated me upon my success. The simple truth proved to be that I had converted most of my hearers to my views.

I cannot better convey an idea of the results of the meeting than to quote a letter which I found in THE ONEONTA HERALD when I arrived home. I knew nothing of its having been written. It read as follows:

ALBANY, February 25, 1858.

EDITOR HERALD:—The railroad committee of the senate had yesterday under consideration the petitions to repeal the law authorizing town subscriptions to the Albany & Susquehanna railroad.

Mr. Martin of Albany made the opening speech for the petitioners. Mr. Martin was raised in Schoharie county; but having become the cashier of the National bank he had the arrogance to say that the citizens of Otsego and Schoharie counties were "raising the devil in getting schools and railroads, and that the counties of Delaware, Otsego and Schoharie did not make butter enough to grease the wheels.

This forenoon H. Baker esq. of your town made one of the cleanest and most practical speeches ever heard, and his positions were demonstrated by facts and figures. Dr. Brandeth, one of the committee, pronounced his as clear and convincing statements; and as a farmer Mr. Baker has done credit to his fellow farmers and to himself. He received the congratulations of all the friends of the road, and the opponents of the measure writhed and winced under his forcible arguments. The committee held another session this evening. The friends of the road have nothing to fear, as far as the repeal of the law is concerned. With energy and perseverance, the road will be built.

Yours etc.,
S. S. BURNSIDE.

What I have written in these pages of a nature personal to myself must not be construed as being done for egotistical motives, for it is not. I could write no history of the Albany & Susquehanna railroad and leave myself out. For between the years of 1855 and 1869 I spent fully ten years of the hardest work of my life in the forwarding of that enterprise. I did it too, at a lower compensation for the work performed than I had at any previous time since I was nineteen years old. I make this statement to correct an erroneous impression that I made considerable money out of the construction of the A. & S. railroad, for such was not the case. The highest wages ever paid me previous to the cars reaching Oneonta was three dollars per day for myself and one dollar for my team, and my expenses while on the road. Except while my team was hauling material for the trestles I was paid two dollars per day for the day's labor at such work performed by them. Sixteen hours labor every twenty-four would not more than represent the average hours labor actually performed, for which I was paid during the progress of the road until it reached Oneonta.

During these years I made no money by using my knowledge in advance of the location of depots or by any other ways of speculating, or on woodlands purchased for ties or timber, ever feeling it my duty to save every dollar I could in proper legitimate way for the benefit of the railroad company. I had promised the people along the line that if we used their money they should have the road. That promise was a daily goad to action to do the most and best possible in my power to redeem it. I made every dollar count to its uttermost to push the road forward, so as to make good my word. No man could feel a greater relief than I did when it was fulfilled.

After the railroad was in operation to Oneonta, I resolved to quit it and engage in other business. But after a few weeks travel and rest I was induced to again take hold of the work and assist in reaching Unadilla. For the work performed west of Oneonta I was paid good wages.

The following spring I engaged in bridge building for the public and in covering railroad bridges. During that year I actually cleared more money than during all the previous years while engaged in pushing forward the railroad, and my labor was much less exhaustive. In the fall of the following year, 1867, the company finding they were not likely to reach Harpursville in the time required to obtain the state aid then due, again sought my help. I took the management of the work in hand, and some days before New Year's the track was ready for the cars to that station. For this work I was liberally paid. To accomplish the task required about two months of continued, excessive push. It was always a source of satisfaction to me to accomplish a job promptly on time. It has almost invariably been my fortune to do it. I suppose it is attributable to the fact that I was born on Friday, the luckiest of all days.

APRIL 28, 1892

THE STRUGGLE FOR THE RAILROAD (PART 2)

When I switched off from the subject of the repeal of the law of 1857 to my personal efforts before the senate committee I did it to keep in connection certain things which I thought best to say. I will now return to the finding of the committee.

Its chairman, Dr. Brandreth, and his associate, Mr. Darling, made a strong report against its repeal. Mr. Hubbell made a minority report in favor of repeal. The majority report was sustained and the law was saved.

During this contest I began to fear that the enemies of the road, even among its stockholders, were as numerous as were its friends; and at once set myself to learn the facts. I, of course, personally knew many of them, and by an examination of petitioners' names on the repeal papers, I learned enough to satisfy myself that some course must be early adopted to counteract such adverse influence. If not, at the officer election their combined strength might wind the company up.

Always knowing that one's plans had better be matured in his own mind and kept to himself, I acted upon that system. In the meantime, I learned as far as possible who were our enemies and who were our reliable friends in our county. I then set to work to carry into execution the measures I had concluded best to adopt. The consent of most of the eastern towns in our county had the previous year been nearly perfected. Those still remaining were immediately finished and the proofs made and filed as required by the law. In May, 1858, the county judge appointed the town railroad commissioners. My appointment was dated May 5th, and Carlton Emmons and Stephen Parrish were my associates for Oneonta. The date of the report of the senate committee upon the subject of the repeal was dated March 17th and the town commissioners appointed the May following.

After they had been appointed for the towns of Oneonta, Milford, Maryland, Worcester, Decatur and Westford, I obtained a list of their names and in the forepart of July I called a meeting of them by writing each and inviting them to meet at Oneonta the 13th day of July, 1858. Nearly all the commissioners responded to my invitation and were present. We met in the ballroom of the Susquehanna house. I called the meeting to order and stated to them that I had made the call especially for the purpose of suggesting the propriety of forming ourselves into an organization for the express purpose of enabling us to act in concert in all matters pertaining to the interests of the railroad, and explaining to them the probable future strength of such commissioners upon future elections of directors, etc.

All at once assented to the wisdom of the proposition, and I was elected the president of such association and Mr. E. R. Thurber of Worcester its secretary. Power was given me to call the members together at any time when I thought the interest of the railroad demanded such a meeting. I, however, disclosed nothing of my thoughts of the use for which I then was confident the first call would be made, but resolved to be in readiness for actions in any emergency.

Early the following November Senator Ramsey came to Oneonta by stage, called on me and wished me to take him to Morris the following day. We started early in the morning. When nearing where the Morris road leaves the Otego creek valley, he asked me, "is there a direct road from Laurens to Morris?" I answered in the affirmative. "Then we will go by Laurens," he said, and I continued up the valley. When nearing Laurens I asked him "Where shall I drive?" Being answered, I soon hauled up before their store door, but the parties were not in town.

We then started on our way to Morris. As we were passing the old cotton manufactory he said to me, "I may as well tell you my business. I have learned that our enemies out number our friends among the stockholders, and I fear at our approaching officer election they will combine their forces and wind us up."

My reply was, "I have known their strength for months past and have been preparing for it, and have my plan matured." "What is it?" was his eager enquiry. I explained to him that the six towns above named should subscribe for the amount of stock for which the towns had signed the consent. And that the railroad company accept their bonds for the ten per cent and bind such subscriptions as so much cash. Then I assured him the proxies of such town commissioners for over $300,000 would give our enemies a dead cold lay out.

"Can it be done?" was his quick enquiry. My reply was "It can," and explained our organization and its aims. "Then we will drive to New Lisbon, at Hard & Peck's, for dinner, as I want to call on them." We went to Hard & Peck's store, took dinner with Mr. Hard, had a very pleasant visit and returned to Oneonta before night.

I immediately issued a call for a meeting of the railroad commissioners of the six towns to meet at Roseville, November 25th, 1858, asking at least two of the commissioners to be sure and be present as important business would come before them, and that unity of action in them all would be imperative. I gave time to be sure of all receiving my letter.

At the appointed time we met at the hotel of Andrew Dunham, each town being duly represented. Then and there in secret session was by us transacted, business which forever quieted the hopes of the enemies of the A. & S. railroad, so far as winding it up was concerned.

After organizing, with Mr. Thurber as secretary, I stated the object of the call, and caused to be offered a resolution that the town railroad commissioners immediately subscribe for the amount of stock for which the towns had given their consent and sign the ten per cent bonds to pay our first installment and bind our subscription. It was unanimously carried.

I then explained that two or more new directors were to be elected and suggested that we here name them. Immediately my name was offered as one. I at once arose and asked the mover to withdraw it, and asked the privilege of naming Jared Goodyear of Milford and Peter Cagger of Albany as the two new directors, explaining the reasons for their addition to the board. That was also carried.

I then stated my plan for state aid, and Mr. Goodyear was instructed to bring the matter before the new board of directors, and if approved by them to have it carried into effect. This was also approved. We then prepared our proxies for carrying out our plans, and after arranging for our immediate subscriptions, adjourned. Andrew H. Platt of Maryland is the only one of the town commissioners, I remember as now living who was present. Stephen Parish of this village went up with me. I had, previous to the first day of November, already secured the signature of over ten per cent of our town bonds, myself afterward signing the coupons. I personally saw that the subscriptions were made and the bonds duly forwarded to the office at Albany.

As arranged, Mr. Goodyear with our proxies attended the directors' meeting, the men we named were elected, and our idea of the state aid fully approved. I had, in 1857, when Mr. Ramsey was in the senate, written him, and also Mr. Peck, a friend from Broome county, in the assembly, my views upon the matter. Mr. Ramsey in his reply to me under date of January 28th, 1857, thus answers my letter: "Your suggestion is a very good one, but the constitution expressly forbids the loan of the credit of the state. We probably have no hope of obtaining aid from the public except in the manner we have been endeavoring to." He alludes to the town bonds, and follows by stating his efforts to establish their constitutionality.

Although I had by letters in the newspapers tried to create interest in state aid, I did not succeed until after the election of directors as above described. But when the matter was thus brought out, Mr. Ramsey adopted and approved the measure, and was indefatigable in his efforts for its success.

The matter was brought before the incoming legislature, and in April, 1859, a law was passed granting $200,000 to aid in constructing the road. Two days after its passage, April 16th, it was killed by Governor E. D. Morgan's veto.

It was unexpected and came with deadening effect, as he was thought to be friendly to the enterprise. It was indignantly received all along the line. Meetings were held in all the villages, and expressions of disappointment were universal. A large meeting was held at the hotel of John M. Watkins in Oneonta, April 23d. Dr. Samuel H. Case called the meeting to order, and after some very appropriate remarks by him, Turner McCall esq., was made chairman of the meeting and Jacob C. Deitz its secretary. On motion of L. L. Bundy esq., a committee of five were appointed by the chair to draft resolutions expressive of the sense of such meeting. L. L. Bundy, Andrew G. Shaw, Nelson Ballard, Samuel H. Case and Munson R. Watkins were appointed such committee.

NOTE: In the first paragraph of last week's article $3,000,000 should have been $300,000, and in the third, Joseph H. Ramsey, *inspector*, should have read *director*.

MAY 5, 1892

THE STRUGGLE FOR THE RAILROAD (PART 3)

After the appointment of the committee on resolutions, at the meeting mentioned in last week's HERALD, H. Baker was called upon for a speech, a synopsis of which, two and one-half columns in length, appeared in the next issue of THE HERALD. Speeches were also made by L. L. Bundy, S. H. Case, Addison J. Nowlen and Turner McCall esq.

At the next session of the legislature a bill was passed which at the completion of thirty miles was to give the railroad company three hundred thousand dollars, at the completion of another thirty miles $200,000, and another thirty $200,000 more, and at reaching Binghamton the balance of $1,000,000, as provided for in said bill. This was passed in April, 1860. It was immediately vetoed by Governor Morgan.

He was again nominated for governor, but the friends of the railroad laid him on the shelf and elected Horatio Seymour in his stead.

April 3d, 1863 an act was passed granting from the state $250,000 when the Albany & Susquehanna railroad shall have been completed to Cobleskill, $250,000 more when completed to Oneonta. The time for such completion was stated in the law. When it was found to be impossible to reach Oneonta by the time named, on March 18th, 1865, the time was extended one year. March 27th, 1865 an act was passed granting $250,000 if Colesville was reached in compliance with certain provisions in the law. This was the last act granting state aid to the railroad making the sum received from the state $750,000. No doubt had Governor Morgan signed instead of vetoing the second bill passed while he was in office, the road would have been completed to Binghamton three years earlier than it was, and at a saving to the company of more than the entire sum named in such law, and the public a gain of a vastly larger sum. The effect of these vetoes was to greatly delay the work in its progress, as money was the all important factor in its prosecution.

I had been appointed land agent for the obtaining the right of way from the line of Schoharie county westward, as well as general agent in all matters towards the forwarding of the work, purchasing of tie materials, etc. The cost of right of way was comparatively light, of lumber for fences and of ties reasonable. Ties from Oneonta east to Central Bridge cost about 25 cents each, from Oneonta to Bainbridge about 32 cents and from there to Binghamton about 35 cents each.

The progress of the railroad had been very slow, while the labor performed by its friends had been immense. It had taken from 1851 to 1865 to get the iron laid to Oneonta. It was opened to Otego, January 23d, 1866, and to Unadilla March 19th, 1866, to Sidney October 23d, the same year.

Tracklaying was resumed in the summer of 1867 and by the middle of October 1867 the cars were running to Afton.

November 1st I took charge of the work between Afton and Colesville by request of the company to push the work to completion by January 1st. There was a ravine at Reid, about three miles west of Afton, of 300 feet in length, to be trestled, three heavy cuts to be excavated and bridge over the road and a creek at Nineveh to be erected. The earth work and bridge were under contract and the work progressing.

I immediately purchased timber for the trestle, made the plans and drafts and on the 6th had the work in progress; I also put new life into the grading contractors. On the 8th Messrs. Wentz and Ramsey came to the work and wanted me to erect and engine house and blacksmith shop at Colesville, two section houses at Nineveh and one at Afton, and a water tank building between Afton and Nineveh, all of which were to be done before the end of the year, except the water tank building. In addition I was to provide the ties and telegraph poles from Afton to Colesville. All of this was completed and the first train ran over the road the Christmas day preceding the new year of 1868. It required the making of long days' work and a continued vigilance to keep all in motion and accomplish so much in so short a space of time. During the time I also attended to the supervision of our lime and cement works at Howe's Cave, and the counting and paying for ties all along the line of the road eastward from the tunnel to Central Bridge. One who has never had a trial does not know what push a live man can put into a host of others when circumstances demand it. I had not been on hand a week before the contractors were having a large amount more of work done by the same force, and new life and hope was diffused into all the work. Words of encouragement and praise worked wonders, and the weather was favorable, there being no snow until after New Years to impede our work.

At the completion of the work to this place I ceased my labor for the railroad company, except the counting of ties and occasionally doing some other desired business like settling for damages and other like work. During all these years I had practiced when railroad company money was lacking to use my own so as to keep the credit of the company in my department always at par. No man was ever allowed to wait for his pay for labor, for materials or land damages beyond the time agreed. Sometimes the company would be several thousand dollars in arrears to me for such advances. I noticed that at a figuring up with Treasurer Phelps on March 20th, 1866, there was due me from the company the sum of $8,905.17. This maintaining of first class credit by promptness is of inestimable value for success in all business transactions; but particularly in railroad building.

By great effort on the part of the directors of the road it was finally completed so that the grand opening to Binghamton was celebrated the 12th day of January, 1869. During these eighteen years intervening between the organization of the A. & S. railroad company great and important changes had taken place in our country. The travel and transport from east to west and west to east had increased to large dimensions. It was at once seen that this road was in a way to form not only a trunk line for such transit, but also a local road of superior importance.

That it was to be an important factor in the business of the country was at once manifest. In a moment the managers of the Erie thought it a prize of too much importance to be left ungobbled. And effort to such end was made. To tell its story would require many pages, more than I have already consumed thus far in its history. I have at my disposal the material to give a full account of the whole affair. If I should think best to give its details, I will do so in an entirely separate chapter or series of them. After passing through that memorable portion of its history, and having for a while been under the management and direction of the governor of the state, in February, 1870, a lease of it was made for 99 years to the Delaware & Hudson Canal company. By this arrangement all the stock owners were made sure of a good interest on their stock, and occupants of the road of a valuable franchise and possession.

For more than twenty years under such management has the importance of the enterprise to the public been demonstrated, as well as the able and wise management of those having its control.

I have followed up the construction of this road only in this cursory manner. If a full history of it is to be given I will have to return, and in a more particular manner describe the various labors and trials which I passed through before reaching Oneonta.

In 1857, as I have before stated, Richard Franchot was chosen its president, and W. L. M. Phelps its secretary and treasurer. When Mr. Franchot was elected to congress, Mr. E. P. Prentice was again chosen as president of the company.

In the summer of 1863 the road was opened to Central Bridge or rather to the easterly side of the Schoharie creek, to where Schoharie Junction now is. The opening was a great day. Many from along the line went to attend the event. The train which brought the excursionists also brought a carload of freight in a new box car, the first one owned by the company, for a Mr. Wetsell; and I was designated by the president of the company to fix the price and receive the pay for the freight. So I suppose I collected and paid into the treasury the first freight money received by the company. Certainly the first received at that station. Many persons in Oneonta will remember Mr. Wetsell, as he was express agent here for a year or two after the road reached this place.

During the following year the road was pushed through to Cobleskill. It was then that the company received the first installment of state aid. During the month of May, 1864, Mr. Goodyear and myself purchased a tract of land of Mrs. Sawyer, near where the heavy ravines were in the town of Richmondville. I at once let the job of cutting the hemlock trees and peeling the bark as soon as it could be done. Mr. Ramsey, Mr. Goodyear and myself had previously counseled upon the matter and concluded it best to trestle those deep fills, well knowing it to be impossible to reach Oneonta by the time named in the state aid law without trestling, even if money were plenty, because of the amount of materials needed to make the fills, and none suitable near at hand. Money was also lacking for such work.

MAY 12, 1892

THE STRUGGLE FOR THE RAILROAD (PART 4)

I was requested by Mr. Ramsey to attend the directors' meeting July 1, 1864, and advocate before the board the idea of trestling the ravines. I had prepared in advance of such meeting to give a fair demonstration of the gain in cost and in time by such trestling, over the attempt to fill with the material within reach.

After hearing my views a resolution was offered to trestle a part of them, leaving the amount to be done to the judgment of Mr. Wentz, the chief engineer. While the matter was being discussed I retired from the directors' room to the engineer's room. The matter of trestling was strongly opposed by the president, Mr. Prentice, and one director, they opposing trestling to the best of their ability. After much discussion by them the vote was taken and the resolution strongly carried.

For reasons I will not now explain, I was confident that the interest of the railroad would be advanced if some other man was acting as its president. I was extremely anxious for the resignation of Mr. Prentice. Seeing the effect of the trestling resolution upon him I resolved to add another straw, hoping it might produce the desired result.

Early in the previous month of May, while purchasing ties and right of way in Nineveh I found that a contractor named Devereaux had failed and absconded, leaving his men unpaid. Of course I knew that the company was liable for thirty days for such unpaid labor. Mr. Hobbs, as attorney for the men, had already made bills for labor for the sum of about $1,600 and had presented them to William Wentz of Binghamton. I at once called on Mr. Hobbs and learned that quite a portion of such bills were in part paid in groceries out of Mr. Devereaux's grocery store, but as he "could not learn the amount so paid, he had made them out for the work performed during the last thirty days and thus presented the claim to Mr. Wentz , the resident engineer at Binghamton. He assured me at the same time that if I could manage to obtain the books he would withdraw the bills sent in and send in the true sum due each man after deducting the amounts the men had received. I managed to find the key to the store and we corrected the bills and found the sum actually due the men less than $600, instead of $1,600 as presented.

As the time was too short to return the bills to Wm. Wentz at Binghamton, I took them and promised to serve them upon Chief Engineer Wentz at Albany within the time required to make good their claim. I at the same time promised Mr. Hobbs that I would meet him at Unadilla on the 24th of the month and pay him the money due the men. I must here state that Mr. Hobbs was a highly honorable and honest man.

On reaching Oneonta I found Mr. Wentz and Mr. Ramsey both at Mr. Ford's. I served the papers and informed them what I had done. All approved and commended my action, and they promised to send me the money in time to meet my promise to Lawyer Hobbs, which was but three days ahead. On the 23d Mr. Ramsey wrote me a letter from which I make the following extract, "Mr. Prentice is opposed to paying them. So you see we have got to take the responsibility and see the men paid, and rely upon the justice of the directors in the matter. I think you had better raise the money and pay them. It is possible Mr. Prentice may change his mind in relation to the matter, if he does I will write you."

Before this came to hand I had used my own money as agreed. I was soon afterwards informed that when Mr. Prentice learned that I had paid those men, his remark was "Then he shall lose it." Be that as it may, I had no fear of losing my pay for I well knew I had saved money for the company by the transaction, and had besides done what was right by the men. I was actuated in my wish for the resignation purely for the good of the railroad company and its success, but resolved to use this as the lever to accomplish the desired end.

As soon as the trestle resolution had been carried a director came to me and informed me of the result. I asked him to offer a resolution that the money I had advanced to pay the Devereaux men be credited to me on the books of the company and to draw interest from the time of its payment by me. He returned to the directors' room and offered such resolution and it was carried with no objection except that of Mr. Prentice.

It had the desired result. The president arose, walked into the room where I was, seated himself at the opposite side of the table from where I sat, and wrote his resignation and returned to the directors' room and presented it to the board. I glanced at his pen as he wrote and was confident that it was his resignation. In a moment Mr. Courter came into the room much excited and said, "Oh, Baker, why did you not leave this Devereaux matter till some future time? It has so maddened Mr. Prentice that he has resigned."

"Has it?" said I, "then you move to have his resignation laid on the table for future consideration." He returned and did so or caused it to be done, and thus the matter rested. Mr. Goodyear being the vice president he at once commenced to fill the position. It was arranged that Mr. Wentz should meet me at Richmondville the 6th and we would perfect the arrangements about the trestles. I presented a plan for them; he adopted it except he threw out two long braces I had arranged for in each bent, he being confident they would be abundantly strong with those two sticks omitted in each bent.

The grading of the road bed through the town of Richmondville east of the depot had been finished, leaving these four ravines aggregating something over 1,600 lineal feet to be filled. Each end of each ravine had been filled as fast as the material would reach, leaving the slopes of an angle of about forty-five degrees. I had to trestle down these slopes and across the ravine and up the opposite slope of each one. The shallowest ravine was 45 feet deep and the deepest 72 feet, the remaining two about 65 feet each.

Mr. Goodyear and myself arranged that the railroad company should have the land

and all the material cut from it at just its cost price, which we had purchased for the purpose of these trestles, and also other purchases we had before made for supplying ties.

I got the materials, tools and men together and made a beginning on the trestle known as the Lawyer trestle the 11th of July, 1864. I for the first two weeks kept a force of men still peeling hemlock trees. I had previously had 400 peeled but was confident that I would need the lumber of very many more and kept up the work as long as the bark would peel.

I bargained with Alonzo Mumford of Portlandville and Joseph Richards of Oneonta to work as foremen on the work, both able, trusty men and superior mechanics. Mr. Mumford remained with me through the entire work. Mr. Richards having work elsewhere remained with me but about seven weeks. When he left I filled his place with William Decker of Richmondville.

It was the business of Mr. Mumford and his assistant to layout the framing of all the timber and seeing to the work being perfectly done. I paid Mumford three dollars per day, other mechanics from two to two fifty and laborers at other work from one fifty to two dollars according to their worth. I had a splendid lot of men, suited exactly to the various parts of the work upon which they were employed. Some of the time I had nearly sixty men in my employ. I paid them every Saturday night, and notwithstanding the high wages paid, I kept no man who did not earn all I paid him.

Immediately upon trial I learned what particular part of the work men were best fitted for, and there they were kept. As each bent was duplicate of the previous one except in height, they soon became experts in their work.

To raise and put in position those heavy posts many of them sixty feet in length and eleven inches in diameter at their smallest end, was no small matter. They were mostly framed round as they grew in the tree, if we could thus haul them to the work. A number of those in the highest trestle we were compelled to hew before the teams could handle them, having over a mile to draw them to that work.

The sills and paling pieces were only flattened. The caps were all hewed square and were 14 feet long and 14 inches square. The track stringers were hewed 14 inches square and were each 24 feet long. I kept a force of men in the woods continually hewing timber, men and teams hauling, others framing, raising and preparing foundations. No part of the work was suffered to drag. The weather was extremely favorable for such work. No rain fell from July to December during working hours to stop our work until we finished the framing and raising them about the middle of December. While the drouth was a serious one for farmers, it was to our advantage, but I had to pay about thirty dollars per ton for all the hay we fed our teams.

Wherever the ravines were over sixty feet in depth I raised a foundation of stone so that not a post was spliced in all our work. We accomplished all without an accident to either man or beast. Had we not trestled those ravines I can not tell what would have been the future of our road or the result with our town subscriptions, as most of the bonds of our towns east of Otego were absorbed in the work before reaching our county with the iron.

My strong point in pushing forward work was my ability to judge of the fitness of a man for the work to be done. As I was anxious to push the work as fast as possible I set every man who applied at work, if I thought I could make him earn the sum I paid, and was myself the judge of his worth. Early amusing incidents occurred by men attempting to palm themselves off as mechanics, who knew nothing of such work.

MAY 26, 1892

THE STRUGGLE FOR THE RAILROAD (PART 5)

One morning soon after commencing on the first trestle, and Englishman and an Irishman called upon me for a job. They had each a few tools, and both claimed to be mechanics. I had just had hauled and rolled up ready for squaring, a large log, twenty-four feet long and large enough to square twenty inches. I had just with my spirit level put a vertical and horizontal line upon each end crossing each other as near the centre as possible.

I said to them "You may score and hew that log, and I will talk about the price of work when I see what you can do." The Englishman was a lank, loose jointed, pale looking man, the Irishman being a robust, strong, ruddy looking fellow, each appearantly about thirty-five years of age. The Englishman gave his name as Tommy Dutton, and the Irishman as Thomas Curley.

Dutton was a ship carpenter and understood his business. A better man never exsist at any kind of work I tried him. The other, I doubt whether he ever used a carpenter's tool of any kind in his life. I immediately saw he could do nothing as a mechanic, but I was confident that such muscle could be made useful in the right place. Seeming by accident to pass him I said quietly to him "Pat, if you want to work I have a pick and shovel which I think you could use, but I see you know nothing of carpenter work."

"Faith sir, you are right, I will try the tools I know how to use." I got him a pick and shovel, and he was as much at home as Tommy was with his long handled, awkward-looking ship carpenter's axe, and proved excellent help. One morning, just daylight, I was going alone to hat we called Canado trestle, and soon a young man came running up to me from behind and accosted me with: "Boss, can you give me a job?" "What can you work at" was my inquiry. "Oh! I am a carpenter! I learned my trade of my father," was his reply.

He was a strong looking man about twenty-two years of age and looked smart and appeared honest and active. I told him I wanted a man to hew timber and would set him at work immediately. By this time, we were at the work, and I called a young man, told him to get the tools and go with this man and score and hew those sticks, some half a dozen or more which he had helped roll in place for hewing the day before. This young man was the son of a carpenter in my employ, and had been with me for a number of weeks. He was a superior scorer, but claimed not to know how to use a broadaxe. They went down to where the logs were stacked and he lined a stick, got into it and scored one side and then said to my new carpenter, "You may now hew this side while I score the other." He took his broadaxe, got on top of the log on his knees and attempted to thus hew the stick. Jim seeing him in danger of cutting his legs every move he made, called out to him, "Hold up there, wait till I call the boss," started after me. He laughingly, but truly, told of the skill of my new man, and wished me to go down and see him use the broadaxe.

It was but a few rods distant but behind a clump of bushes, out of sight from the trestle. I took a good man to hew with me and on arriving, found my new carpenter standing on the log, broad axe in hand awaiting our coming.

"I thought you said you were a carpenter, and knew how to hew," I laughingly said. "Really, I must own I never saw such an axe used in my life," was my reply. "I was in want of work and thought I must pass as a carpenter to get a job." "Well this man will do the hewing and I will give you a job at which I think you will succeed," was my reply. I set him to handling stone, work which was suited to his skill, and he proved an excellent hand and remained with me until all the trestles were up.

I then let the job of pre-sawing the track stringers to Tommy Dutton and J. H. Carter, by the lineal foot, to be by them done as fast as needed for the work. They thus sawed some 5,000 lineal feet of 14 inch hemlock timber, making two sticks 7 by 14 inches each. I put packing blocks of one inch in thickness and bolted these together and dowled them on the caps of the trestles to support the ties for the rails. I so laid them that each joint had a whole piece by its side the joints meeting on each cap.

I will go back to the time of commencing the second trestle, the fore part of August. I was confident of having the grading completed through Worcester and Maryland so as to reach Onhonta with the track during the year 1861. Judge Westover, thinking the trestles more than it would be possible for me to perform, thought that he would surprise me by sending for a superior mechanic of his acquaintance to come as an assistant, so that I could have two of them under way at the same time.

His man came and was around the work looking on for two or three days. I often spoke to him as I did to all the strangers who often called, and I wondered at his staying so long, but concluded that he was an acquaintance and guest of some of my men, and he soon passed from my mind. After the trestle were all up and the Judge had become better acquainted with me, he told me story of the stranger, and how he came to make his long visit.

Had I known it at the time I would gladly have made him useful, as for fully four months, I, to forward the trestles in the time desired, did the work ordinarily accomplished by four men from June to January.

After standing around seeing our way of doing the work, and the clocklike perfection of its performance, he told Judge Westover that he dare not undertake to take charge of such a job for he did not believe any other man in the world could do such work in the manner and with the success and labor that we were doing it. That after three days observation of our way of framing round timber, he was unable to learn how he did it, and, too, in such exactness and perfection.

Had I have known of his desire I could have initiated him into the mystery in a few minutes and no doubt made him useful help. Framing round timber where every joint is cut on a bevel, and every waling piece put on with a lock joint, as were those was truly a mystery, and I suppose Alonso Mumford who had the special charge of laying out the bents after I had given him their respective heights, was shrewd enough not to allow him to observe the secret of my process. I however had no desire to conceal my way of doing the work. It was of course a great puzzle for a man to stand by and see four round posts framed and raised with every cut on a bevel even to the tenons on their ends, and the cap put on them and all the waling pieces (gerts some call them) put in place in a lock joint and bolted, and all come into position perfectly.

It however was all plain to any one who could see the whole process. I first made draft board of dry, well-seasoned matched lumber large enough to draw a perfect bent 60 feet height and of the width wanted, on an exact scale of one inch to the foot. I then made patterns of one and one-half inch lumber of the exact length between the shoulders of the posts and the shoulders of the paling pieces, with a cross or head piece firmly secured to each end at the right bevel for the shoulders of the tenons or gains to be cut in the posts. These head pieces were rounded out on the lower so as to easily fit upon the largest post I should need to frame. On each of these end pieces was marked vertically a center line.

I first placed upon top of the slope properly bedded on cross bed sills, the first sill upon which the track stringers were to lay. I then obtained with my level the exact height of my first bent of the trestle, first having placed the sill as it was to lay, its center line exactly twelve feet from the center line of the first sill laid. The level gave the vertical distance between the two sills. The measure on the draft, the length of the posts by my adding the grade increase which was about one and one-half inches.

JUNE 2, 1892

THE STRUGGLE FOR THE RAILROAD (PART 6)

I made two patterns, one for the outside and the other for the middle posts, as they slanted opposite ways and were of different lengths, but the same pattern answered for both sides of the respective posts. The posts being rolled upon the framing skids and sawed off square at each end, just the length from end to end of tenon, they now had with a spirit level a vertical and horizontal mark made on each end which crossed each other at the average center of the stick at right angles. A chalk line was then struck upon the top of the stick from end to end on the center line, as was marked on its end. The pattern was then placed on its top the right distance from the top end of the post for the shoulder to the top tenon, with its end center lines exactly at each end on the center line on the posts, and the shoulder of the tenon, and the gain at the other end of the pattern accurately marked; the width of the gain was measured and marked and the patterns moved down the posts and the next, waling gains marked, until the lower one of the bent was reached, the remainder of the posts being now accurately measured for the lower shoulder. The end of the pattern also gave the exact bevel for that.

The posts were then turned one-fourth over and a center line again drawn on its top, the distance for the depth of the gains and thickness of tenons were measured from this center line and the shoulders of the gains and tenons accurately marked by a short pattern made for such purpose or a carpenter square. We used the pattern for greater speed in the work. The tenons and gains being marked, its opposite side was laid out like its first, and its fourth like its second. The center line being the points worked from, the timber when framed was perfect, if there was proper care in doing the work. The blind inside shoulders of the lock joints were always cut at an exact vertical line so that the waling piece locks were all framed square across them. But they as well as the mortices in the caps and sills were all laid from a center line, and the face of the timber faced by a spirit level. Any observing mechanic will at once see that round and tapering or crooked timber can be truly and perfectly framed in this manner and all the work come together as well as if every stick was square and perfect.

Having placed the first bent just as the grade and line demanded all the others were established by that. All that was necessary was to place the next sill in its exact distance to its center line from the first, and perfectly level lengthwise. Then by finding how much lower it was from the first if going down a slope or higher if going up a slope, the vertical length of each following bent was obtained and its exact length of posts as before from the draft. All these trestles were on a grade which elevation had to be provided for in each bent. All I asked of the engineer was a stake placed at the center line on each side of the ravine where he wanted the top of my trestle, and its center to be when completed. So perfect did I do the leveling and get the length of my bents that when completed the trestles were as level and true as if on continuous sills, and all of one length. I never trusted to anyone but myself to obtain the length of the posts of a bent on the whole work. The perfection and strength of the work was a mystery to every one and many were the compliments I received from different railroad engineers on the success in their erection. They required considerable over a million feet of lumber in their construction. The bolts used in them were made under the direction of R. C. Blackall of the Albany shops at that time and he also furnished me the heavy tackle used in the raising of those immensely heavy posts. In the framing it will be seen that each succeeding bent in all that work was but the duplicate of its preceding one varying only in their heights. And by work in the framing from the top downwards, all the work was thus uniform. All the work of raising was done by men on the top of the trestles, the fall of the tackle winding on a windlass. I constructed a machine for the raising which was moved forward as the work advanced bent after bent. The men who did the raising were all on top of the completed work. Soon after commencing work two experienced bridge builders came and I employed them. One was named Jack Ange and the other Thomas Lamb. It was their special business to put the work together. This was the only dangerous part and required cool heads, void of fear. To be clinging to and putting in position timbers from forty to seventy feet above the ground is work which could not be safely trusted to a novice.

 I was ever good-naturedly careful to have my men all understand that no liquor could be used by them while on or around any of my work. One day Tom Lamb went to Cobleskill and so forgot himself as to get tight. On sobering he felt so ashamed that he told his companion, Ange, that after such a spree he dare not look me in the face again. He was the coolest bravest man in danger I ever saw. I saw him knocked off a timber one day fully sixty feet above ground. By a spring he caught another some ten feet distant, threw himself upon it, climbed up a post and resumed work as if nothing had happened. I filled his place with another man. All these trestles being on an upgrade the erecting was commenced at their lowest end so as to work up hill instead of down. One reason why the thing was so much of a mystery to the uninitiated was no doubt that my draft board was always kept in the tool house, a shanty building erected at the beginning of each separate trestle. When not being used its face was always turned to the wall to prevent its being marred; and I presume it was seldom seen by strangers or in fact anyone but myself. I have been thus particular in my description of the building of this work, not only for its success, but also as others may sometime wish to construct some important work from unwrought timber.

 Before the fall came, the directors found it impossible to get the earth work ready for the continuation of the track and proceeded to procure an extension of the time by legislative enactment for reaching Oneonta. By this time the company began to think or rather act as though they thought what I undertook was bound to succeed and they offered me the track laying from Oneonta to Cobleskill, where it had rested for the most part of a year.

As I was extremely anxious to reach Oneonta at the earliest possible moment I consented when offered to lay the track. The condition was that I might associate with myself an experienced track layer, and that we would be at Oneonta by the first day of October, provided the roadbed was ready for us. But if for want of roadbed or material, we were delayed, two days were to be added to our time for each one we were so delayed. The first week of May was the time fixed for commencing the work.

The grading between Cobleskill and Richmondville had been mostly completed the previous fall and as I had the trestles completed and the track stringers all in place, that five miles was ready to lay as soon as the frost was safely out of the roadbed. The cut through the rock just west of Richmondville station was not ready for the track. There were several places between there and Oneonta where a large amount of grading was still to be done.

JUNE 16, 1892

THE STRUGGLE FOR THE RAILROAD (PART 7)

We commenced track laying at Cobleskill with a light force of men and were at Richmondville with the iron laid May 25th. We then laid the side tracks. The road bed not being ready, I set part of one force helping grading and the balance of our men making gates for the farms eastward towards Albany. This was done to keep the men in work until the rock cut was ready for the track.

During the preceding winter I had cut and piled on the land purchased about 1,400 cords of wood and had had 30,000 railroad ties hewed and delivered, and 5,600 lineal feet of track stringers pit sawed and put in place on the trestles; besides counting and paying for all the ties delivered between Central Bridge and Oneonta. Altogether it made a very busy winter's work. I had 30,000 ties piled in one place near the Waldorf trestle, about one and one half miles easterly from Richmondville. A larger pile of ties one seldom sees in a life-time.

They were for use between Richmondville and Worcester, as I had been able to buy but few along that part of the line. I also had cut and hauled to the saw mills in Richmondville, hemlock logs for a large amount of fencing, some 200,000 feet. The logs were from the lands we had purchased there for trestles and ties.

June 14th, at night, I received a messenger call to go immediately to Albany. The train was held at Cobleskill until I could arrive there. At Albany I found the directors in session awaiting my arrival. Mr. Northrup of Centerville explained the reason of my being sent for. He wished to know if it would be possible for us to reach Oneonta with the track by the first day of September. The company then owed Mr. Daniel Drew of New York city $250,000 borrowed money, which was due September 1st, and they had received notice that the money was wanted at that time. If we could get the track finished by that date, they could then obtain and use the state aid then becoming due for such payment. Could we do it; and if so what bonus would we ask?

I well knew the straightened circumstances of the company and for what especial use the $250,000 had been borrowed and that their anxiety could not possibly exceed mine, either to pay the money to Mr. Drew or to be in Oneonta with the track at the earliest possible moment. The delay at Richmondville had already carried our contract time past the middle of October with a fair prospect of a still farther extension by like causes. Two heavy cuts still remained to be finished between Worcester and Schenevus, besides other work of various kinds on the line to Oneonta.

After a moment's thought my reply was "give us the interest on the $250,000 for the time we save it for you, and we will do our best to be in Oneonta by September." Of course my offer was instantly accepted, as its terms cost them nothing. They then put the charge of the grading into my hands to control exclusively, giving me power to manage it all as I thought best.

All the company was to do was to have the iron, spikes and chairs on hand as fast as we wanted to use them. All else was to be done by me. The company furnished the engine Delevan and conductor Ottman and his men to do our transporting in delivering material as needed for the work. On making my proposition known to Mr. DeGraff he said "It is an impossibility, but I am with you to do my best to aid you. If you think the thing possible, I will leave its management wholly in your hands." A better man for such a work than DeGraff there never lived. He had been in my employ the previous summer for nearly two months on the trestles and I well knew his executive ability in carrying out one's plans. He was a man of great physical strength, as well as fine a man as ever need live.

The coming evening we spent a short time in my detailing to him my plans. About that time five men had just come to work for us, among whom were Mike and Bill Dorsey, men whose names are now familiar all along the valley. I in a very short time saw these new men were men who understood railroading and would be able aids in our work. I had previous to starting the track laying had made by Henry Mosher & Sons at Oneonta, two truck wagons of my own design for the express purpose of distributing ties. I had that day as I returned from Albany bargained for a third one to be made by a Mr. Palmatier of Richmondville and to be ready for use in one week.

I had long known that liberal wages and a lively interest in the work at which they are employed was the main factor for success in a hard job. We at once increased the wages of our men on an average about twenty-five cents per day, with extra pay for extra and night work. It was understood by all that each man was employed expressly for work and was to do his best. We had our cars for boarding and lodging our men. They were under the especial care of Mr. and Mrs. Jacob Shafer, excellent folk for such a position. Our men were regularly and well fed on the best of muscle producing food. Among the food used, well-cooked beans were never lacking, my experience being that for laboring men at hard work nothing else equals them.

Our men too, were kept as much as possible from the use of spirituous liquors as years of observation had convinced me that they were an enemy to continuous daily extra effort; and should ever be avoided where such is desired. The result of our system was that we soon had a lot of men who could perform more track laying in a given time than any I ever saw. Mr. Samuel Terrill of this town is one who worked for us all the way from Richmondville to this place.

As we progressed from station to station, Mr. Lane and his men followed and ballasted up the track ready for use and the company at once commenced running trains and doing business. At the cut near the Griswold farm house, between Worcester and Schenevus, we were delayed about two days for roadbed. I had early doubled the force on that cut, working night and day, and thought it would be ready for the track by the time we arrived, but at the last moment one gang struck and thus the delay. We were again delayed at Maryland two days for iron and spikes, but with all the delays and rain and bad weather, on the 24th of August we were on the depot grounds at Oneonta with the track. We were on Saturday, the 26th, at the Susquehanna house, treated to a fine dinner by Messrs. Morris & Place who kept what was then the best hotel in Oneonta; truly a dinner fit for kings.

With that set of men, had there been a road bed ready and the materials on hand, I would unhesitatingly undertake to lay a mile of track every day possible to work to the Pacific ocean, and been sure of doing the job. In addition to the wages earned and paid our men, we paid most of them additional sums as presents, ranging from five to thirty dollars each, according as we thought they deserved. Among our men, Mike Dorsey was one to whom we were very grateful for his ever efficient aid. Had not our men took hold of the work with us, with a determination for its accomplishment, the task would not have been possible within the time.

On Tuesday, August 29th, 1865, the grand opening was held. It was a great day for Oneonta. For over fourteen years, since the formation of the Albany & Susquehanna Bailroad company, had we worked, waited and hoped for this final day of consummation and triumph. It had arrived and all were rejoiced.

The state commissioners formally accepted the road, the state aid was paid and Daniel Drew received his money promptly on time.

All our town bonds from the towns east of here and our own had been used before reaching Oneonta. I had delivered over the last $10,900 of ours to Mr. Ford the day we laid the first rail in this county at the Worcester town line. It was between the 15th and 20th of June. No anxiety of all my life equalled that I had to reach Oneonta with the road and fulfill my promise. In this case there seemed to be a very strong party who were determined the road should never be built. Our money had been used and hence my anxiety. No money would ever induce me to again put myself in a position of such responsibility. Had our road failed and our money been sunk in it, and my promise broken, my life would have been ruined. To forfeit my word under such circumstances would have destroyed all its future, no matter how long it lasted. But fortunately I had been spared to see my promise redeemed and all made right.

There was in this triumph other greatly compensating things. When obtaining the vote of Milford three men who were bitterly opposed to the road stood on the town tax roll for more than one-fourth of its amount. That must be overcome before we could even start for their consent. One of these men while I was canvassing for consent in Portlandville followed from place to place to try to induce his neighbors not to sign the consent to take stock. He assured them if ever one cent tax was laid upon the town towards the building of the road, that their firm, Steere & Windsor, would take all their capital and themselves out of the town. I respected the men and did not doubt the sincerity of their opposition, but we must have the consent of Milford.

When about $10,000 in amount of the property necessary remained unobtained it seemed utterly impossible to obtain the remaining sum. In my dilemma I called on the late David Wilber, showed him my books and asked his aid. He carefully looked over the names of those remaining whom I had not obtained, got into my carriage with me and in less than two days we had the necessary sum and names and a good margin besides. He seemed to take pleasure in aiding me and utterly refused any compensation for the service he had rendered. I ever appreciate his timely aid.

JUNE 23, 1892
THE STRUGGLE FOR THE RAILROAD (PART 8)

The next season, as has been explained in a former chapter, a tax was levied on the towns to pay the interest on the 10 per cent of the bonds of the six towns, of which Milford was one, and the sum of $280 was entered into the tax roll of that town for such use. True to their threat, Messrs. Steere & Windsor made immediate preparation to move out of town. They moved first to Cherry Valley and next to Hallsville in the town of Springfield.

In April, 1863, when Mr. Goodyear and myself were returning from Albany, after the passage of the bill which finally gave us state aid, as the stage drew up to the door of the hotel at Hallsville, Mr. Windsor seeing me on the stage, immediately came and asked me step into his room in the hotel with him, at the same time telling the driver not to leave until I returned. In his room I found Mr. Steere. They told me that seeing me on the stage they had resolved to embrace the opportunity to right the great wrong they had done me personally and also to the Albany & Susquehanna railroad by their opposition to it.

They assured me that I was right and they wrong, and asked forgiveness for personal injury they had done me, and that they both hoped that they should live to see the Albany & Susquehanna railroad completed, which they had so strongly but honestly opposed, and that they had seen their error and were glad to personally confess it to me whom they had so hotly opposed.

A like case occurred with Mr. John Edgerton of Franklin. While I was canvassing that town for its consent, he with others (he the moving spirit), rode all over that part of the town I had not canvassed to prevent a favorable vote. Such was his influence in town as to make the obtaining of the consent impossible. When the road was completed to Colesville and a meeting held at Wells Bridge to consider the question of a depot at that place, Mr. Edgerton was there as one of its advocates. On meeting me he immediately acknowledged that he was wrong in his opposition to the railroad and of his town's aiding in its construction, but above all of his personal abuse of me in attempting to obtain the vote of his town and the unfair part he took in the matter and that if it was possible for me to forgive him he wished me to do so. These and other like acknowledgements I am sure were not lost on me.

The value of the enterprise to this valley as well as the localities through which the road passes would be hard to conceive. But its influence for the future good of the country is beyond estimate. Its benefits are to increase with the passing years. Its coming effect as an important factor in transit is beyond human calculation. With all such enterprises they bring to each community some evils with their benefits, but when the balance is struck between benefits and injuries, evil and good, the preponderance will ever be found largely in favor of the latter, even if we leave its financial gain entirely out in the estimate. Railroads have had and exercised an entire revolution in our whole country since the commencement of their construction.

I would fail of my duty did I not add another chapter on railroads and their builders. Oneonta has a just and commendable pride in the success of such enterprises; and particularly so where individual efforts of its citizens has aided in carrying to final completion such important public works.

For a long term of years after the benefits, importance, influences and necessity of railroads had been known and enjoyed east of the Mississippi river, no one was found to undertake the construction of one which should join the East with the West; the Atlantic with the Pacific. Parker, Carson and Fremont had each in turn with a host of others crossed the vast area lying to the west of the Mississippi and to them all this large desert expanse, together with the Rocky mountain ranges, had ever presented inseparable barriers for the success of such an undertaking.

For fully twenty years before a move had been made toward its commencement, its necessity had been canvassed and its benefits set forth, and its final construction prophesied before any farther advance than words orally and on paper had been made towards its construction.

During the latter part of the decade of 1840 gold was discovered in California. Such discovery lost none of its promises of rapidly made wealth, by the stories which came from the Pacific slope to the quiet homes of the citizens of the Atlantic States. Golden visitors loomed up in many minds and this El Dorado of rapidly made wealth called forth many an enterprising stalwart pioneer for fortune.

At that time there resided in the quiet village of Oneonta, a man in the prime of life, being then not far from thirty years of age, a man by the name of Collis P. Huntington. He was in trade with his brother Solon, and the firm were doing a prosperous business in the old stone store now owned and occupied by the Mendel Brothers. He was a man of good nature, powerful physique, keen and sharp, wide awake in every matter pertaining either to the business of the firm or of the public at large. He was loved and appreciated by his townsmen; and upon the forming of a fire company and obtaining a fire engine he was made its first high officer.

In 1849 the gold fever had so far mastered his mind that he decided to go to California and learn for himself the business field which that renowned state offered to his Yankee enterprise. On the route to the land of gold by the way of the Isthmus of Darien, he like others was destined to delay and disappointment, but by his good health, good care of himself and attention to the wants and cares of others, he finally found himself at the golden gate with more money than he had when he left home and all bills paid.

He at once commenced to become acquainted with the country, to learn if possible to him the most profitable field of labor. His ambition was to succeed in what he undertook, but he looked for such success only as the reward for his own well-directed labor and choice of location.

San Francisco was then too far from the mining region to be the best apparent opening for his contemplated business. Sacramento offered far better promises. From that point he could command the mining trade of the near by mountain regions to the best advantage. At that point he could obtain his goods quicker and at less cost of transport, and could thus offer better bargains to his customers than from any other observable locality. He at once selected this place as the field of his future labor. Being conscious of his own powers of endurance and application to business and void of fear, he by his superior foresight was able to carve out a fortune, when others more timid would have been sure to fail.

California society at that time was composed of a heterogeneous mass of citizens. Many of the people, probably a majority, were honest, temperate and quiet people, while the rest were composed of the worst elements in all the land. Being as they were unrestrained by either local law or social influences and the vice restraining power of the better half, the female portion of society, these were truly perilous times. Men, who while under the restraints of their home and surroundings were supposed to be and were upright and moral, amid such scenes as these, soon were on a level with the worst and on a fast road to ruin. Thousands who made vast sums of money easily and rapidly would squander a fortune in a single night.

Such had been the training and such the moral rectitude of Mr. Huntington that he was able to pass through all this chaotic social state and come out like those of old who went through the fiery furnace without even its smoke upon their garments. Where thousands failed he stood firm and erect.

His restraining moral influence was carried into all his business. His clerks and employees were by the terms of their contracts to keep themselves entirely out of the streets at night. Good rooms were provided for them in the upper story of the building they occupied as his store and their meals were furnished at his own table; and books and papers were freely furnished for their use. In this manner he was able to retain the best and most reliable help, and to keep them from the dissipating temptation which everywhere surrounded them.

No wonder this very course he proposed was one to command and secure success. He applied the means to deserve it. The very ones to win it. Next door to him was the store of Mark Hopkins from Lockport, New York. E. H. Miller was his partner. Hopkins and Miller had formed such partnership and theirs had, too, been a success. Huntington and Hopkins of course became first acquainted and then fast friends.

In 1853 Hopkins retired from the firm and came east. Hopkins, stay in New York was short and he returned to California, no doubt anticipating the consummation a partnership with C. P. Huntington. In May, 1854, such partnership was formed, which continued without a ripple until Mr. Hopkins' death. During all these busy years no difference of opinion ever occurred, or unpleasantness arose in any possible way to mar in the least their joy, or their success.

JUNE 30, 1892
C. P. HUNTINGTON AND THE CENTRAL PACIFIC (PART 1)

Few men can for years conduct a business amounting to so many hundreds of thousands of dollars of which such can be truthfully said. These men, and other like them, established and fixed California as a free state. This union of sentiments of California's best men, was the germ from which sprang the important union which finally resulted in the completion of one of the most important enterprises ever carried to a successful termination.

Means of transit is the most important factor in the development of any state or country. Without these its progress is of a necessity slow and circumscribed. The necessity of a means of connecting the Atlantic states with the then comparative new Pacific slope began to dawn on the law making power os the national capitol at Washington.

In 1851 Senator Gwinn gave notice in the United States senate of the introduction of a bill for the construction of a railroad to the Pacific. In 1852 senator Douglass reported a bill upon the same subject. California had the same year passed an act donating the right of way for such a railroad through that state. In 1853 congress made its first appropriation of $150,000 for the purpose of making a survey, the matter to be under the control of the war department. In 1854 three more surveying parties were sent out and $190,000 voted towards the cost of such survey.

In the meantime the states as such were making moves in the matter and before 1860 no less than eighteen states had passed resolutions to aid in such an important enterprise. Thus the importance of the contemplated road grew upon the public mind until the tocsin of the alarm of war sounded from Fort Sumpter in Charlestown Harbor throughout all the length and breadth of our land.

Then, above all other times, was the importance and necessity of such a railroad apparent. It needed bonds of steel to unite in the strongest of ties the interests of all liberty loving people. Great necessities and great occurrences usually call forth minds fitted for such momentous occasions. Many minds were turned towards this subject, and among them was that of C. P. Huntington. Mature thought convinced him that the insurmountable obstacles in the way of such work must and would yield to the skill and perseverance of true American genius when fully awakened to the importance of such improvements.

Just at that time a civil engineer by the name of Theodore D. Judah, appeared in Sacramento and at a public hotel announced that he had discovered a line by which a railroad could be constructed over and across the Sierra Nevada mountains, and desired to secure aid for its survey. Mr. Huntington, after hearing what he had to say made no suggestion or public offer of aid, but afterwards, privately, asked Engineer Judah to call upon him at his store and he would there talk over with him the subject of his investigation. The following evening the call was made.

After listening attentively to all he had to say, Mr. Huntington asked as to the probable cost of such survey. He was answered, about $30,000. Huntington then told him he would find six men who would stand the expense of such survey, and the interview closed. In the evening after business hours had passed, Messrs. Huntington and Hopkins discussed the matter fully in all its various bearings.

The discussion finally resulted in C. P. Huntington, Mark Hopkins, Leland Sanford, Charles Crocker, James Bailey, E. B. Crocker and Engineer Judah to do unitedly the work of making such survey. After a careful examination this resulted in the formation of the Central Pacific railroad company, under the general railroad laws of California with a capital of $8,000,000 to construct a railroad from the navigable waters of the Sacramento river to the bounds of the state of California.

The five men who organized the company were Huntington, Hopkins, Stanford, Crocker, Bailey and later E. B. Crocker. This was in 1861. The survey and location were carefully made, Huntington himself personally climbing over the rocks and sagebrush and thus securing by his personal examination the best possible line. He also went carefully over all the examinations and estimates of the cost of such road. While riding in the stage from Oneonta to Richmondville a year or so after, I heard from Mr. Huntington many of the particulars of this personal line exhmination.

Maps of the road were at once made, and Huntington and Judah started for Washington to lay the matter before congress which was then in session. Huntington took with him from his associates an unlimited power of attorney to do and act according to his own judgment and binding them equally with himself to all bargains he saw fit to make.

Huntington in his own way laid the matter before congress so plainly and clearly that the railroad act of 1862 was passed and became a law. By this act the Central Pacific railroad company entered into an agreement with the government to construct a railroad from the navigable waters of the Sacramento river to the easterly boundary of California, having also the privilege of building eastward until it met the Union Pacific. That road was also to have the privilege of building westerly until it met the Central Pacific.

To aid in the construction of such railroad the government was to donate every alternate section of land, the sections being designated by odd numbers to the amount of five alternate sections to the mile on each side of the track. The title to such land to be vested in the company when it should have completed forty consecutive miles of the railroad and telegraph, and on completion of said section the secretary of the treasury should issue to the company bonds of the United States, payable thirty years after date, bearing six per cent interest to the amount of bonds per mile as follows:

From the western base of the Sierra Nevada mountains, $48,000 per mile for the distance of 150 miles eastward, and between the mountainous sections at the rate of $32,000 per mile. The company was to complete fifty miles of the road and telegraph line within two years of filing their consent to the provisions of this act, and fifty miles each year thereafter. The entire line between Sacramento and the Missouri rivers to be completed so as to form a continuous line of railroad and ready for use by July 1st, 1876.

No sooner had the necessary legislation been obtained than it became necessary to inspire confidence in others to enable the company to carry forward this vast work. The first struggle encountered was the possibility of such road, the second, the necessary congressional legislation. The third and still harder task still remained, that of obtaining the necessary means to carry forward this vast undertaking.

Forty miles must be completed before the company could receive any of the government bonds. To push forward the work it became necessary for the company to themselves become personally responsible for the entire sum needed for the first forty miles of the road. Mr. Huntington knew their ability and at once announced that he would sell none of the company's bonds for anything but cash and that he would pay cash for all the materials he might purchase. On this basis the work progressed.

So exact were they in all their payments that the company was never thirty days behind with the payroll, a thing that can seldom be said of any previously constructed railroad. One of the most serious obstacles to this work was that all the material for the road, except the ties, must be transferred 18,000 miles by water around Cape Horn to reach the place for their use.

This compelled the company to have a year's supply continually in advance on its way of transit. He managed these large shipments in a way so quiet as not to excite a rise in freight or price of material by any act of his. At one time he had twenty-three ships chartered to transport supplies before the ship owners were at all aware of his wants. Had each manufacturer or ship owner known in advance of his needs a vast difference would have been made in the cost of material and also in the cost of their transport.

The officers of the Central Pacific were: Leland Stanford, president; C. P. Huntington, vice president; Mark Hopkins, treasurer. During the first year Messrs. Judah and Bailey withdrew from the company, receiving back all the money they had advanced.

JULY 7, 1892
C. P. HUNTINGTON AND THE CENTRAL PACIFIC (PART 2)

The year 1863 saw twenty miles of the railroad completed and it was continued until it reached New Castle, 31 miles. The state of California, to aid the work, donated to the company $400,000 and later it assumed and paid the interest on $1,500,000 for twenty years. After reaching New Castle it was found that some other than the common contract system must be adopted for doing the work. A company was formed called the Contract and Finance company, the railroad stockholders themselves being the company.

The first act of congress in relation to the road being found imperfect in its workings in many particulars, two others were passed, one in 1864 and another in 1866, amendatory of the act of 1862. During all his efforts before congress, it is confidently stated that Mr. Huntington never tried to buy a vote or influence any man to vote for his measures upon any other grounds except their actual merit. He says he ever considered a vote a sacred right, not a commodity for sale or purchase.

Wadsworth was reached with the road in July, 1868. This place is 192 miles from Sacramento. Three years had been used between New Castle and Wadsworth. The next 500 miles to Promontory was built in less than one year. This was an immense work, considering the distance that all the material used had to be transported.

At this point the rails of the Central and the Union Pacific were brought together May 10, 1869, about seven and one-half in advance of the time fixed by congress for a union of the two lines of road. Its completion was a grand triumph for its constructors, particularly for Mr. Huntington, who had been the main inspiration of the work. Others, of course, are entitled to the details of its construction.

Before the road reached Promontory, Mr. Huntington had arranged to buy the 50 miles between that place and Booneville table, and to make the depots of the roads at that place.

This vast enterprise even if its end had come at its accomplishment would have forever stood as without a parallel in the great enterprises of the world. But its completion was but a small part of its mission for good. In fact it was but the beginning. It opens up to the world a vast country before useless and valueless. In fact, worse than valueless, because it separated the improved east from the progressive west. Bu this not only opens up all this intervening country, but at the same time it unites these two extremes. Its benefits are incomputable and are to continue at an increasing rate in the future.

The greatest individual triumph in this vast work I conceive to be due to our former townsman, C. P. Huntington. But few men possess the power of mind over mind, will over will and mind over matter, that is demonstrated in the construction of the Central Pacific railroad. In a world possessing so many millions of people, it would be hard to find so important a national enterprise consummated so nearly as was this by individual effort. It stands alone without a parallel.

When nations are imperiled, great generals usually arise. When public financiers are wanted, with a nation's combined wealth to back such enterprises, competent men are seldom wanting. But in an enterprise where every opposing obstacle is to be removed, or overcome by the efforts of a few and under the guidance of one, the case is far different, and it is a pleasure to record such successful works of perseverance to completion and final triumph.

But this is a case where the world at large is benefited, whether the enterprise proves to be a source of gain to its projectors and builders or not. The railroad will continue to do its work long after the company who pushed the road to its early completion have ceased all their cares and toils. But their works will live and continue their mission for the common good.

I should be pained to believe that men who had given their labor and imperiled their fortunes and spent years of their lives in the pushing forward of such an enterprise to final success, had done it without a full and fair financial reward. Such compensation, except the satisfaction of success, is all that is generally received for such public benefits during the life of its constructors. I have long observed that it easier to curse than honor those whose acts deserve praise.

Few men of common sense would engage in such vast works, if mere dollars and cents were their only hope and aim. They take hold of and accomplish them from a higher and more noble end and aim. It is that they may benefit their race. That they may develop new sources of industry, open new fields of labor, create new means of gain, make places of poverty and obscurity yield wealth to a nation and enrich its individual members. It is to give access to forests, mines of metal and coal, quarries and hidden treasures which minister to human want and a nation's good. It is to open new fields of agriculture, cover the hills, valleys and plains with happy homes, waving grain, ripening fruits and grazing herds as the rewards for care and industry. It is to open manufactures and turn the dormant resources of the country into fields of labor and wealth. It is that roads, churches, schools, villages and cities may spring up where naught but waste and desolation had ever before reigned unmolested and supreme. These are a few of the motives which to most men of such enterprise loom offer up continually before them as a stimulant and partial reward for their labors, their money and their personal efforts. With no higher reward than the food one eats and the clothes he wears, he has but a meagre compensation for his toils.

From our personal acquaintance with Mr. Huntington we feel confident that wealth was but a secondary consideration in commencing and pushing to completion this vast work. His whole life's history bears testimony of such fact. The many public and private gifts he has made are conclusive evidence that such was the case. The gifts to the Presbyterian church in this place, the Memorial church at Harwinton, Conn., the library building and library at Westchester, N.Y., the Huntington Industrial school at Hampton, Virginia and many other acts of public benefits give an insight unmistakable of the true motives and promptings of his active business life, its end and aims.

Well may Oneonta should be proud to be able to name such a man as one of its former citizens. Well may we rejoice at his success and prosperity. By such men is humanity honored amid the human race dignified and enobled. By them are the prosperity, progress and success of our nation and people perpetuated and secured. Collis P. Huntington was born at Harwinton, Connecticut, October 22d, 1821. His father, William Huntington, was a man of large stature, being six feet, two inches in height and well-proportioned. His mother was a woman of rare worth. To her early teachings and influence no doubt was the son indebted for the noble qualities and principles which has characterized the main acts of his successful life.

He was never in the habit, then as common as now, of indulging in the use of spirituous liquors and tobacco. A habit, which if men would stop to count the probable cost of its use through the average period of life, would find fewer votaries than now.

In politics he is a Republican, true, square and outspoken at all times. On questions of finance, tariff, coinage, on other measures upon which the policy of the party is so distinctly marked, he is ever to be found sound and unwavering in its principles, believing them to be those which tend to the common good of our people.

So far from an anxiety for public notice or notoriety he has ever shrunk from it and as far as he possibly could avoided it. After I had commenced to pen these scraps of history, I wrote him asking him to favor me with a few notes as I wished to devote a few pages to a record of his noted and successful career. My letter to him was written the 4th of November, 1891. On the 8th I received from him by mail this very characteristic reply.

23 Broad St., New York City,
Nov. 6th, 1891.

To Harvey Baker, Oneonta, N. Y.
My Dear Sir:

Yours of the 4th informing me that you are preparing scraps of history of Oneonta and vicinity is received and that you would like to say something about myself personally, although quite a number have written my biography and some of these seem to know all about me—and something more.

I am very busy and hardly have time to prepare anything of the kind that you propose. If I can lay my hand on something that comes anywhere near the facts, I will send it to you. With kind regards,

Very truly yours,
C. P. HUNTINGTON

On the 18th day of November I received the following letter and the book named by express. It was a superbly bound volume, containing sketches of Huntington, the Vanderbilts and Oakes Ames and to that volume am I indebted for most of the main facts contained in these two biographical chapters.

23 Broad St., New York City,
November 16, 1891.

To Harvey Baker, Oneonta, N. Y.
My Dear Sir:

I have sent you to-day by express a book published by the Bancroft Histori-society society in San Francisco, which gives some account of myself. I have not had time to read it and perhaps never shall, although I expect to. So after you have got through with it you will please return it to me. Perhaps you may get the information you desire out of it. If not I will see what I can do further.

Very truly yours,
C. P. HUNTINGTON

I made such use of this fine work as I thought space would permit and the 30th of the month I returned it to its owner. It is a biography which I wish could go into the general trade and be read by every citizen of our country. From its appearance, however, I think that only a limited number of copies are intended to be published.

The great misfortune of our age is that the true worth of an active man is seldom known and appreciated during his lifetime. His loftiest motives are constituted to selfish aims and ends. The personal sacrifices he makes and the work he performs are overlooked or underestimated even if its own developing power enriched not only himself, but a host of others, and proved to be a boon to his country or worldwide extent and inestimable value; even if it is to increase for all coming time—that its success is robbing somebody is more apt to be the reward accorded than the true honor so justly deserved.

JULY 14, 1892
THE LOCATION OF THE RAILROAD SHOPS

With this chapter I will close my labors upon the A & S railroad construction. After opening before described at Oneonta, I felt the need of a season of rest and took a trip of several weeks' duration, in which I visited Ontario (upper Canada), the central and western part of our own state, the oil regions of Pennsylvania and the bituminous and anthracite regions of that state.

On returning home I found the railroad company making preparations to push the track towards Otego and Unadilla. Mr. Wentz called on me and engaged of me my track laying tools. I recommended to him Michael Dorsey as a suitable man to take charge of the westward track laying.

The first day of November, 1865, I again engaged to purchase the ties and assist in pushing the track westward to Unadilla, at four dollars a day and expenses, and immediately commenced on the work. I soon had men both east and west engaged in getting out ties and delivering them on the line of the road. The track westward from Oneonta, for the first and most of the second mile, was laid with hemlock ties left of those I had made in Schoharie county the previous winter. The gap westward to the mouth of Mill creek was filled with ties purchased in Maryland. At Mill creek I purchased several thousand of Adam Horton.

I succeeded in obtaining ties by a continued effort and getting them on the track as fast as needed, and the iron was finally laid to the Unadilla depot, and the opening held there on March 19th, 1866. It was no small matter to have hewed and hauled upon the line of the road nearly 60,000 ties and used between the first of November and March first, but it was accomplished, but by far more different parties than there were thousands of ties.

The summer of 1866 I engaged in the building of town bridges, and also the covering of the railroad bridges from Schenevus to Otego, some eight in number. I took David Van Schaick as partner in the work on the railroad bridges. We were to put on the plates, rafters and to cover the sides and ends of them all. I also had the work of building the pile and timber ice breakers of the two river bridges in Otego at the same time.

While covering the bridge at Colliersville, on the night of the 13th of September I was called up by Mr. Lane about midnight at Kniskern's tavern, with a request from Mr. Wentz to purchase the ties to continue the track from Unadilla to Sidney. He wanted 5,000 more than they had on hand.

Hoppicking and county fairs and work of various kinds crowding everybody, looked like a hard undertaking in addition to the work already on hand. But by noon I had several men hewing ties. I found about 700 already hewed but still in the woods at Maryland, which I purchased. The following day I bought a tract of land of Orlando Quackenbush of Otego, and taking my men from the ice-breakers and adding a few more to assist them, I had the ties at the railroad within two weeks' time and the track was completed to Sidney October 23d of that year.

In the fall, having completed the work contracted December 1st, I again engaged in procuring ties to use in furthering the track from Sidney to Afton, at the same wages as the previous year. I also that year, 1867, was engaged in forwarding the work of the Howe's Cave lime and cement company, as its superintendent and head officer, and also the covering of the railroad bridges at Sidney and between Sidney and Bainbridge.

I had then purchased and was engaged in clearing off the swamp lands between Main street and the railroad and making the foundation of Mechanic street in Oneonta village across these lands. Nights after the train on which I usually returned came in, I would stop a while at the work on the swamp and street. The result was I was taken with a swamp fever, which for about three weeks in September kept me upon my bed under the care of my favorite physician, Dr. S. H. Case.

S. R. Barnes and Wm. N. Roberts, with myself as its chairman, had the previous fall been appointed by the county board of supervisors as committee to prepare plans for a county jail and jailer's house for Otsego county at Cooperstown. The committee visited several jails in this and other states that fall before making their report, which also consumed considerable of my time.

October 31st I was sent for to come to Albany on the next train. Just off my bed and still weak, I responded to the call. I found the railroad directors in session on my arrival. I was immediately informed that my especial aid was wanted to complete the road to Harpersville before the first of the coming year. When the last $250,000 of state aid was promised its terms were that the road should be completed to that place all ready for use, as specified in the law, by the first day of January, 1868. There was now only two months and a large amount of work remained to be done. A ravine at Reid's, about three miles west of Afton, of some 300 feet remained to be trestled, a bridge across the road and creek the east side of Nineveh to be erected and a large amount of grading was to be done.

I was asked my terms to put up the trestle by the linear foot for the timber used in its construction, or my price to work for them by the day, as formerly. In a moment I named a price for the trestle complete, they to furnish the bolts, or ten dollars and expenses if I worked by the day. After making the offer I immediately retired from the room. Within five minutes I was recalled and told to at once commence for them by day and that all the work was to be entirely under my charge and that I must have it done on time.

I returned to Afton on the next train and purchased a grove of pine timber and had men at work before night cutting and preparing it for the trestle. I called on the grading contractors, both of whom were my acquaintances, and put new life into their work, and also saw and started a new pace in the bridge contractor.

November 8th, Messrs. Wentz and Ramsey called on me at Scott's in Nineveh at evening and wished me to erect an engine house 100 feet in length, at Harper's station, a blacksmith shop at the same place, also to build two dwellings about one-fourth of a mile east of Harpursville station, and one west of Afton and the building and support for a water tank at a spring about half way between Afton and Nineveh, near Chamberlain. Mr. Wentz had the plans for them all with him. I at once consented, and before night the next day work was commenced on them all.

I had already many thousand more ties purchased than were needed for the track. I pushed all the work with vigor. The weather was favorable but part of December very cold. On Christmas day all was complete and a train with the officers of the company and their friends ran over the road to the station. This virtually ended my railroad work. Early in February all undertaken was completed.

During a number of years past we of Oneonta had been interested in another question, that of the center points of the road and the erection of its repair shops. When the road was first started, and its final location to pass at Colliersville, a bargain was made with Mr. Goodyear, fixing the division point and shops at that place. He was to donate to it all the lands needed for such purpose.

We of Oneonta were extremely anxious for their location at this place. Many were the talks had between Mr. Ford and myself upon the subject. Mr. Goodyear had large real estate interests here, and I always considered that a favorable argument when talking with him upon the matter. That his opposition to their location here was overcome is proven by the fact that I obtained a written contract from him for the land wanted for a round or engine house at this place, if such could be found suitable for the purpose upon his premises here. It was obtained on the 4th day of November, 1869. On Saturday (two days thereafter) Colonel Coryell, assistant to Mr. Wentz the chief engineer, was here for the express purpose of making the selection of such lands, and stopped over the sabbath with me. As no site on Mr. Goodyear's lands of necessary size for round house and shops could be found, no location was selected.

It will be remembered that that fall and following winter occurred the memorable fight in which the managers of the Erie attempted to gobble up this new trunk line road. The efforts of Gould and Fisk to accomplish such end, which commenced in June, 1869, and which ended in the courts, and the road passing into the hands of a receiver and finally being run under charge of the governor of the state, is a matter of history which will not soon be forgotten. On the 5th day of February, 1870, the lease, or sale, of the road was consummated by which the road passed into the possession of that powerful and rich corporation, the Delaware & Hudson Canal company.

In the early summer of 1870 the immediate erection of an engine house had become indispensable. The old engine house I erected at Harpursville in 1867 had been moved here and re-erected just east of the Main street crossing, but it was only a temporary substitute. In the fore part of the month of September some of the officers and employees of the railroad company came to Oneonta to look over the place to see if a suitable site for a round house and perhaps other buildings could be found. Mr. Ford and myself were anxious that if possible they be located near the depot grounds, or as near them as was practicable.

I had before decided in my own mind that their present location was the only eligible site, but resolved not to call notice to it unless it became a necessity. As the road had but recently come into the possession of the Canal company, they were, of course, not familiar with the formation of the country about our village, and we wanted everything as near the village portion of our town as possible.

After the lands from Main street to the John I. Couse farm east had all been carefully examined and no favorable site found and they were about leaving the line, I suggested that they examine the line west, to which they assented. I immediately took them to the present location of the railroad buildings. At once all was changed. One of them exclaimed "This is just the spot! Why did you not bring us here before?" The site was by them pronounced all that they could wish. Early in September the first board of D. & H. directors of the road was chosen.

Under the date of September 10, 1870, I received a letter from Albany from which I make the following extracts:

> "An engine house to be located somewhere on the line of this road is agitated again, with positive proof that it will be settled upon before the week ends. The location of the engine house can no longer be delayed. My choice of location is west of Oneonta on that level place that you and I looked at. I told Mr. Dickson that the ground was already prepared as far as grade was concerned. He asked me how much land could be got and I told him 20 acres, if needed. Now, Mr. Baker, this is a very important time for the interests of Oneonta, for I feel safe in saying that where the engine house is located, so will the shops be. No road ever prospered with its general shops located at the far end of it. What you are to do is to be prepared to meet the officers of the D. & H. C. Co. at Oneonta next Wednesday, the 14th inst., with a good liberal offer of land at the point you and I looked at, west of your village, on the land about level with the track, if they wish for it."

This letter was of five pages in length and strictly private, else I would give it in full, with the name of its distinguished author.

The officers were met and the offer made and on the evening of the 16th of September, two days later, a public meeting was called for the purpose of raising the necessary funds and purchasing and presenting to the company the twenty acres of land, which Mr. Wentz had that day surveyed as a site for the round house and shops.

The money was soon raised, the land paid for and the question of the location of engine house and shops thus fully settled. Hon. John Cope was chosen the treasurer to consummate the matter and pay for the lands. I find in my diary of the date of the 22d that I spent the day with the committee in raising the balance of the funds, and that on the 23d we took the deeds of the owners of the land purchased. On the 24th proposals were received for the erection of the first half of the southern engine house. Mr. Bridgeford of Albany was builder, he being the lowest bidder for the job. The stone, lime and cement used in its construction as well as in most of the buildings there since erected, was furnished by the Howe's Cave lime and cement company.

From that half of the first engine house since has arisen one of the finest and best equipped railroad plants in our state. This collection of fine buildings and excellent machinery, with its corps of first class mechanics and superior and experienced foremen and superintendents, is the result of the liberality of our citizens who aided in the purchase of the lands given the company and of the noble men who assisted us in the choice of their place of location.

I trust such action has been alike beneficial to the D. & H. Canal company, and to the village and community at large. It would be impossible to give an approximate estimate of its advantages to us for the past while their good for the future is beyond computation. Such wise and judicious outlays of money and labor are of untold value to the communities so favored. It is but a matter of duty on our part as officers and citizens of Oneonta to aid in every possible way the interests of the D. & H. C. Co.

Since the railroad passed into the hands of its present owners I have been but little in its employ. In fact, I have done no work for it except to render Mr. Wentz a little aid in some matters during the first three years of the decade of 1870. I have not even made the acquaintance of its managing officers. But my interest in its continued prosperity will remain unabated so long as memory of the past remains and anticipations for the future good of my adopted county endures.

The following editorial comment appeared on page 5 of this same issue of the Herald:

The chapter published on the third page this week closes Mr. Baker's papers so far as they relate to his labors in securing the Albany and Susquehanna railroad in this valley. They were penned only after earnest solicitation on our part and our regret is that he has not more fully detailed his labors in connection with that important work. His efforts for a railroad, which commenced with his first taking up his residence in this town, were continued with unabated zeal, by conversation, by articles in the public press, by speeches and personal efforts until, after a score of years the work was accomplished. No matter how great the opposition, his efforts were unwearied; and, without detracting in the least from the well-earned honors of such men as Eliakim R. Ford, Col. W. N. Snow or Dr. S. H. Case, it may safely be said that for no small share of the benefits which "progressive Oneonta" now enjoys through the construction of the railroad it is indebted to the labors of Harvey Baker.

AUGUST 4, 1892

BIOGRAPHICAL SKETCHES OF ITS OLDEST INHABITANTS (PART 1)

Without some permanent landmarks one is not aware of the changes which are taking place around him. One would hardly believe that not an industry was pursued by the same parties and in the same place in our village where it was fifty years ago. The same rule applies to resident citizens. Not a family now exists in the same house with the same heads in our corporate limits that did when I first came here. The same also applies on the entire river road on its north side from Sidney to East Worcester, a distance of fifty miles.

It was fifty-one years in February last since I first came to Oneonta. It may not be uninteresting to its citizens to know who were its residents and where they lived at that date. Such will enable its present population to note the changes which have taken place during these intervening years. Most of them, however, so far as streets and numbers of population are concerned have occurred within the past few years.

In the following papers I intend to give every resident of the village then within the bounds of our present corporate limits and also include the tier of farms on the south side of the river at the same date.

This completed, with the notes I may make upon individuals, I will then give our schools, churches, newspapers and such other local matters as I may think worthy of record.

These will be followed with short biographies of some of our pioneer settlers who still have posterity among our citizens.

I am also urged to give a sketch of my own early life. Should I conclude to do this, I may mix that chapter in among those which I consider far more interesting than one can possibly be to the average reader of these papers.

Should my readers not tire and my own time permit, I will then give a sketch of the pioneer settlers of other towns within our county and in the valley of the Susquehanna river and the Schenevus creek.

When I came to this valley from my native county, Broome, I had letters of enquiry in relation to the Johnson water wheel's from nearly every mill owner from Bainbridge to Colliersville. They were furnished me by Nelson Johnson, the inventor and patentee, and my business was to ascertain their need in the mills in this region.

My first acquaintance with Oneonta dates with the early part of February, 1841. I left home on fine sleighing. It remained good until my arrival at Unadilla. From that place I found the sleighing very poor, the road being bare nearly half the way.

I arrived at the old McDonald house then kept by David Sullivan, about sunset and put up for the night.

E. R. Ford was then trading on the south corner of Main and River streets. I called at the store the following morning to enquire where I could obtain a saddle on which to ride to Colliers. I was directed by Mr. Ford to Mason Gilbert, a hatter, who resided about twenty rods south towards the river.

He loaned me a good saddle and leaving one of my horses at the inn, I rode the other to Colliersville. The weather was warm and pleasant and had been the two preceding days.

I found Collier and Goodyear both at home and bargained with them to rebuild their mill in Milford and warrant it and made a written contract with them. I still have the original. I was there served with a fine dinner, my horse well fed and groomed and when I offered to pay my bill not a penny could I induce them to accept.

The frost was coming out of the ground so that it required much care on the part of my horse to select ground strong enough to support both his and my weight. He sometimes went down nearly to his knees in the soft ground.

I stayed the second night at Mr. Sullivan's, and returned home by way of New Berlin, Norwich and Cincinnatus, having business at the two latter places. I found excellent sleighing from West Oneonta to my home.

I came the second time to Oneonta March 25th, with a load of water wheels and my kit of tools. Stayed that night at Angel's tavern as I came on the turnpike by the way of Gilbertsville.

The next morning went up to Colliers and at once commenced work on his mill. About the 6th of April a flood came and the 8th I was compelled to cease labor on the mill on account of high water.

I went across the river to the shop of Henry Dietz and there made five sets of water wheel patterns before it subsided. While there at work one day William Dietz, then a boy, (the father of the wife of Professor Henry Bull of Oneonta) came to the shop and informed us the pickerel were plenty in the streams on the flat towards the mouth of Schenevus creek.

I had a small rifle which I took when out, and Mr. Dietz the last time I saw him only a few days before his death, told me that I shot in less than one hour as many pickerel as he could carry. That kind of fish were both plenty and of large size in the Susquehanna river and its tributaries at that time. The following spaing 1743 I shot several in a small pond then on a farm owned by Henry Wilcox of this village. The largest one weighed four and three-fourths pounds. It was the largest fish I ever caught. I do not remember shooting a fish since that time.

I repaired Collier & Goodyear's Oneonta saw mill in the month of May. During that time I examined carefully the village and the surrounding country, and learned the names of most of its inhabitants. I then thought that no place I had ever seen had such fine and inviting scenery as did this locality, and the many places I have since lived, and numerous other places seen, has only tended to confirm such early formed conclusions.

I will now proceed to give my recollections of its inhabitants, commencing at the farm of Hunton Parish now owned by Georgo Parish on the south side of the river. Mr. Parish was then and for many years thereafter a successful farmer on that farm. The same house now the farm house was then his home. Lightning in those times as well as now, sometimes came uncomfortably near the homes of people. I remember hearing it told that it came down the chimney of Mr. Parish's house when his wife was standing near the fireplace passed under her foot, tearing the sole from her shoe, and left the house without serious injury to either the house or its occupants. Mr. Parish soon after my acquaintance with him purchased one tier of lots off the Maynard farm, thus enlarging his own.

The Almiron L. Maynard farm was the next farm east of Mr. Parish's. It included at that time the portion south of Mr. Parish, the Dye farm and the present David Orr farm. The easterly fifty acres of the Orr farm was sold by Mr. Maynard that year to Mr. Joseph Crandall. Mr. Crandall afterwards sold it to Mr. E. R. Ford. I purchased it of him and in the decade of 1860 I sold it to its present owner Mr. David Orr. The Orr farm was sixty years ago was known as the Mickle farm.

The year 1841 Col. W. W. Snow built a house for Mr. Maynard on his farm, the one for a number of years past occupied by John Scramling and family. About 1850 Mr. Maynard sold his farm in parcels to a number of different individuals, myself being one of its purchasers. With that and subsequent purchases, 160 or more acres of it came into my ownership, which I sold to Mr. Orr.

AUGUST 11, 1892
BIOGRAPHICAL SKETCHES OF ITS OLDEST INHABITANTS (PART 2)

John Fritts owned and occupied the next farm east. The house in which he resided is the same one now occupied by his daughter and granddaughter. He was not only a good farmer and citizen, but also a noted hunter. He seldom suffered a season to pass without one or more successful deer hunts. He was also a successful bee hunter. The bees were never keen enough to evade his Diogenes-like search. He was one of the moving spirits and original owners of the Oneonta and Franklin turnpike.

The next farm east was then owned by Jonathan Brewer and family. He and his wife are dead, but all the members of his family are still living, and all but one reside in this town. The farm is now owned and occupied by C. H. Baker. On it for some years after the close of the revolution remained two Indian families, a history of whom was some time ago published in THE HERALD. It was written by Pem. Dunham, a grandson of Jonathan Brewer and wife. It was a valuable historic article. The buildings on the Brewer farm have nearly all been rebuilt since it passed from the possession of the family. A willow tree stands a short distance above the house, which is said to have been brought from down the river as a walking cane while the farm was still in Montgomery county, and stuck in the ground where it now stands.

The next farm east of the Brewer farm was then known as the Andrew Parish farm, where he with his family for many years resided previous to his purchase of the E. R. Ford farm, now the property of the Scramling family and of Hunton Parish. In 1851 it was owned and occupied by Ephraim Parish. It was afterwards divided and Nicholas Alger purchased that part which is now the Amsden farm. The house where Mrs. Amsden now lives was erected in 1842 by Wm. J. Smith for himself as a residence, he having previously purchased a lot of a few acres of the Parishes where it stands.

The Morenus farm, the next one east in 1841, was the home of Jeremy P. Morenus and Martin Morenus. The widow of Thomas Morenus, Jeremy's father, resided with him. Thomas Morenus was one of the pioneer settlers in this valley. He was a soldier in the Revolution. He was for some time a British prisoner in Quebec. The exact date of his first settling here I am unable to ascertain. Some say that it was before and others say that it was directly after the Revolution.

His son Jeremy died March 27th, 1884, aged 85 years. He was a strictly honest man, a man whom one could rely upon every time. He was a soldier in the war of 1812 and was for some time a prisoner in New York during that war. I will relate a specimen of his honesty. Some time after L. S. Osborne or Shepherd & Osborne commenced business in R. J. Emmons stone store, I was there one day when Jeremy came in with a dinner plate in his hand. He gave it to Mr. Farmer, the clerk, with this remark: "When we opened the package of plates we found 13 instead of 12, the number I paid you for. I thought best to return it immediately before it was forgotten." I had considerable dealing with Jeremy during his lifetime and I ever found him a perfectly honest man. His death was hastened by being thrown from a wagon. He was very active until near the time of his death.

His mother lived with him until her death, at which time she was nearly one hundred years old. The next farm east was the Francis Brewer farm. It formerly embraced all the lands now included between the Morenus and the farm now owned by Mr. . Williams. Francis Brewer was one of the pioneers in this vicinity. He built his first house upon the hill near the woods, upon the farm where he resided for some years. He afterwards built the house and barns torn down by the writer in 1859, when he built the present buildings upon that part of the farm now known as the Youngman farm.

I well remember Francis Brewer, having had many conversations with him of old-time events. I remember his telling me that the first time he came here they were making maple sugar at the corner of Luther street as late as the fifteenth day of May, that the flat in that part was then covered with large maple trees. There used to be a wrought nail factory upon the bank of the river, nearly north of the barn on the Brewer farm. Some of the old foundation timbers remained there when I owned the farm in 1859.

Elias Brewer had a farm east of that owned by Francis, his father. It was formerly part of the Francis Brewer farm. He, with his family, resided there in 1841. Asa Brewer a few years later built the house now owned by Sarel Hudson. Asa for some years owned about sixty acres of the westerly part of the old Brewer farm.

The present Williams farm was then owned by John Hackett, the father of the John Hackett now residing still farther east on the river road. The Williams farm is the one named in a former paper as the Joachin VanValkinburgh farm; upon which the portion of General Clinton's army on the boats bivouaced in 1779, when on their way to join the army of General Sullivan at Tioga.

Just easterly of Mr. Hackett's farm house stood an old blacksmith shop in which worked one Hillsinger and sometimes Anson Hawkins. A house stood a little east on the opposite side of the road, occupied by the family of the blacksmiths. At a later date it was the home of Mrs. Simerson, a daughter of Francis Brewer. She died but recently at a ripe old age.

On the next farm lived the family of George Swart. Sessions' barn occupies its site. His (Swart's) old house recently stood on the north side of the road nearly opposite that of Frank Sessions, the present owner of the George Swart farm. On the westerly side of the farm, where the present one stands, was an old plank school house which must have been built during the previous century if appearance gave correct indication of its antiquity.

The farm east of and adjoining was owned by William Swart, the brother of George and the two next small houses near by and on the north side of the road were occupied by two sons of William Swart sr. These three dwellings are all gone and a newer one occupies the place of the old farm house. The farm is still owned by a descendant of the Swart family.

The adjoining farm east of the Swart farm was owned and occupied by Aaron Brewer, the great grandfather of Frank Sessions. He early lived on the farm and there died. His only daughter married William Hackett, eldest son of John Hackett above named. This old Aaron Brewer farm was one of the first settled in this vicinity, by Elias Brewer, the father of Aaron.

On this farm for many years after the Revolution was kept a tavern by the Brewers, and the place became noted for military trainings, the small flat west of the house on the south side of the road being cleared of its stumps and used as a parade ground. The Brewer were quite numerous and many of their descendants are numbered among our citizens to-day.

Erastus Blanchard married a Brewer and lived the next house east on the opposite or south side of the road. His farm was originally a part of the Elias Brewer farm. Erastus in those days was one of the best business men on that side of the river. He was honest, trusty and reliable and had a memory which would retain a long string of accounts and dates with perfect exactness, as the writer well knows by actual experience.

This Blanchard family deserve a short notice. Their mother, Mary, was a sister of Conrad Wolf. James Blanchard married her nearly a hundred years ago and they settled on a farm between the Wolf farm (the present George Swart farm) and the Ouleout creek about two miles north of the latter. They raised a family of eighteen children, sixteen of whom grew to manhood and womanhood and proved worthy citizens. Many of them and their descendants still reside in this vicinity.

A story is told of their early life worthy of record. One summer afternoon one of their children strayed into the cornfield and fell asleep. Not awakening and among so many not being missed, he lay out all night. In the morning when the matter came to the knowledge of the father, he mildly said to his wife, "Mother, hereafter nights we must count them and see that they are all in, lest a like accident again occur."

AUGUST 18, 1892
BIOGRAPHICAL SKETCHES OF ITS OLDEST INHABITANTS (PART 3)

The farm adjoining the Brewer and Blanchard farms was owned and occupied by Hontice J. Couse and family. He had a large farm and was in good financial circumstances. He was a fine looking man of commanding appearance. He raised a family of five daughters, some of whom with their posterity still live in this vicinity. This is the last farm I will name on the south side of the river, as it is farther east than its corporate limits now extend upon its northerly side.

This tier of lots comprising the farms named was all formerly in Delaware county, the Susquehanna river previous to 1822 being the county line. When the town of Huntsville was formed this tier of lots was taken from that county although the fact that the law took off further east than that town extended, was not known to the inhabitants living east of the David Orr farm for more than fifteen years afterwards.

We will now return to the corporate limits at their westerly bounds on the north side of the river, and come up River street easterly with our record. I wish I could picture with my pen the present village of Oneonta as it is photographed in memory at that date.

In our village charter passed February 23d, 1885, the boundaries of Oneonta are described as follows: "All that part of the town of Oneonta, Otsego county, New York, lying within the following described boundaries, to wit: Commencing at the northerly bank of the Susquehanna river at the southwest corner of lot number one hundred and sixty-five in Wallace patent and running northerly along the west bounds of lot number one hundred and sixty-five to the head or north line of the patent; thence easterly along the said line of the patent to the northwest corner of lot number one hundred and eighty-four in said patent; thence southerly along the west bounds of said lot number one hundred and eighty-four to the north bank of said river; thence down the northerly bank of said river to the place of beginning, shall continue to be known as the village of Oneonta, and as such shall have perpetual succession, etc."

The first charter of the village covered a much smaller area, of which I shall speak in a following chapter. That the lands now embraced in the corporate limits in 1841 were almost exclusively farm lands will be readily seen as I proceed. But now quite a village extends both east and west of its present bounds.

I will commence at the corporate limits on the north side of the river, coming up the river from the west. The first house I remember was then just built and it was the one standing directly opposite the road leading from the Parish bridge to the River road. It was then occupied by William J. Smith, its builder, but during the year was purchased by Isaac H. Peters, and was his first place of residence in this town.

The next house was that of Conrad Wolf, the same house still standing and the one in which Mr. Wolf and his wife resided until her death and as long as he kept house afterwards. East of Mr. Wolf resided Jacob Farrington senior, the father of the present Jacob Farrington of our village. His wife was Conrad Wolf's sister. The old Farrington house has within a few years been rebuilt.

On the adjoining farm east, in 1841, the time I name for all these present described places, resided a farmer and millwright by the name of Charles Spoor. He purchased the farm of Andrew Parish. One of the things he used to name was that he paid Mr. Parish a thousand dollar bill on the purchase. Mr. Spoor had for many years worked at mill building in Georgia and Alabama, and his stories of southern life and customs were very interesting. The house then standing and occupied by Mr. Spoor has been removed and is now the first house north of the railroad crossing on the east side of Fonda Avenue. A fine new dwelling was erected on its site by Celey Wood esq. some years ago. The farm which is still unsold is the property of H. A. Fonda.

What is now known as the chapel was the next house. It was owned with the farm by the Rev. J. W. Paddock, the installed minister of the Presbyterian church. He removed during the summer to the Bennett house, which I shall describe later. His family consisted of his wife, one son and three daughters.

Next came the home of Andrew Parish. It stood in front of where the Scramling residence now stands. It was purchased and removed by M. N. Elwell and converted into No. 34 River street and No. 45 Main street, where in the latter Mr. Elwell still resides. This farm had but a short time before been the property of Eliakim R. Ford and he set out the fine rows of maple trees which stand upon both sides of the street as it crosses that farm.

The house now owned and occupied by Henry Wilcox was just being vacated by its former owner, Mr. Lawrence Swart, and Gideon Ray, the father of James Ray and grandfather of Mrs. Dr. Manchester's mother, was moving into it in March, 1841. Messrs. Collier and Goodyear had exchanged the farm since known as the Ansel Barnes farm west of the Cooperstown Junction for it, and Mr. Ray was its first occupant after it came into the possession of Messrs. Collier and Goodyear. The house, where Alderman Samuel Coon now resides and owns, was then a one-story house upon the same farm. In it the writer's father and mother moved in the month of October, 1841 and lived until May 1st, 1842, it that fall being the only unoccupied house in the present corporate limits.

Upon the south side of River street, about where Burnside avenue now is, was an old ashery building which had been used for the manufacture of pot and pearl ashes in former years. It was soon after torn down.

Mrs. James McDonald, the third wife of James McDonald esq., of whom I shall speak more fully hereafter, occupied a house which stood near where the old Squire Shaw house now stands.

The next dwelling was the old James McDonald tavern, which was built by him in 1810 and opened as a public house in 1811. It was in 1841 kept as an inn by David Sullivan. Mrs. Sullivan was an excellent landlady, everything about the house and table being the picture of neatness and order. The food was always of the best and prepared by skillful hands. I boarded with the Sullivans several weeks at different time and my recollection of every incident of such residence with them is pleasant to remember.

This old tavern building should not be passed without a brief record. The building was well built and is still a good house and if suffered to remain will be for many years. It was the site of the post office from 1817 to 1829, during which years its proprietor was Milfordville's postmaster. After Mr. McDonald's death in 1834, Mr. John M. Watkins commenced his long term as mine host in that hostelry. He was followed by William Fairchild as its landlord, then came David Sullivan. When vacated by the Sullivans Mrs. James McDonald was its keeper for a couple of years. Isaac Brewer was its next landlord. He was succeeded by Henry Dunham. Next came James Ray who I think was its last occupant as a keeper of a public house.

About 1853 it was purchased by Rev. Erastus Westcott and fitted up by him as a residence. Rev. John Smith was its next owner and occupant. Ephraim Parish and son became its next owners. At this writing it is still owned by the Parish family. For a number of years it has accommodated two families and it is doubtful if a better paying dwelling can be found anywhere of its age and lightness of expense of repairs.

The highway, always until changed to a private residence, ran across the present yard close to the corner of the building, and the other branch of the road east where the mill house now stands leaving a large green in the space between. The old road passed up through the mill yard and around where the Shellman shops now stand. Where the Florence block, the Hackett and Elwell residences now stand and the street in their front was an impassable swamp, in which numerable frogs held nightly concerts and daily light songs during the entire part of the warm season. After the grading of the railroad across it, Mr. Elwell cut a ditch to let off the surface water. I then purchased it and completed its reclamation.

AUGUST 25, 1892

BIOGRAPHICAL SKETCHES OF ITS OLDEST INHABITANTS (PART 4)

The next house northerly to the tavern on the west side of Main street was an old frame house which stood back of the swamp above named. It stood where the easterly part of Elwell's garden now is. It was occupied by Wm. W. Snow and family. A lane passed from the street from where Mendel's gate now is to the Snow house and the barn beyond. It has ever been a wonder to me why that swamp of nearly three acres in extent, should for a hundred years have been suffered to remain, when a drain of two hundred feet would have made it dry land, at a cost of ten or fifteen dollars.

On the high ground north of Fairview street stood the house now known as the Peters house. It was owned and occupied by Sylvester Ford and wife, the parents of E. R. Ford. They were an aged and very fine couple, respected and loved by all.

Mr. Ford kept a large fine cow. In the winter time he used to lead her to the mill race to water. To prevent her slipping he had her shod sharp like a working ox, and she would walk off on the ice with her head up, as if conscious of her safety from slipping.

The Nathan Bennett house came next. It was the same one recently moved back by Mr. Lacey. It stood where his two new ones now stand. It was occupied by Mr. Bennett in the spring but during the early fall Dominic Paddock moved into it. I well remember attending his donation party there in the late fall month.

The stone basement house now owned by Hon. W. L. Brown was that season being erected by Timothy Sabin. He moved into it that fall. I shall say more of Mr. Sabin hereafter. The Dr. Joseph Lindsay house was then the same as now except its occasional repairs. It was occupied by the doctor and his family. It consisted of his wife, John, Jacob, and Sally Ann.

The doctor to a great extent had ceased the practice of medicine. He was the pioneer physician in Oneonta having moved here in 1807. He was a man of superior education and in 1841 was engaged in teaching a select school composed mostly of young men. He was always busy even in his advanced age and almost always when out doors wore an overcoat. One day I met him on the street with a rake and fork on his shoulders going to the hayfield. He was always social to us young men and greeted us kindly when we met. It was in the afternoon and a very hot day.

After passing the usual salutation, I said to the doctor, "Would you not be more comfortable this hot day with your overcoat off?" "Why, no, Baker, it is as good to keep the heat out in a hot day, as to keep it in on a cold one," was his reply. I could but smile at his philosophy, but no doubt in his case it was correct. He was a thin spare man not overburdened with hot blood.

I shall ever remember Dr. Lindsay with feelings of reverence. His wise counsel to me in his old age was of inestimable value. I had for three consecutive winters about the close of the decade of 1840 suffered intensely with a pain in my stomach. It usually began with the commencement of cool weather in the fall and lasted until warm weather in the spring. I counseled with the best physicians in the state but none could or did tell me the difficulty or its cure.

The pain would begin in from one to two hours after eating and continue until the next meal. Eating would at any time stop it as long as the food remained in my stomach. But I had ever rigorously observed only at meal time to eat, and had no idea of keeping my stomach continuously grinding food.

Some physicians advised me to chew tobacco. Others to smoke it. But only three years old I had taken a bit of it in my mouth and I had decided that the one bit was enough for my lifetime. I, too, had seen the force of the tobacco habit on others, and thought I had rather risk my pain than that disgusting filthy habit.

One day meeting the doctor I thought I would state my case to him and did so in as few words as I could. He heard my story and then enquired, "You always drink cold water as a drink, do you not" I answered in the affirmative. "Cease drinking cold, and use warm drink with your meals. Drink liberally and quite warm." At his, to me, singular advice I made no reply but looked him in the face. He proceeded: "I think your trouble is the excess of gastric juices in the stomach. They are too strong and when food is out of it, they gnaw on the coats of the stomach. Warm drinks will reduce them. Cold ones will not. Try the warm ones and see the effect."

I, the next meal, drank liberally of weak but warm tea and to my joy was immediately cured. It was as speedy as the most successful Christian scientist' best work. More than forty years have passed and during all those years his counsel has proved correct. A number of times I have tried to return to cold drinks without warm ones at my meals and after a few days the old pain would return. Even now if after eating I feel any uneasiness in my stomach a drink of warm water soon sets it all right.

Dr. Lindsay has many descendants in this vicinity. Among them are his grandsons, Loomis J. and Dudley M. Campbell of this village. Both these men have achieved worthy and commendable distinction as scholars, teachers and authors. The former, especially, will long be remembered for the compilation of the best dictionary in the English language. They have a library of rare works which it would be hard if not impossible to duplicate.

The Angel tavern, called by him the "Oneonta House," came next with its sheds and barns. It occupied the entire corner from where the Amsden blacksmith shop now stands around to the office of the Evening News. It was then kept by Mr. Angel. I staid there over night in March on the second trip I made to this valley.

Mr. Angel was a man whose memory and history ought to be preserved. I regret that I do not know more of it. He was a carpenter and joiner by trade and an extra good mechanic. The old Presbyterian church building in Oneonta was his work. The church records of Milford show that in 1805 Ezekiel Follett and William Angel contracted with the trustees of the church to finish it before the 19th of January, 1807. It was completed in advance of the time named.

Some of the best early mechanics in this town and Milford were the apprentices of William Angel and learned their trades of him. Among them were Munson R. and John M. Watkins.

Mr. Angel was among the first promoters of the Oneonta and Franklin and the Charlotte turnpikes and was a charter director in each of them. His prophecies of Oneonta's future which I have myself had from his own lips, mark him as a man of almost miraculous foresight.

He married for his second wife in 1837 a Mrs. Gates, a widow lady, the daughter of James McDonald esq., and the sister of our present townswoman, Mrs. Andrew Parish, who at an advanced age resides at No. 14 River-st. Mrs. Gates was the mother of Gen. Theodore Gates of the late war and of the wife of Judge Erastus Cook, late of Brooklyn, N.Y.

Mr. Theodore Gates entered the army under Col. George W. Pratt of the Ulster guards as first lieutenant-colonel. He held that position when I saw him near Centerville with Colonel Pratt and his regiment in March, 1862. After Col. Pratt was killed he took the command and soon rose to worthy distinction in our country's service. His work called the "Ulster Guards," published in 1879, I consider the best history of the war I have ever seen. He is still living in New York city, but I am told is in very poor health.

William Angel was appointed postmaster in Oneonta and held the office from May until December 1841. The office during that time was kept in the west front room of the Oneonta House. Mr. Angel died November 12th, 1841, aged 62 years.

The next house easterly of the Oneonta house, was the Otsego house, as it was then called, standing upon the opposite side of Chestnut street from Angel's tavern. It was then kept as a hotel by Elihu Brown.

In my paper of the "Baird block," in giving the name of Brown's predecessor, I gave the name of Griswold; I have since learned that it should have been John M. Watkins. He was the successor of the Emmons named in that paper, and kept it for two or more years; years later he was again its landlord as stated.

John M. Watkins attained a high reputation as landlord and his wife as landlady. They had many years experience at that business; they first kept the McDonald house, then the Otsego house at two different terms, and twice the Oneonta house; the last time for many years its owner. Then for some years the American, on State street, Albany.

While in the latter house, an incident occurred which clearly demonstrates their ability and resources in a case of emergency. One morning, before beginning to get breakfast, the cooks all struck and left the kitchen. The house was full of guests. The occurrence was at once reported by Mr. Watkins to his wife, in her room up stairs. She promptly said, "I will fill their place until new cooks can be obtained." Then with a daughter, she went to the kitchen, and with the aid of such help as remained had a fine breakfast on hand at the usual hour; and all went on as smoothly at the hotel as if nothing out of the ordinary had happened. The guests did not even know of the ripple in household affairs. New cooks were immediately obtained to fill the places of the strikers. In all my acquaintances with married people, I never saw a pair who equalled Mr. and Mrs. Watkins in their love and affection for each other—noble qualities of worthy citizens!

Elihu Brown left the hotel about the close of the year 1841. He moved to Rondout in 1842. He was the starter and promoter of the stone age in Oneonta. He commenced it in 1836 and during the following years he erected the W. S. Fritts house, the R. J. Emmons store, the Ford mansion and store, the Huntington store, and the Sabin store basement. He was for those times quite a noted builder. I once met him after he had resided a number of years in Rondout.

The Roderick J. Emmons stone store then used as a stove and hardware store, was the next building east. It is the same building now undergoing such thorough repairs by its present owners, the Cornell Brothers. This was the first of the stone stores erected by Elihu Brown, who became famous as starting and continuing the stone age in Oneonta.

Mr. R. J. Emmons, besides his store was also at that time running a foundry it being the first one started in Oneonta village. Joseph Tabor had, however, for a number of years carried on one on the Otego creek where the Culver foundry now is.

SEPTEMBER 1, 1892
BIOGRAPHICAL SKETCHES OF ITS OLDEST INHABITANTS (PART 5)

Close to the east side of the Emmons store stood the old Jacob Deitz store. It was in 1841 occupied by Messrs. Clyde & Cook as a general merchandise store. The Mrs. L. L. Bundy brick store is on the same site. Enos S. Brown was Clyde & Cook's successor. The next building was the old Jacob Deitz house, recently the residence of Mrs. L. L. Bundy. It was occupied by Mr. Slingerland and family, he having married the widow of Mr. Deitz and the family of Mr. and Mrs. Deitz there resided. The barn on the old Deitz farm stood where the Tobey and Brown block now stands. It was low land at that place and in the spring time a miniature pond of water usually occupied the south or front yard of the barn.

The building now owned by the United Presbyterian church stood where the Central hotel now stands, and was the residence of R. J. Emmons of the stone store before named. At that date not even a foot path extended along the north side of Main street between the Deitz and the Emmons houses.

Then came the office and residence of the late Dr. Samuel H. Case, one of Oneonta's best men, citizens and long life physicians. I had intended to devote some space to a biography of Dr. Case, but the superior one by Dr. Lathrop of Cooperstown, published in THE HERALD of July 21st, 1892, will be read by all its patrons and it does much better justice to the memory of that noble man and physician than possibly could my pen. I trust every reader of THE HERALD has given it careful perusal.

Just east of Dr. Case's residence stood a building which was built for an Episcopal Church. It was occupied for such purpose.

Next came the new stone mansion of E. R. Ford. It was erected during the years of 1839, '40 and '41. Mr. Ford, immediately after the purchase of the Frederick Brown farm, commenced the erection of that dwelling. He had all the pine lumber for its inside finish sawed and for several months sunk under water before its being air seasoned for use. The house still stands and I hope long will as an evidence of his design and forethought aside from the persevering toil of its erection. The land all the way from the stone house to the present site of the Free Baptist church was farm land and farmed by Mr. Ford. I shall devote more space to Mr. Ford in a future paper.

A small house stood on the corner of Main and Maple streets, then occupied by John M. Watkins. On the opposite corner where Vosburgh's house now stands was a large two-story shoe or chair manufactory. Its occupants were Nathan Graves and Robert Riddle.

The next building stood well back from the highway and was occupied by Wm. H.

Schofield as a cooper shop and residence. I think the building had been made of the former wagon house of Simeon Walling, the one erected by the man Keech as named in a former chapter. Mr. Schofield had a long sign over the gateway which passed from the street to his shop. The Schofield firkins had a high reputation among the farmers at that time.

Mr. Schofield is the only mechanic who was carrying on business in town in 1841 who is still engaged in the same business. In fact I do not remember any business firm of that time which in any continuous form exists unbroken until this date. William McCrum was at that time learning his trade with R. W. Hopkins, and is still in the same business at which he has become rich, but he is the only other man that I can call to mind still living in the corporate limits and pursuing the same business that he was fifty-one years ago.

The next dwelling was that of Joseph Walling. It was the old red tavern house of his father, Simeon Walling of Revolutionary times. The name and memory of both these ancestors of our honored townsman, J. R. L. Walling, is ever dear to all who had the pleasure of their acquaintance or ever with their personal history. When Joseph Walling in 1854 erected his fine brick residence, the first built in this village, the old frame house was removed to East End and is still doing service as a good dwelling.

The next dwelling was the house still standing at the southwest corner of Main street and the Yager Hill road. It was at that date occupied by the late Rev. John Smith and family. He was then the distinguished and successful pastor of the First Baptist church of this place. He was the father of our present townswoman, Mrs. Henry Wilcox, of River street. Elder Smith and family were for many years my next door neighbors and every memory of them is pleasant to recall.

The next house was in March, 1841, occupied by David T. Evans. Almost directly before its front door stood a mile board of the Catskill Turnpike company, the railroad of those times. Dr. Evans soon moved to near Ford's store and opened a tailor shop in its second story front rooms. The doctor soon commenced the practice of veterinary surgeon and soon secured a good practice and remarkable success in the profession.

He was one of the most interesting conversationalists of his time. His numerous and captivating stories of things of his own experience and observation ought to have been preserved to pass down the pages of history not only to perpetuate his memory, but to add to the instruction and entertainment of future generations. He recently died at a ripe old age.

SEPTEMBER 8, 1892
BIOGRAPHICAL SKETCHES OF ITS OLDEST INHABITANTS (PART 6)

Crossing the turnpike road and returning westward the first house within the present corporate limits was the one now standing first west of Otsego street. It was occupied by Sylvenus Smith, who had a tannery west of it back towards the Oneonta creek.

West of the creek on the high table land stood the residence of David Yager, the father of David J. Yager esq. Several of his descendants still live in town.

David Yager was an early settler in Oneonta. He first purchased and improved the farm up the Oneonta creek, which is still known as the Yager farm and now owned by W. Babcock esq. When the Yagers first came to town some years prior to their final location here, on going up the Oneonta creek while all was yet primeval forest, they found encamped on that farm a large party of the Mohawk Indians. They left, thinking Indians to numerous and whites too scarce for a suitable place for a future home.

There stood a small house where the Catholic church now stands. It now is a part of the parsonage, being removed from its former site.

The Mrs. Reynolds house was just then being built by Mason Gilbert. It was not finished or occupied.

Then came the Presbyterian church, the oldest church in town. Dr. Joseph Lindsay was that season teaching a select school in the upper front rooms in the church. I well remember the first time I saw the venerable doctor accompanied by a number of his pupils. Dr. Joseph Lindsay came to this place in 1807. The particulars and peculiarities of this distinguished old gentleman were some of them named in the last chapter.

The next building was known at that time as Ford's horse barn. It stood back of the creek near where the back end of the Reynolds & Wilcox block now stands. Silver creek at that time passed down through the low lands and found its way into the mill race at the east end of Barn hill.

Then came the Brockway house which stood on the present site of the Westcott block. It was then occupied by Sylvenus Noble and family.

A house stood where the Dr. Hamilton residence now stands, which was occupied by Mr. Noble and son Charles as a shaving and toilet soap manufactory and also by S. B. Beach as a manufactory of Beach's famous shoe and harness blacking.

The old Dr. Evans house which is still standing was occupied both as a residence and an office by a Dr. Knapp, D. T. Evans moving into it that fall and opening a tailor shop up stairs in the northwest front corner room of E. R. Ford's stone store as before stated.

The residence of John Tanner the distiller came next and stood where the McCrum and Saunders block now stands. His distillery stood directly back of Ford's store, about where the Press office and Luther's cabinet ware rooms now are.

Ford's stone store stood where the Ford block now is. It was then just being finished and was first occupied in March, 1841.

Westerly of Ford's store stood the wagon and blacksmith shop of Turner and Horace McCall. I am not positive whether they were occupying it in 1841 or not, but I know they were a short time thereafter. Just back of that shop was the foundry of Roderick J. Emmons. It stood below the bank on a level with Tanner's distillery. A sweep horse power was used to give the blast for melting iron at the foundry.

The motive power used at the distillery was supplied by the water of the Ford spring and also from Silver creek. It was carried in troughs and a ditch around the bank and applied to an overshot wheel, and thus power was obtained to propel the millstones to grind the grain used in the distillery. Silver creek was at time a durable stream the year round. The following year, 1842, the dwelling and distillery of Mr. Tanner was purchased by Bedford Chamberlain of Maryland, and the Tanner property passed into his possession.

In 1841 Mr. Chamberlain was running a distillery in Maryland which stood where the David Wilber saw mill now stands. Gilbert Campbell was his distiller. In the flood of February 1842, the distillery and grist mill adjoining were washed away and Mr. Chamberlain and Mr. Campbell exchanged Maryland for Oneonta as a place for business and future home. James Pendleton had a blacksmith shop which stood just back of where the west end of the First National bank block now stands, west of it stood a building occupied by Jacob P. Vanwoert as a tin shop and stove store. He had married the year previous and had just started new in the tin and stove business. He lived in a part of the same building.

I remember that in 1842 W. W. Snow was his partner in the business and that I bought a parlor stove of them that fall. The building was afterwards moved father eastward and owned by Stafford Van Woert, and for several years occupied as a tin and stove shop and store. It was burned with the other buildings in the big fire of July 27th, 1881.

Next came the Solon Huntington store. The same building is now occupied by Samuel Mendel and brothers as a store, one of the oldest and most reliable firms in the county. Separated only by a stairway west of it was the stone house erected in 1836 by William S. Fritts and occupied by him as residence and tailor shop. John B. Steele, attorney at law, had his office in the upper story. A. G. Shaw was his clerk and student.

The brother of Mr. Steele was killed at or near Andes in Delaware county in the anti-rent war. I was at Andes the day previous to that bloody tragedy and all was quiet and serene. Counselor Steele married the eldest daughter of Dominie Paddock and soon thereafter moved to Kingston, Ulster county. He was afterwards an M. C. In the fall of 1841 Wm. S. Fritts was appointed as postmaster to succeed William Angel. He was a fine penman, a good officer and worthy citizen, besides being a first class tailor.

The Reynolds building recently burned was the next building west. It was then owned and occupied by Timothy Sabin as a store. He at the time was postmaster and the office was kept in the store. Silas Sullivan was his clerk. Sabin rebuilt his store that year. It stood off the bank and was reached by a plank bridge from Main street. He had a safe built in the northeasterly corner of the front wall of its foundation. Many of our citizens will remember noticing it after the building was burned in March, 1888.

SEPTEMBER 15, 1892
BIOGRAPHICAL SKETCHES OF ITS OLDEST INHABITANTS (PART 7)

Next west was a vacant lot which contained the noted spring, that was by many anticipated to have much to do with the future growth and prosperity of Oneonta at an early date. It had years before been reserved in conveyances especially for public use. But in 1829 E. R. Ford had purchased one half of it and in logs conveyed a part of it to his residence at River street. I used water from the same logs until they failed some three or four years after my residence was erected on the southwest corner of Main and River streets.

Next west was the home of Potter C. Burton. The house was built by Mrs. Burton's brother in 1835 and purchased by Mr. Burton the following year. Mr. Burton was from 1835 until his death a resident of this village. He accumulated by his industry and economy a fine property. He was a superior mechanic, a good financier, a kind parent and husband and a worthy citizen.

Westerly and adjoining the Burton building was the Cook and Brown store. The firm was composed of Samuel J. Cook and Adam Brown. In this building on its second floor was at that time published the Oneonta Weekly Journal. More of this paper will appear in a later chapter.

The Cook and Brown store building formerly stood on the southeast corner of Main and Chestnut streets. It was formerly occupied as a store by E. R. Ford before he removed to the south corner of Main and River streets. Mr. Angel moved it to make room for his enlarged hotel. This and the Burton building were off the bank and were approached over a wide plank platform. In the fall of that year Mr. Cutshaw built the retaining wall and filled in between the street and buildings. A portion of this wall is still standing on the premises of the writer who for the past forty years has owned the Burton premises.

The old house west of Goldsmith's store was the next building. All the blocks from the Burton building to it as well as this house were burned October 14th, 1891. In 1841 it was occupied as a dwelling by John Cutshaw and family. That year he moved the old school house which formerly occupied the site of the Ford stone store, to his lot on Chestnut street he had purchased of Enoch Copley. George Bixby moved it for him by the job. It now forms the south wing of his home at No. 56 Chestnut street.

The building next was the one now known as the General Burnside house. In 1841 it was the home of Charles Cushing as a dwelling, and also of Miss Lena Bennett as a tailor shop. A few years later it was owned and occupied by the late Woodbury K. Cooke as a law office and dwelling.

No other building was reached until near the saw mill. The old house still standing was built by Joseph McDonald about 1808 and so far as I can learn is the oldest house on the corporation. It belonged to Collier and Goodyear and was then occupied by Samuel McCrany. He and his son John were blacksmiths and their shop stood nearly in front of the house just on the edge of the sawmill yard. In the fall of 1841 I ironed a light sleigh in their shop which still annually does service. The old blacksmith shop was moved north a year or two later to just east of where the line of the railroad passes Main street. A man by the name of Dix was its first occupant after removal. Stafford Potter, a distinguished hoemaker, was its next occupant. His hoes had a wide fame all the country round. After Mr. Potter the Moshers were its occupants. When the railroad was built the old shop disappeared.

Between the old McCrany house and the mill pond stood a small house occupied by the sawyer. His name was Snyder. A daughter of his a year or two later caught the small-pox and had the disease in that small house amid a large family and not one of them caught it. Dr. Hamilton was their physician. He at once inoculated the family for the kine pox with the result named.

This house was the one which in the decade of 1820 was removed from the southwest corner of the lot where the Baird block is now being erected. As soon as the Snyder family vacated the house I tore it down. That was done in February, 1844.

The old McDonald saw mill stood about sixty feet east of the old miill foundation now standing. I built a new one on the present site in 1843. The grist mill is the same with additions as in 1841. I repaired it and added another run of stone, new waterwheels and bolts in 1843. The two store rooms, as wings, have been added since, also the driveway in front. They were the work of Mr. Elwell, its occupant for nearly forty years. Just below the grist mill where C. C. Stewart's plow shop now stands, was a small frame house which was occupied by Caleb Bennett, the miller.

The next building was a wool-carding and cloth-dressing establishment. It was occupied by William W. Snow. He had in his employ James Van Valkenburgh, a grandson of the Joachim Van Valkenburgh named in connection with General Clinton's passage down the river, in chapter three of these papers. He married the daughter of Elias Brewer—made a man of distinction and served one or more terms as a member of our state legislature.

With the old clothing shop the buildings on the east side of Main street close as they were in 1841.

Upon the west side between the river and River street the first building going north was Mason Gilbert's hat shop. It has since been changed into a residence and is the property of Richard Ruland, who now occupies it. Next comes the former residence of Mr. Gilbert.

The building next north now owned by A. C. Wolcott was occupied in 1841 by two fine looking young ladies by the name of Mariom. They were milliners by occupation.

Then came the Orrin Adams house. It has been removed to the back end of the lot and is now the property of Mrs. O'Neil.

In 1841 it was occupied by John Reynolds, the father of our present townsman, George Reynolds of Grand street. John Reynolds was a man who must not be passed by without notice. He was one of the most useful of men. In cases of sickness or death, in those times of need when acts of kindness and aid are most wanted and appreciated, he was without his peer. No matter the time of day or night, no matter how pressing his work, no matter how inclement the weather, he was ever ready to respond to such a call. Many are the memories of his kindly aid by the former citizens of Oneonta. Such kindly acts continued unabated during his life. For some years he was my near-by neighbor, only a few rods distant. My second one south. I speak from actual knowledge of his personal worth. He was a trunk and harness maker by trade and did honest work with the best of material. Such men and such citizens lift up and enoble the human race. He died in Oneonta July 20th, 1857, aged 55 years. His wife still survives him and is remarkably active at the advanced age of 93 years.

Next north of John Reynolds came the old Ford house, then occupied by William F. Raymond. He had but recently purchased it. He was the joiner who did the wood work of the Ford stone mansion. I purchased of him the site of my house and he was its boss builder in the fall of 1841 and winter of 1842. It stands a few feet south of the old Ford store. The north side of the store was about thirty feet north of the north end of my present home, a home I have occupied since May 1st, 1842. The store was twenty-six feet in width. Mr. Raymond and myself moved it across Main street and converted it into a machine shop. It was burned down November 20th, 1875.

The old Ford residence has been rebuilt and is now the home of D. L. Hecox esq. He has erected several other buildings upon the old Ford Property.

I have now named every building I remember except some barns which were upon River and Main streets, within the corporation limits in 1841. I will now proceed in like manner upon the other streets.

What is now called Maple street and is a fine popular thoroughfare, was then called Bronson lane. Mr. Bronson being the owner of the land upon the east until it reached the Walling farm. His was the only house I remember as standing upon it not already named on Main street. It stood near where the houses of Messrs. Benjamin and Butts now stand. Another house stood on top of the hill north of the Normal school building, which was occupied by Daniel Sullivan. It was a log house mostly surrounded by woods.

Up the Oneonta creek road the only house within the bounds of the corporation limits lived Daniel Gifford. His house stood over across the creek and was approached by a road which ended at his residence. The first house up the creek road was that of Abram Houghtaling, the father of Mrs. Gifford. He lived just out of the corporation limits.

SEPTEMBER 22, 1892

BRIEF BIOGRAPHICAL SKETCHES OF ITS OLDEST INHABITANTS (PART 8)

Chestnut street had the same name in 1841 as now and was practically upon its present site. On its easterly side after leaving Main street the first house north of the Otsego house was a small building standing near where the Morris Brothers' store now stands. It was owned by Samuel B. Beach and occupied by Caleb Lake, a barber. Next came the shop and cabinet warehouse of Robert Hopkins. In this shop our townsman, William McCrum, learned his trade. He was an apprentice with Mr. Hopkins at that date. Mr. Hopkins was an excellent mechanic and citizen. Where the Miles residence now stands then was the dwelling of Samuel J. Cooke, who at that date was in trade with Adam Brown. Mr. Brown was the son of Frederick Brown, the former owner of the E. R. Ford farm.

Next came the residence of Solon Huntington. He purchased it of Timothy Sabin in 1840. Robert W. Hopkins' house was north of that of Huntington. It occupied the site of the present Methodist parsonage. His garden was where the new brick church now stands. Mr. Hopkins was famous for a good garden.

A colored man by the name of Ben Petrie lived in a small house about where George Baird's north line now is. His mother who lived with him was known as aunt Dinah. A small house also stood just north of where N. I. Ford now resides. It was occupied by Chester G. Cross, a wagon maker by trade. The N. I. Ford house was built that year by a Mr. Jenkins. A short time after he sold it to Elisha Shepherd, father of Mrs. Ford.

About where Eseck Blend now resides was the home of a family by the name of Morrell. Mrs. Munson Watkins, who lives with Leroy Hackett on River street, was of the Morrell family.

Returning to Chestnut street, Eli Derby lived where the John Pardoe place now is; Daniel White, the father of Anthony White, once resided there. A barn stood near where Hon. James H. Keyes' garden now is. The house on the north corner of Chestnut and Academy streets was the next. It was owned and occupied by Hezekiah Watkins, the father of our townsman, Timothy D. Watkins, and of Abiatha H. Watkins of Cooperstown. Hezekiah Watkins was a noted stage proprietor in those times when stage coaches filled the place of present railroad cars. He was an excellent business man and a worthy citizen.

The house on the opposite corner of what is now Academy street was then owned and occupied by Adam Brown. It was afterwards purchased by P. C. Burton and was his residence until he erected the fine mansion in which Mrs. Burton now resides.

The adjoining lot south was owned by William S. Fritts. It was then occupied as a residence by Mrs. Knapp and her son, Wm. J., the editor and publisher of the "Oneonta Weekly Journal." In its upper westerly room Miss Herrick had a school. She afterwards became the wife of William Miller esq. of North Franklin, father of the late Colonel Miller.

Caleb Potter, the father of Mrs. Jacob Brown, owned and occupied the next building, lately the office of the Daily News. He was a cooper by trade and an excellent citizen.

The Oneonta hotel shed and horsebarn buildings filled the remaining space to the hotel building.

What is now called Grove street was the Church street of those days and only extended north to the present northerly line of Academy street. Its only buildings on its west side was the school house which stood where Goldsmith's house now is, and the James Pendleton house which still occupies its former site on the corner of Grove and Academy streets. On its easterly side was the Baptist church, and the sheds on its north and east side. The barn still standing back was there then as now except its age.

On the corner of the street which is now the east end of Academy street, was a house, the one still standing on the southwest corner of Academy and Grove streets. It was occupied by George Bixby, the father of our respected townsman, Edward Bixby, late of the firm of Bixby & Miller. George Bixby was a mason by trade and was for many years a resident and respected and useful citizen of Oneonta.

This ends the list of buildings as I remembered them within the present corporate limits in 1841, with the names of their occupants with but few exceptions. There were many citizens whom I remember whose names do not appear as occupants of dwellings. These were mostly boarding at the hotels or in private families, or where more than one family occupied the same residence.

The merchants on the south side of Main street in 1841 were: Cook & Brown, Timothy Sabin, Solon Huntington and Eliakim R. Ford. Those on the north side were Clyde & Cook and R. J. Emmons.

Physicians: Dr. Joseph Lindsay, Dr. Knapp and Samuel H. Case. Dr. Case is the only one I remember as practicing to much extent. James Pendleton and Samuel McCrany were the blacksmiths. Cabinet ware, R. W. Hopkins; foundry, R. J. Emmons; distillery, John Tanner; tailors, W. S. Fritts, D. T. Evans, John Cronkite; harness maker, John Reynolds, coopers, Wm. H. Schofield, Caleb Potter; boots and shoes, Smith & Carpenter; wagon maker, C. G. Cross; shoe maker, Darius Brewer; builder, Wm. F. Raymond; painter and chair maker, George Andrus; wool carding and cloth dressing, Wm. W. Snow; tinsmith, J. P. Van Woert; jeweler and silver smith, Potter C. Burton; hotel keepers, Wm. Angel, Elihu Brown, David Sullivan; editor and printer, William J. Knapp; miller at grist mill, Caleb Bennett; saw mill, sawyer, David Snyder; clergymen, Rev. J. W. Paddock, Rev. John Smith; toilet and shaving soap manufacturers, Sylvaus Noble and son; harness and shoe blacking, S. B. Beach; farrier, D. T. Evans. For land surveying Ira Emmons esq. was the surveyor. He resided in the east part of the town. Hezekiah

Watkins was the stage proprietor and mail contractor for most of the lines in this region of the country. Oneonta was a noted stage center.

When I left Broome county for Otsego, Oneonta was apparently a place of more life than was Binghamton. That place for years had the advantage of a canal without increase of business or life. But when the Erie railroad made its advent into Binghamton its actual life and growth began.

So too with Oneonta. Its advance dates back really to the completion of the Albany & Susquehanna railroad. From that date its growth has been sound and progressive. It will so continue, its locality is favorable for such growth. It is by nature a center point. It may not really be styled a natural place for the location of a village, but it is one for the concentration of business and where business centers other inconveniences are soon overcome.

As a location for health, for proper drainage, for variety of locations for residences, for beauty of scenery, for interesting surroundings, for a natural business center, Oneonta has few superiors. It is destined in the near future to become a prosperous city. Already the advantages of city life without its annoyances are enjoyed by the inhabitants.

Soon other railroads and other business avenues will be opened. They cannot much longer be delayed, the business of the surrounding country demands them, and such imperative demands seldom remain long unfilled. Ours is a growing progressing country, its future is to exceed the past with an expanding ratio. Such is ever the developing power of progress. There is no place for stand-still.

Our state has seen and recognized our location and its advantages. It has observed its prospect for future development and located here some of its most necessary and as well as important institutions. It has built an armory of no insignificant kind or dimensions. It has erected, equipped and set in motion one of the finest Normal schools within her bounds.

Oneonta's citizens too are alive and active. The spirit of progress, advancement and improvement is among them almost universal. Such fact is everywhere apparent. No better place for residence, business, or social advantages need be sought than can be found within this immediate vicinity. Industry, economy and good business management in any of its varied forms receive as good reward as do like kinds of business in any other locality where as good advantages can be obtained.

The value of real estate is continually and steadily on the increase. And well may it be. Improvements are continually going forward in an increasing ratio. Much may be anticipated, expected, and surely realized, in the future growth and advancement of Oneonta. At least such is the belief of one who has been its citizen and resident for more than fifty years.

SEPTEMBER 29, 1892
THE TOWN OFFICIALS OF ONEONTA (PART 1)

I am requested to give a list of the supervisors who have from the first of our civil organizations, been the head officers of this vicinity.

I suppose the person making the request was not aware that he was asking an impossibility. But no doubt it will be of interest to a large number of readers of THE HERALD to learn what can be correctly reported of our early town organizations.

While all this region was in Montgomery county, on March 7, 1788, a town was formed called Otsego, which town embraced the larger county of portion of what is now Otsego county. Of course that new but extensive town must at that date have contained many inhabitants.

Almost fifty years had passed since the Lindsay patent had been granted for 8,000 acres of land in the region of what is now the towns of Cherry Valley, Springfield and Roseboom. We must also bear in mind that in 1770 a patent had been granted by the English crown, known as the Otego patent, which patent still is the foundation of the titles of most of the lands now comprising the towns of Oneonta and Milford. The terms of that grant were, that at least one family must be settled within two years of its date, upon every thousand acres of its arable lands contained within the 69,000 acres of the patent.

We have reason to believe from the best sources of information we can obtain, that such terms were practically complied with, for the validity of the grant was sustained and its title not questioned. If such be a fact there must have been quite a population in this region at the outbreak of the revolution.

That such was the case we have abundant evidence, but, unfortunately, we are unable to obtain a record of either their names or of their early history except of a very few. We in our town have the names of Henry Scramling, Stoughton Alger, Joachim VanValkenburgh and there were others whose names I am unable to learn. But the fact of such settlers is established by the diaries of Van Hovenburgh and Beatty of the army of General Clinton, when they passed down this river in 1779.

Such fact of early settlements in the Susquehanna valley is further established by the map and account of the raid of Colonel Butler from Fort Defiance (the middle fort on the Schoharie creek) in September, 1778. Colonel Butler, with his army of 260 men, cane by the way of Harpersfield to Colliers, there crossed the river, went down through this place and down the river to Ouaquago.

They burned the Scotch settlement at the mouth of the Ouleout creek, the village of Unadilla on both sides of the river, with the grist mill and saw mill and also all the buildings of the Tory settlements below Unadilla to where Windsor now stands. A detailed history of these events will be found in the history of General Sullivan's Indian expedition, published by order of the state senate in 1887. The publication of that work has rescued from oblivion many important historical facts in this region of the country, which without its record, would have been forever lost to the world.

The fact that the larger part of these settlers who came previous to the revolution were loyal to the British crown, and of course by our people called Tories, is established beyond doubt. At the beginning of the war many of them joined the British army. Those who were not Tories were obliged to seek safety by fleeing to their former homes. Among those who fled to the protection of our lines in the Mohawk valley were the Scramlings and Algers before named.

It will be remembered that the Colonel Butler I have named as leading the raid down the Susquehanna river, was Col. William Butler, formerly of the 4th Pennsylvania regiment. He was one of General James Clinton's army who went down the Susquehanna river in 1779 to join the army of General Sullivan at Tioga. General Clinton was a native of Orange county and the father of Dewitt Clinton. I make this explanation as the names of Butler and Clinton are, by those not familiar with our history, often confounded with like names of prominent officers in the British army.

Had these pioneer settlers left us a record of their names and of their civil organizations we would be rejoiced thereby, but if such a record was kept it has not been preserved for our satisfaction or information. My grandfather on my maternal side, early after the revolution became a pioneer in this valley, having settled in what is now Bennettsville, in the town of Bainbridge, while that town bore the name of Jericho. I have in my boyhood days heard many of the traditions of the early settlements of this valley, particularly of Unadilla. I am glad to know that the facts learned from General Sullivan's Indian expedition confirm so many of these traditions that I am constrained to believe them all virtually correct.

After the town of Suffrage had been formed from Unadilla, which occurred on the 5th day of February, 1796, soon thereafter notices of a town meeting were posted, which was held at the house of Isaac Collier, now Colliersville, Tuesday, April 5th, just two months after the formation of the town.

I will copy the names of all the officers elected at that town meeting, as by so doing a better idea may be formed of our early official organization. It will also be noticed that the list contains several names of those who were former residents of this immediate locality.

James Moore was elected our first supervisor. He was also re-elected each year thereafter to the same office until 1806. The name of the town was changed from Suffrage to Milford in 1800, so it will be noticed that Mr. James Moore was supervisor of Suffrage so long as such name existed for the town, and also the first six years of the town of Milford. Henry Scott was elected town clerk, John Moore, Joel Stoddard and Aaron Brink were elected commissioners of highways. John Bevins, Joseph Culver and Samuel Whitmarsh were elected assessors; James Westcott and David Hamlin were elected overseers of the poor; John Felton jr. and James Westcott were elected constables; David Cully, Henry Scott and James Moore were elected poor committee; Samuel Bidwell was elected poundmaster; Lemuel Sergeants, Samuel Doolittle, Aaron Brink and Daniel French were elected fence viewers.

OCTOBER 6, 1892
THE TOWN OFFICIALS OF ONEONTA (PART 2)

There were nine road wards or districts in town. I will omit the bounds and names of path masters or overseers, except the 5th, which was the ward through this corporation. It commenced on its east end at Houghtailing creek and extended down Main and River streets to the town line. The town line was the Stoughton Alger farm, later the Ward farm and now the Bingham farm.

The Oneonta creek was then called the Houghtaling creek, as the father of the late Abram Houghtaling was an early settler on the farm first above the Gifford farm up the creek. Aaron Brink was the first overseer of this highway ward.

In 1807-8 James Westcott was supervisor. In 1809-13, Ezra Adams was supervisor. In 1814 John Moore was supervisor, 1815, John Dietz. In 1816-17, John Moore. In 1818, John Badger. In 1819-24 Peter Collier was supervisor. In 1825-26 Jacob Dietz was supervisor. From 1827 to 1830 inclusive Peter Collier was supervisor.

In 1830, April 17th, the town of Oneonta was formed, taking therefor a portion of each of the towns of Milford, Otego, Huntsville and Davenport, and the year following it commenced electing its own town officers.

The first town meeting was held in the new town of Oneonta at the house of Thomas D. Alexander on the first day of March, 1831, Eliakim R. Ford and Robert Cook present, being justices of the town. After the opening of the meeting by proclamation it was resolved:

1st. That there be three assessors elected for said town.

2d. That there be four constables elected for said town.

3d. That there be four poundmasters chosen for said town.

4th. That an amount equal to the sum which may be distributed to said town from the common school fund be raised by tax for the support of common schools in said town.

5th. That the sum of one dollar per day be allowed to the fence viewers of said town.

6th. That five per cent be allowed as the compensation of the collector as his fee for collecting the taxes for said town.

7th. That all circular and partition fences in said town shall be at least four feet and six inches in height.

8th. That widows who have no land shall be entitled to let their cattle run at large in the public highways from the first of April to the first of December.

9th. Resolved that the annual town meeting shall be held on the first Tuesday of March.

The following were the officers elected at this meeting: Supervisor, William Richardson, (he was also elected in 1832-33); town clerk, Adam Brown; justices of the peace, John Dillingham, Jonah Northrup and John S. Yager; assessors, John Van Woert, John Fritts and John T. Quackenbush; commissioners of highways, Isaac Shepherd, Ansel Marvin and William Angell; overseers of the poor, George W. Smith and Samuel Carpenter; collector, Hiram Shepherd; constables, Hiram Shepherd, David Sullivan, Emanuel Northup and Robert Cook; commissioners of schools, Obediah Gifford, Peter Dicks and Joseph Walling; inspectors of schools, Samuel H. Case, Washington Throop and Amos Cook.

Omitting the overseers of the highways first elected in Oneonta I will now proceed to give the names of our supervisors in the order of their election and terms of service:

1834-5—William Angell.
1836-8—Samuel Betts jr.
1838-9—William Angell.
1840—Samuel H. Case.
1841—William W. Snow.
1842—Timothy Sabin.
1843—Carleton Emmons.
1844-6—Eliakim R. Ford.
1847—Enos S. Brown.
1848—John M. Watkins.
1849—Carleton Emmons.
1850—Jonathan Brewer.
1851—Luman S. Osborn.
1852-3—Carleton Emmons.
1854—James F. Dean.
1855—David J. Yager.

1856-7—Samuel H. Case.
1858—Harvey Baker.
1859—Silas Sullivan.
1860—Hosea A. Hamilton.
1861—John Cope jr.
1862-3—Stephen Parish.
1864-72—John Cope jr.
1873-4—William W. Snow.
1875—George Scramling.
1876-7—William H. Morris.
1878—Walter L. Brown.
1879-80—Henry G. Wood.
1881—J. R. L. Walling.
1882-8—Walter L. Brown.
1889—Deforest Wilber.
1890-2—Henry Bull.

The list given comprises twenty-six different names during the existence of the town of Oneonta. It also contains eight which cover the time we were embodied in the towns of Milford and Suffrage. We were in towns under those latter names thirty-four years. And under the name of Oneonta sixty-two years.

I regret my inability to add the names from 1788 to 1796 to my list. But I have already gone back of what the town of Otsego can do by its town records. Their records were burned many years ago, about 1825, and of course the older ones, while the town was in Montgomery county, were also destroyed.

Why the town of Unadilla has not preserved their records since the close of the revolution I cannot divine. But they do not assume to go back even to the formation of the town. That town was formed the 10th day of April, 1792, but the record only goes back to 1796.

OCTOBER 13, 1892
MILITARY ORGANIZATIONS OF ONEONTA

Oneonta's military record will require but a short chapter. The first of such record found in the adjutant general's office which comes near our locality is of the date of 1806. At that time Matthew Cully of Milford was made lieutenant colonel in the Sixth regiment, and Alfred Carfts of Otego, now Laurens, was made captain. These two commissions bear date, March 19th, 1806.

I have now before me the commission of John McDonald as Captain of an infantry company, which was the first company of militia ever formed in this town of which I can find any record. The commission bears date, February 29, 1812. Joseph Mumford was lieutenant colonel. I found the original records of the same commission the office at Albany. It was signed by Daniel D. Tompkins, as governor and "commander-in-chief of all the militia of the state of New York, and admiral of the navy of the same." These commissions passed the state secretary's office the 10th day of March, 1812, Anthony Lamb, secretary. This organization of infantry seems to have been continued. The company roll of 1828 shows Eliakim R. Ford its captain, David Marvin lieutenant and Jacob Newkirk ensign. This roll is under date of September 1st, 1828, and is in Captain E. R. Ford's handwriting. John M. Watkins was first sergeant, William Smith second sergeant, Leander McDonald third sergeant and Clark W. Baker fourth sergeant. The roll contains forty-one names of officers and privates.

The roll of 1831 shows David Marvin as captain and John M. Watkins as ensign. This roll contains fifty-eight names as attending drill September 4th, 1831.

John M. Watkins was commissioned captain of the company to date from August 25th 1832, but this commission was signed by Governor W. L. Marcy and Adjutant General John A. Dix, the 5th day of January, 1833. The roll of September 3d. 1832 contains eighty-eight names of which sixty-three were present at that drill.

Among the list I find the names of most of the old citizens of this region of country. Jacob Morrell and Sylvanus Smith were fifers. Jacob Hillsinger and Henry Smith were drummers. Among the privates we find the names of John Cutshaw, Levi Tarbox, Abram Blend, Aaron Ford, Joseph and James Fern, Henry Yager, David and Daniel Sullivan, Frederick Bornt, besides many other familiar names and old citizens of this vicinity. Joseph Walling was first sergeant, John D. Yager second, Harvey Carpenter third, and Peter Yager fourth. Solomon Yager was first corporal, Chauncey M. Brewer second, Oliver McDonald third and David Yager jr. the fourth. In 1834 John M. Watkins resigned his commission which was accepted as follows:

STATE OF NEW YORK,
BRIGADE ORDERS.
SPRINGFIELD, March 22d, 1834.

Brigadier General Walter Holt has accepted the resignation of Captain John H. Watkins of the 60th regiment, 2d brigade and 16th division of infantry of the militia of this state, and he is hereby at his own request honorably discharged from the said office.

WALTER HOLT
Brigadier General 2d Brigade, etc.

This shows sufficiently the standing and position of the military of Oneonta at that early date. It also shows that its commanding officers were at the time of receiving their commissions comparatively young men. John McDonald was commissioned captain at the age of 27 years. He was the eldest son of James McDonald and was a man of fine physique, well educated for the times. Mrs. John M. Watkins and Mrs. Andre G. Shaw were his daughters. He was born in 1825.

John H. Watkins was born in 1806. He was commissioned captain at the age of 26 years. His residence was in this town from his birth until his death except the few years which he spent in the Merchants' hotel in Albany. He died April 25th, 1890, in his 84th year.

It will not be interesting to follow our military organizations farther previous to the late war of the rebellion nor the various enlistments from this town in that war. They have been recorded in our country's late history. We will therefore skip the intervening years from 1835 to 1875 in our military record.

The Third Separate Company was formed August 5th, 1875, with Henry G. Wood as captain. Captain Wood's commission bears date of July 26th, 1875. The general order for the organizing of the company was issued August 10th, 1875, Franklin Townsend, adjutant general. This company is known as Third Separate company infantry, 28th brigade, 6th division, national guard of New York. At its organization it had 103 members, including officers and privates. Its first officers were men who had earned fame in the great war of the rebellion. Captain Wood was an officer under Generals Custer and Sheridan in the cavalry. He was an able and competent officer, well versed in military tactics and also in civil affairs as a private citizen. He was highly honored by the people of Oneonta. They elected him supervisor in the years of 1879 and 1880. He was in June, 1879 made by the board of supervisors one of the building committee of the new court house then decided to be erected for Otsego county.

The first lieutenant of the military was William H. Morris, the second was Nathan Hemstreet. Simply the names of the first three officers of the Third Separate company are alone enough to warrant its success.

To such an extent had this company inspired the public confidence that in 1885, on Thursday, the 18th of June, the corner stone of a state armory was laid and the work completed that year. The public spirited people of Oneonta by private subscription the year previous purchased the site for the armory and conveyed it to the state. The result was the erection and sustaining of a state armory and drill room and shooting hall, which are alike an honor to the state and also to the village of Oneonta. The building occupies a prominent position on the eminence on the north side of Fairview Street, at a point where it is in fair view of all the travel upon the line of the A. & S. railroad as well as from the public highways approaching the village.

Captain Walter Scott was the second commissioned captain of the Third Separate company. His commission bears the date of September 28th, 1886. Under the command and able management of Captain Scott the company has lost none of its prestige and high moral and military standing. It ranks high among the military organizations of the state.

The presence of properly officered and thoroughly drilled military organizations is becoming yearly more necessary for the safety of the public peace and the preservation of our American free institutions. Without the aid of such restraining power our civil authorities would often be compelled to succumb to the violence of mob rule, and anarchy be left to usurp the place of law and order. But with a well drilled military force within easy reach its moral restraint is so powerful that its more efficient and stronger force of arms is seldom necessary for the public security and welfare. It is the duty of every good citizen to honor and aid the country's military organizations. No one can tell the moment its force will became a public necessity, a restraining power otherwise unobtainable.

Skill in the use of arms has ever been among the most necessary and most powerful agencies for the preservation of the public peace. Sharpshooters at long range have ever been the dread of all contending belligerent forces. The side having the most skilled marksmen always possesses a decided means of advantageous success. Hence the necessity of the continual and successful use of arms, as skill in marksmanship only comes by long and persevering practice. Under the able and practical training of Captain Scott, one of the best shots in the Empire state, the Third Separate company has acquired an enviable and distinguished reputation in such practice which enables it to rank high among the best military marksmen in the country.

The recent call for military aid to preserve peace and protect life and property at Homestead in our neighboring commonwealth of Pennsylvania, and still later in our state at Buffalo, are but samples of the state of anarchy and disorder which are at any moment likely to occur under the unwise guidance of associations of men who undertake to trample the rights of others and of the public into the dust and to supplant private rights and liberty with disorder and anarchy.

Without such military organizations to aid our civil force very often the thoughtless mob would rule and neither property or life be safe even in our well governed state. But since railroad and other corporations are barred by state statutes from themselves organizing and employing an armed force for the protection of their property or that of others under their care from destruction, it becomes imperative that military companies composed of true loyal men be within easy and speedy reach in every case of need.

The recent case at Fire Island is not without its lesson. When men become so void of all feelings of humanity as to be guided entirely by selfishness and to leave their homes and cross wide areas of water to prevent their suffering, starving fellows from landing from a poor, storm rocked ship, compelling women and children to suffer for want of sleep, of food, of warmth, as well also as able bodied men like themselves, if in no other case the importance of military power here becomes apparent. When common feelings of humanity have left a human form, such form has no more use in our civil compact. Its mission is completed. Oblivion should alike cover it and its memory. Should Governor Flower pursue each and every participant in that disgraceful melee, excepting no one, from a judge or lawyer down to the oar puller of the poorest skiff until every one of them was utterly banished from our land, he would receive the praise and approval of every loyal citizen of our state.

Our common good demands that there be no abatement in our love of country, our loyalty or our military zeal. The safety of our free institutions and their perpetuity depends upon the loyalty of succeeding generations. When personal selfishness assumes command of public affairs all is lost. The higher and nobler principles of liberty and humanity must ever continue to prevail if freedom and frree institutions are to be preserved.

Oneonta and the vicinity within reach of its military protection are to be congratulated. Well may they feel proud of such an organization. It is alike a guaranty of safety and peace to it and all its surrounding country.

OCTOBER 27, 1892
ONEONTA VILLAGE INCORPORATION (PART 1)

The first incorporation of the village of Oneonta was obtained in 1848. Application was made at the June term of the court of sessions of Otsego county, "in the matter of the incorporation of Oneonta village, in the town of Oneonta, county of Otsego, in which, upon the petition of Samuel J. Cook, Worthington Wright, Collis P. Huntington, Samuel H. Case and others, on reading and filing a surety, census, notice of application, etc., *** on the report of Horace Lathrop, James R. Angell and H. G. Harding, dated August 15th, the county judge, James Hyde" ordered that an election be held and a vote taken for or against such incorporation.

The order named the 14th day of October for such vote and the hotel of John M. Watkins as the place of holding such election.

Such vote was taken and the certificate of the inspectors of such election, who were John McCrany and E. C. Hodge, shows that "the whole number of votes given at such election was eighty-two, of which the number having thereon the word 'yes' was sixty-six and the number having thereon the word 'no' was sixteen."

Of all the eighty-two names contained in the above named poll list the following still live in Oneonta village, viz. Andrew G. Shaw, D. J. Yager, John Cutshaw, H. A. Hamilton, William McCrum, Orlando Sullivan, Timothy D. Watkins, Harvey Barnes, Wm. H. Scofield, Harvey Baker and DeWitt Ford. C. P. Huntington resides in New York city. I remember no others who then voted that are now living.

After a careful examination of the list I can remember but a single voter within the corporate bounds whose name does not appear on the list now before me. That one name is that of William H. Olin. Why he did not vote I cannot assign any satisfactory reason, for he was the active party in obtaining the incorporation. The certified poll list becomes a part of the official incorporations papers. It was a move of much importance to our people, and my recollection is that nearly every legal voter cast his vote either for or against the measure. The completed papers of Judge Hyde, the clerk's certificate and the map and bounds of the incorporated tract, all bear the date of October 27th, 1848.

It will thus be seen that the affirmative vote of sixty-six of our citizens decided the question of our incorporation as an incorporated village, which was affirmed by Judge James Hyde at the date above named.

Oneonta's first village election was held December 2d, 1848. The following are the names of the officers elected: For trustees, Eliakim R. Ford, Hezekiah Watkins, William Bronson, William S. Fritts, Samuel J. Cook; assessors, John Cutshaw, Elisha Shepherd, Ephraim C. Hodge; village clerk, William H. Olin; treasurer, Andrew G. Shaw; collector,

John McCrany; pound master, Solon Huntington; street commissioners, Collis P. Huntington, Harvey Baker, Hosea A. Hamilton.

The poll list of the village election showed that 28 votes were cast and E. R. Ford was the only candidate who received the entire 28 votes. The town inspectors again acted as inspectors of this first officer election. E. R. Ford was by the trustees made the first president of Oneonta village.

William H. Olin (the late Dr. Olin) was then a rising young lawyer in Oneonta and on March 7th, 1849, it was resolved and adopted to levy the sum of fifty-six dollars and five cents upon the taxable property within the incorporation for the purpose of paying William H. Olin the necessary and proper expenses of procuring the incorporation. This resolution was indorsed by E. R. Ford, president.

I remember that I did not myself favor so early an incorporation. I thought we ought to have at least twice as many voters before we chose especial guardians over our affairs, but of course I submitted to the will of the majority.

We had already a fire organization and a small fire engine and C. P. Huntington was foreman of the company. I will relate an incident that occurred about 1845 or 1846. The fire company, under the command of their foreman, came down to the mill race between the saw and grist mills for practice, as was often their custom. After practicing for some time throwing water in various directions, some one proposed to try the stream on the grist mill window in its westerly gable. I was then half owner of the mill property with Messrs. Collier and Goodyear and had it under my charge.

Mr. Huntington himself had the hose pipe in hand and asked me "Shall I try it?" "Yes, fire away, I will risk the window," was my prompt reply. No sooner said than done. The sash and glass were shattered in an instant. "Don't throw water in the mill, as I have grain there," was my immediate appeal, but the position was so oblique that scarcely any water entered it. A bin of from 100 to 150 bushels of wheat was nearly under the window but it received no damage. Mr. Huntington offered to pay me for the window, but I assured him it my risk not his. The quickness of its destruction was a source of much satisfaction as well as surprise to the fire company. Our townsman, William McCrum, was one of the fire boys who had hold of the engine brake at the time. "How's the grist mill window and the bin of wheat?" was the inquiry I often heard for some weeks after the incident when I happened to meet one of the boys. Mr. Huntington made a splendid head officer for a fire company.

The second corporation election was held March 7th, 1849. The poll list is not preserved but the inspector's list is. Eighty-three votes were cast. Eliakim R. Ford, Hezakiah Watkins, William Bronson, Samuel J. Cook and Err W. Bennett were elected trustees. John Cutshaw, David T. Evans and Ephraim Hodge were elected assessors. Hosea A. Hamilton and Harvey Baker were elected street commissioners; Solon Huntington poundmaster, by 83 votes.

The third officer election was held March 10th, 1850. E. R. Ford, H. Watkins, James T. Wild, S. H. Case and E. W. Bennett were elected trustees; W. H. Olin, clerk; John Mc-

Crany, collector; Solon Huntington, poundmaster. On the 16th day of September, 1849, the trustees leased of Solon Huntington "a piece of ground for the purpose of being used as a pound lot and also a passage or driveway thereunto for the said village for the full term of twenty years in consideration of one dollar."

This pound lot was located nearly where the Windsor hotel barns now stands. The lease covers a full page of legal cap and is signed and sealed by the trustees and Mr. Huntington. At a later date the first village prison or lock up was erected upon this lot. It was a structure of stone.

At the election of 1851 Eliakim R. Ford, Harvey Baker, John T. Wild, Err W. Bennett and Hezakiah Watkins were elected trustees. D. W. Ford was elected clerk, David J. Yager, treasurer. An especial election was held April 9th, 1851, at which the following resolutions were passed:

> *Resolved*, That the sum of fifty dollars be raised by tax in the incorporated village of Oneonta upon the taxable property therein to defray the expenses of building one or more reservoirs in said village.
>
> *Resolved*, That the sum of thirty-five dollars be raised by tax in the incorporated village of Oneonta upon the taxable property therein to defray the expense of purchasing some engine hose to be used in the extinguishing of fires.

Eighty-five dollars contrasts considerable with the thousands raised now.

At the election March 3d, 1852, Harvey Baker, S. M. Ballard, John McCrany, John M. Watkins and William Bronson were elected trustees; A. G. Shaw, clerk; D. J. Yager, treasurer; E. B. Shove, collector; S. Huntington, poundmaster. A tax of twenty-one dollars and ninety-nine cents was voted for this year.

NOVEMBER 3, 1892
ONEONTA VILLAGE INCORPORATION (PART 2)

As no previous mention of by-laws is made I suppose the following, prepared by the president of the board, were the first by-laws published and in force in the village:

SECTION 1. All persons are hereby commanded to observe the following by-laws, under the forfeiture of the penalties thereunto annexed, to be collected by the trustees of this village for the benefit of the same.

SEC. 2. To keep all places where fire and ashes are kept safe from exposure from accident, and to make such improvements for security against fire as the trustees may direct on their examination of the premises. Forfeiture for not complying with the above, three dollars for every twenty-four hours after being notified by the trustees that such premises are unsafe.

SEC. 3. Not to obstruct the street or sidewalk by allowing or leaving any obstruction therein. Forfeiture, $2 for every offence.

SEC. 4. Not to run or trot any horse for a horse race or trotting match in any street or lane. Forfeiture, $2 for every offence.

SEC. 5. Not to play any game of ball, quoits, wrestle or fight in any street or lane. Forfeiture, $3 for every offence.

SEC. 6. Not to ride or drive on any sidewalk, except to cross the same. Forfeiture, $1 for every offence.

SEC. 7. Not to suffer any dirt, or filth of any kind, to remain on the sidewalk or in the ditch opposite your premises. Forfeiture, $1 for every twenty-four hours such nuisance is suffered to remain after being notified by one of the trustees to remove the same.

SEC. 8. Not to allow any sheep, swine, horses or neat cattle to roam at large in any street or lane. Forfeiture, $2 for every offence.

SEC. 9. Not to burn any shavings or other substance within eight rods of any building, except between the hours of seven and eleven a.m. Forfeiture, $2 for every offence.

SEC. 10. Not to explode or ignite any arms, fire-balls, rockets, crackers or other fire works within any street or lane without the consent of a majority of the trustees. Forfeiture, $2 for every offence.

SEC. 11. Not to exhibit any shows of any kind, circus, caravan, or other exhibition of natural or artificial curiosities, without the written permit of a majority of the trustees and complying with such regulations and paying such sums as they shall prescribe and exact. Forfeiture from $10 to $20 for every offence.

SEC. 12. Not to permit any show, circus, or other exhibition on your premises, unless such permit has been first obtained from the trustees. Forfeiture, $5 for every offence.

HARVEY BAKER, President,
JOHN MCCRANY,
S. M. BALLARD,
WM. BRONSON, Trustees.

Dated at Oneonta, this 19th day of April, 1852.

A map of the village as incorporated in 1848 is preserved. It shows the east bounds of the village as then to be the west bounds of the Joseph Walling farm, now the J. R. L. Walling farm. Its west bounds are the east line of the Andrew Parish farm, now the Scramling farm. Its south bounds are the Susquehanna river. Its north bounds are the Otego patent line. This corporation continued in force until April 20th, 1870

At that date an act was passed under the title of "An act to incorporate the village of Oneonta, Otsego county, New York," which was passed at the date above named and Oneonta become an incorporated village by legislative enactment.

The following year, March 14th, 1871, an act was passed which extended the bounds of the corporation to their present limits, as named in chapter Twenty-six of these papers, viz. The westerly line of the Conrad Wolf farm for its westerly bounds and its easterly bounds to be the westerly line of the John I. Couse farm. Its north boundary still remaining the Otego patent and its south the Susquehanna river.

The people of Oneonta, finding the charter of 1870 unsatisfactory, in the fall of 1884 called a public meeting and appointed a committee to prepare a new charter. Harvey Baker was by the meeting appointed chairman of such meeting. The committee held many sessions and prepared the present charter with much care.

The village was divided into six wards and a trustee or alderman assigned to each ward and only two of them are annually elected, so that four members of the previous board remain over each year, thus giving a majority of experienced men continually on the board. This new charter was passed by the legislature February 23d, 1885, which, with some amendments, is still in force.

Few villages, if any, have a better system of local government than has Oneonta, or a better plan for the election of its officers.

Each ward has its member in the board of trustees. They are to be actual residents of the ward, and to be real estate owners and taxpayers, and are thus directly interested in the financial management of all its affairs. Streets, walks, sewers, water courses, lights, in fact all and every matter of public interest is by the charter entrusted to the management of the board of trustees.

So greatly has the village increased in all its departments that instead of an annual tax of $21.99, as was levied in 1852, the levy of 1892 was $26,600.50 for the various corporation expenses of the village of Oneonta for the year ending March 1st, 1892. The report shows the receipts for the year of 1891 to have been from all the various sources

$56,707.34, which sum was disbursed as shown by the various payments set forth in such report, with the exception of the sum of $417.96 shown as balance in the treasury at the date of the report. At the close of the last preceding annual report the balance in the treasury was $20.

The $56,707.34 received during the year of 1891 was composed of the tax levy of that year for $25, 030.20, highway tax $4,109.34, notes $21,808.36, bonds $3,500, walks, sewers, poll taxes, etc., making up the sum total as above named of $56,707.34.

Few villages, if any, excel Oneonta in various sources of public improvements and protection. Its water supply, fire departments, electric lights, gas works, street paving, store sidewalks, sewerage system, horse railroad, schools, both Union and state Normal, newspapers, military company, bands of music, churches, railroad and shops, manufacturies of various kinds, all are notable.

Oneonta as a place of residence has few if any superiors. It is healthy in locality, with a great variety of sites for residences or business places. It is in the midst of an agricultural country. Its scenery is of surpassing beauty and loveliness. A view of the valleys of the Susquehanna, the Charlotte, the Otego and the Oneonta streams must be seen with the surrounding hill-sides to be appreciated or enjoyed.

As to schools, churches, in short in all things which render life enjoyable and existence a source of happiness, Oneonta has few superiors. One can here secure all the advantages of city life, with that of country surroundings in their highest perfection. Pure, invigorating, life-giving air and water are everywhere found. Health, the normal state of all our people; happiness and contentment the end attained. Who ever selects Oneonta as a home and place of business or residence is sure, if he performs his part, of such success and happiness as is ever vouchsafed as a reward for well doing.

NOVEMBER 17, 1892
ONEONTA'S FIRST NEWSPAPERS (PART 1)

Oneonta newspapers come in for a share of notice. The first paper published in Oneonta was by a man by the name of Edward Graves. He came from Cooperstown, where his father was carrying on the jeweler business. He was at that time a young man, and was a cousin of Mrs. Carlton Emmons and Mrs. Aaron Ford.

Learning that such early enterprise had been started I had a letter written to Mrs. Nancy M. Harper of Berrien Springs, Mich., a sister of Mrs. Graves, to learn all possible facts about the paper. Mrs. Aaron Ford kindly aided me in my investigation; so, too, did Hr. William McCrum.

From the information obtained I find that a paper called "The Oneonta Herald" was started in the upper story of the Cook & Brown store late in the year of 1838 or early in 1839, and that Edward Graves was its editor and publisher. Its publication was continued for a year or more, when he sold out his plant and soon after went to Michigan, where he started the first paper published in Cass county in that state.

His sister writes that the last she ever heard from her brother was about thirty years ago, at which time he was on his way from Oregon to California.

The name "Herald" seems to have been a favorite with early Otsego county newspaper enterprises. It was the name adopted by Elihu Phinney when he first started the "Otsego Herald" in 1795, and it still proves a good name after almost century's use in our county.

William James Knapp was the purchaser of Mr. Grave's outfit. He was the son of Mr. and Mrs. William Knapp and a grandson of James McDonald esq., his mother being Mr. McDonald's daughter. She still lives, and now resides at No. 14 River street in this village, at the advanced age of ninety-two years.

Mr. Knapp, when he purchased the apparatus and commenced the publication of the "Oneonta Weekly Journal," was a young man only twenty years of age. The publication was continued in the same building in which Mr. Graves had started the Herald. It was a sheet 24 by 36 inches. Its mechanical and editorial execution gave ample evidence of superior skill and ability.

As I pen these lines I have some eighteen copies of this paper upon my table. The following is copied from No.7, vol. 1, of the date of October 29, 1840:

Oneonta Weekly Journal, published Thursday mornings at Oneonta, N. Y., by Wm. J. Knapp. Terms: To mail and village subscribers. $2.00 a year if paid in advance, or within three months after the date of the subscription; or $2.50 at the expiration of the year. To companies of thirteen or more, $1.50 if paid in advance, or $2.00 at the end of the year. All subscriptions for less than a year to be paid in advance. Any person procuring five subscriptions and sending ten dollars current money to the editor will receive a sixth copy gratis.

Advertisements will be conspicuously inserted for $1 a square for the first three weeks and 25 cents a square for each subsequent insertion. A liberal discount will be made to those who advertise by the year. Legal notices inserted at the rates prescribed by law.

All letters and communications for the editor must be free from postage. Job printing of all kinds executed with neatness and despatch and on reasonable terms.

A good quality of paper was used, and the journal of that early date will bear a comparison without loss with our present like-size publications.

Patent medicines then as now came in for a full share of advertising space, while local advertising shows a very liberal patronage of Oneonta's citizens. Among the merchants advertising in this number were E. R. Ford, Sabin & Carpenter, Cooke & Brown, Bennett & Smith, Clyde & Cook, Snow & Van Woert, W. W. Snow, wool carding and cloth dressing works; Mason Gilbert, hatter; R. J. Emmons, wholesale dealer in hardware and manufacturer of castings, etc.; Potter C. Burton, watches, clocks, jewelry, silverware, looking-glass plates, etc.; R. W. Hopkins, cabinet and chair warehouse and manufactory; C. G. Cross, wagon maker, sleighs, etc.

The Angel hotel, where the Stanton block now stands, was advertised as the "Oneonta House," and the one standing where the Baird block is now being erected was called the "Otsego House," and was kept by Elihu Brown.

Timothy Sabin, postmaster, advertises 34 letters as remaining in the post office for the quarter ending Sept. 30th, 1840.

John B. Steele advertises his law office in the Fritts stone building directly opposite the Otsego House.

The marriage of Horace McCall to Miss. Eliza Yager, daughter of Mr. David Yager, occurred Oct. 25th, 1840, by the Rev. John Smith, also of Hansen Gould to Miss Amanda Ford on the 14th of the same month, by the Rev. Mr. Toller. All the above parties lived and died in Oneonta and will be remembered by many of our present citizens.

The arrival of the packet ship, North America, with 200 Mormons bound for the Mormon settlement at Quincy, Ill., is reported and that 2000 more are named as waiting to embark early the next spring for the same place. We thus learn that Mormonism prospered and gained largely in numbers by foreign immigration over fifty years ago.

This paper also informs us that the commissioners were then engaged in surveying and settling our northeastern boundary between the states and the Canadian province of Quebec.

From the New York city market quotations I note the following : Hops, first quality, 35 cents per pound; butter, best, 15 to 18 cents; lard, 10 to 12 cents; ham, smoked, 10 to 12 cents; cheese, American, 6 to 6½ cents; beef mess, $10.50 to $10.75 per barrel; pork,

$14.75; dressed beef averaged $6.50 per 100 pounds; sheep from $1.25 to $3.50. American flax was quoted at from 6 to 7½ cents per pound; Russian flax, 7½ to 9½ cents; pot ashes $5.25 per 100 pounds; pearl ashes $5.25. These figures will show farm product values 51 years ago of the articles named.

The issue of November 18th, 1841, gives the election returns for the county and state. Levi S. Chatfield, Leonard Caryl and Festus Hyde were elected as members of assembly for Otsego county by an average Democratic majority of about 1,400. The state senate that year stood 17 Democrats and 15 Whigs. The assembly 33 Whigs and 95 Democrats. It will be remembered that Democrats and Whigs were the designating political party titles; until 1856, when a union of free soil electors of both parties was made under the name of Republicans, that cognomen still remaining in use.

Medical advertisements in these old papers eclipse if possible the most skillful effusions of modern times, alike in their names and their wonderful cures.

The Reverend I. Covert's "Balm of Life" is without a rival in all cases of consumption or lung diseases, and is backed by nearly a full column of physician's certificates; sold by Clyde & Cook.

"The Balm of China," a remedy just imported from the flowery Kingdom, where for over 3,000 years it has preserved the lives of the celestial citizens, and has by a missionary just been imported to render immortal so far as lung diseases are concerned all Americans who avail themselves of its wonderful powers of restoring the diseased to perfect health; sold by Cooke & Brown.

"The Lion of the Day," the genuine old Dutch German pills, no cure no pay, are advertised by Timothy Sabin, with a long list of recommendations, and brag enough for a model modern quack. I quote a single paragraph: "The East, the fountain of all light, has opened her vast storehouses and is pouring forth to mortals the precious sap of life and health. When in health we have a full view of the wide-spreading waters of the Atlantic and behold old Phoebus with his mighty fires come forth from the waves of the ocean, and in his blazing chariot commence his daily rounds to pour a flood of light upon the world and wake ten thousand songs to the praise of Him who laid the beams of his chamber in the deep, plants his footsteps in the seas, and rides upon the storm."

"Such is the 'lion of the day.' Doctors with all their boasted science step aside and contemplate the ushering in of a new and eventful era, in which the inhabitants are their own physicians."

The above is but a small part of the bombast booming the "lion of the day." No wonder Oneonta has so long been famous for its health record, since its people mere so early and so highly favored with life-preserving medicaments. When we remember that E. R. Ford sold in his old store, which then stood on the southeast corner of Main and River streets, every conceivable life-giving potion, and, from delivered the mail to all the region round about, as well as in Oneonta, thus keeping all the people informed in all matters pertaining to the general good, the mystery is solved; the secret of universal health is revealed. Not that these remedies were purchased and used. By no means; but that they were bought and kept on hand at all times ready if needed.

How long the Oneonta Weekly Journal was published by William J. Knapp I am unable to ascertain. His mother, Mrs. Parish, thinks he published it about two years. My personal recollection would place the time some months longer. The latest number at hand is dated September 9, 1842 and is number 44 of the second volume.

His health failed and its issue ceased. The press and fixtures were sold, I think by Woodbury K. Cooke, who was then a resident of this village. We were thereafter until 1853 without a paper or printing press in Oneonta.

During the early part of our struggles in starting the A. & S. railroad we were compelled to visit Morris, Cooperstown or Cherry Valley to obtain printed bills or notices of various kinds wanted. In 1852 I had Oneonta's first published by-laws printed at Morris by A. S. Avery.

NOVEMBER 24, 1892
ONEONTA'S FIRST NEWSPAPERS (PART 2)

The second Oneonta Herald was started in the village of Oneonta by L. P. Carpenter in 1853. Mr. Carpenter came to Oneonta from the Freeman's Journal office in November, 1852, and immediately commenced arranging for the publishing of the paper. He issued the first number of the Herald, February 3d, 1853. It was published in the upper story of a building standing very near the present site of T. Willahan's store. It was worked off by hand, the strong arm of Mr. Carpenter himself doing the most laborious part of the work. This was a task he had previously practiced on the Freeman's Journal, the last hand press work on that paper being performed by him. I learned the above facts from Mr. Carpenter personally on the 19th of April, 1892.

The Herald was for the times a very ably conducted paper. At the date of its establishment the opportunities for obtaining intelligence from all parts of the world compared with those of to-day were very meagre indeed. Such, however, was the dilligence and enterprise of Mr. Carpenter that he gave us an excellent paper from its start, and thus it continued during his publication of it.

During the struggle of the Albany & Susquehanna railroad, even during its darkest days, the enterprise found in the Herald an indefatigable advocate and champion. The same was true of every local interest, as nothing tending to our local advancement escaped its ably edited columns.

At the formation of the Republican party, the Herald at once espoused the cause of freedom, and lent all its influence in favor of the exclusion of slavery from the free states and territories north of the Mason & Dixon's line.

The Herald with all its patronage was transferred by Mr. Carpenter to Mr. Geo. W. Reynolds in 1866, who at once assumed its future issue. In November, 1871, Mr. Reynolds sold it to C. S. Carpenter, who continued its publication until 1873, when Messrs. Capron & Johnson purchased it and also the Otsego Democrat and started the united papers under head of the Herald and Democrat.

The history of the Democrat is as follows: G. A. Dodge, July 31st, 1868, started in Oneonta village a paper called the Susquehanna Independent. It was a seven-column sheet, 36 by 48 inches in size, its price one dollar per year, its politics Democratic. It was published under the above named title until its 44th number; May 28th, 1869, when its name was changed to Home and Abroad, under which it sailed for a short time and was again changed the Otsego Democrat.

In 1872 it was purchased of Mr. Dodge by Mr. William H. Jefferson, who continued its publication and management as a Democratic organ until 1873, when it was purchased of him by Messrs. Capron and Johnson and by them consolidated with the Oneonta Herald, as above named, and its publication continued as a Republican paper by its recent purchasers.

They fitted up the Broad street stores in the McCrum & Saunders block and for some years the paper was issued from that spacious suite of office rooms.

In January, 1875, Mr. Johnson purchased the interest of Mr. Capron in the paper and the latter retired. He removed to Norwich, Chenango county, and there assumed the control of the Chenango Telegraph. Mr. E. M. Johnson employed Mr. C. S. Carpenter with himself as associate editor and continued the publication of the Herald and Democrat.

January 12th, 1882, the paper appeared under the proprietorship of Johnson and Yager. It was thus continued until January 4th, 1883, when Yager & Fairchild are named as its owners, and the name of Johnson disappears as that of one interested in its publication and ownership.

January 3d, 1884, the name of the paper was changed to its original and proper name of ONEONTA HERALD, which it is hopeful may be continued during all its future existence. It having been the name of the first paper ever published in Oneonta it is but fit and proper that it should be its last.

May 24th, 1888, new presses and an entire new outfit was provided for THE HERALD by its proprietors and an enlarged sheet of eight pages of seven columns each took the place of its former issues, thus virtually doubling its size without increase of cost to its now numerous patrons.

Under the able management of Yager & Fairchild the paper had yearly and steadily increased in public favor and patronage until it had become not only the best but the most popular weekly periodical published in any rural region of our entire country. For its mechanical execution, for its published matter, for the general variety and interest of its news, for the correctness and reliability of its published statements, it stands without a superior in modern weekly journalism.

The entire ownership and control of THE HERALD by G. W. Fairchild, its present editor and proprietor, dates from January 1st, 1890. For some time previous to, and since that date, its editors have been continually assisted in the management of its various departments by A. B. Saxton.

The reading public have been backward in learning and appreciating the desirable qualities of THE ONEONTA HERALD. It has a patronage alike for the extent and number of its subscribers which is without a parallel in any interior portion of our state. The number of its patrons and the area of its circulation is continually increasing. For the money paid for it no paper excels it in cheapness or in the amount and variety of valuable information furnished its readers.

As an advertising sheet it has few if any superiors in number and extent of circulation. As such it is appreciated and patronized. Its outfit for job work is the best and most approved obtainable. It is kept continually supplied with the best improvements of the age.

A visit to the present HERALD office by one who could contrast it with the rude outfit of 1841, as can the writer, is to behold at a glance the progress made in our civilization; and the inventive genius displayed in the mechanic arts, is an object lesson the force of which can in no other way be so well demonstrated or so easily understood. Long may THE HERALD prosper, alike for the good of its owner and that of its numerous patrons.

DECEMBER 1, 1892
A VISIT TO MCCLELLAN'S ARMY (PART 1)

The American Banner was the name of a paper published in Oneonta in the year of 1853 and part of 1854 by John B. King. It was mainly devoted to the abolition of slavery. Mr. King was aided in the start of his enterprise by Isaac S. Ford of Richfield and other noted anti-slavery men of those times.

Mr. King was a genial man, an able writer and a man of ability, but not being much patronized he discontinued the publication of the Banner in 1854. It was issued while published from the old shop building which formerly stood on the northeast corner of Main and Maple street, near where the Vosburgh residence now stands.

In 1854 G. W. Reynolds purchased of Mr. Ford the Banner press and outfit and started upon it the publication of the Franklin Visitor at Franklin, Delaware county. Smith D. King, a son of John B. King, was the Visitor office's first devil. During the war of the rebellion John B. King was a captain of a New York company. He was captured by the enemy and thrust into the notorious Libby prison where he soon thereafter died from exposure and want.

William S. King, late of Iowa, was a younger brother of John B. King. I made his acquaintance during the political campaign of 1855-6 at the time of the formation of the Republican party. He was then a young man of ability and promise. I did not again meet him until after the commencement of the war.

In 1862 when E. R. Ford, Samuel H. Case, Cornelius Miller, Daniel Dibble and myself visited Washington and General McClellan's army of the Potomac, we found William S. King as postmaster to congress. Mr. King, learning from Col. W. H. Chase that I was in the city, sent an especial message for me to call upon him at the capitol. At that time all passage through the army lines south of the Potomac except on the president's or General McClellan's pass was prohibited. I called on him at his office. Finding that our party wished to visit the army, he at once volunteered to try to obtain for us a pass. He succeeded in obtaining one for our party, and on March 11th we set sail from Washington on the steamer Guy for Alexandria.

Had we been five of the crowned heads of Europe we could not have received more courteous treatment from the officers and soldiers of the Union army than did we during our four days' sojourn on the sacred soil of Virginia and on the government boats and cars.

Arriving at Alexandria we visited the Marshall house, rendered famous by the death of Ellsworth, and then went directly to the station of the Orange and Alexandria railroad. The train was just ready to start for Fairfax station, which was as far as the road was in running order, it having been torn up from that point to Manassas Junction by the rebel army.

Upon showing our pass to the officer acting as conductor we were told to appropriate any place we chose upon the train, which was already heavily laden with army stores and soldiers. We were soon at Fairfax station. From there we proceeded immediately to Fairfax court house to the midst of General McClellan's army of 70,000 men who were at that time bivouacked in that immediate vicinity.

We at once proceeded to Gen. McClellan's headquarters. We there found one of his staff ready to give us any information we desired. He could point out precisely where every regiment or even company in that large army were quartered. Mr. Ford had two sons, Clinton and Raymond, in the army, Dr. Case an only son, Meigs, who was a surgeon in the 43d N. Y. Vol.; Isaac Quackenbush was among the Ellsworth avengers; Albert Baker among the Pennsylvania bucktails, all of whom we wished to visit.

We first visited Quackenbush and Raymond Ford and then directed our course toward the quarters of Surgeon Case, near Flint Hill. That the meeting of our army friends was a happy one expresses it but faintly and conveys no adequate idea of the pleasure it gave us.

The land around Fairfax is rolling, no high hills, no plains. The finest sight immaginable was the camp fires in the early evening in every direction as far as the vision could reach. A sight few of us will ever again witness.

It was surprising to see how quickly Dr. Meigs Case had supper and quarters provided for us. A square tent just the right size was soon up and a bed of hay with plenty of blankets sprang into existence like magic.

We talked until about ten o' clock and then laid ourselves to rest. Daniel Dibble and myself being the junior members of our company, took the outsides of our bed next to the canvas with Miller, Case and Ford between us. Just as we retired it commenced to rain in true Virginia style, but it neither interfered with our comfort or disturbed our rest.

In the early morning while it still rained hard, one continuous crowd of the army was passing our quarters on their way back to Alexandria to take boats for Richmond by the way of the Potomac. One can form no correct idea of an army of sixty or seventy thousand men. To see all one can of such a one in motion is still more grand, puzzling and perplexing. It can be remembered but not adequately described.

About ten a.m. we started on foot, except Dr. S. H. Case and Surgeon Case, who rode on horseback, by the Warrington pike road for Centerville and Manassas, which had but two days before been evacuated by Gen. Beauregard's rebel army. On our way we had become divided, Mr. Miller in company with Mr. Dibble, Dr. Case and son, Mr. Ford and myself forming three separate parties. As we were passing a piece of pine woods about two miles from Fairfax, Mr. Ford and myself being the rear party of our company, we saw a regiment standing by their fires all ready to march at the appointed hour.

Mr. Ford suggested that we go to the nearest fire, about which we saw a number of officers, and make them a call. We did so. Imagine my surprise as we neared them at recognizing Col. George W. Pratt, son of Col. Zadock Pratt, who was in command of the Twentieth New York regiment known as the "Ulster Guards." I at once introduced Mr. Ford to him and we had a very pleasant chat.

His first lieutenant was the noted General Theodore B. Gates of Kingston. He was a stepson of William Angel of this place, whose name I have so often written. He at the moment was away on duty. We had returned to the pike but had not yet passed the grove when young Gates sprang down the bank and extending a hand to each, said, "I know you, Mr. Ford; and you, Mr. Baker." We had neither of us seen him for years, but he looked like the Theodore of old except a little older and in a different garb.

Soon after we left Col. Pratt he had returned and learning of our call had run across the woods to head us off before out of reach. Our visit with him was short but sweet. He was a fine young man and worthy officer. Upon the death of Col. Pratt he succeeded him in command. At the close of the war he was made a general of our state guards. In 1879 he published a work called "The Ulster Guards," which gives I think the best history of the great rebellion yet published. On page 182 of his work he thus describes our visit, speaking of the number of civilians who after the advance of the army rushed forward to view Centerville and Bull Run, he thus describes us: "Among the latter class were Messrs. Ford and Baker of Oneonta, N. Y., both of the gentlemen of large wealth and whom I had known many years before. My surprise at seeing them there and on foot was very great. * * * They had set out from Washington to visit Bull Run and as it was uncertain what moment the army might be withdrawn they resolved to do what the soldiers had done—march—and here they were."

I will here state the reasons for our being on foot and without horse or carriage. I had learned of both soldiers and officers before leaving Washington that to see the army and the places we wished to visit our best and only true way was to be entirely unencumbered with either team or baggage. Such proved to be sound advice. Had we taken a carriage our trip with its present interest would have been an impossibility. Being untrammelled we could go where we pleased.

We were about the first if not the very first civilians to visit Centerville after its evacuation. In fact Dr. Alexander, with whom we staied one night, said we were the first that came. Five more from the west on a pass from President Lincoln came during the night and staied at the same place.

Centerville was a little hamlet with perhaps a dozen houses, its first and most noted citizen being Dr. Alexander, a member of the Alexander family of old who were among the oldest and most prominent of the earlier settlers in Virginia. Alexandria received its name from that family.

The Union army had all left Centerville except the Harris cavelry, a regiment of nearly a thousand men. That night the rebels returned in force from Fredericksburg to Manassas; and the height of Bull Run, which had become impassable by the rain making it an immense river, was all no doubt that saved us and a part at least of the cavalry from a surprise and possible capture.

Centerville at that time was a city of log houses built in regular lines for the accommodation of the southern army. It had sufficient houses to accommodate fifty or sixty thousand men and tents enough for ten thousand more. The army of General Beauregard certainly had comfortable quarters during the first winter of army experience.

DECEMBER 8, 1892
A VISIT TO MCCLELLAN'S ARMY (PART 2)

We went from Centerville to the Bull Run at Blackburn's ford, the battle ground of the first day's battle. We there found Stephen Holden, a former student and teacher in the Franklin Institute. We had seen him in Washington, but he could get no pass until after we had left that city. His father was formerly from Hartwick in this county, but had lived for several years on a fine farm he owned which lay between the wooden bridge on the road from Centerville to Manassas and Blackburn's ford. This ford was on a cross road which extended from the Centerville road to the Warrington pike, before named, the two roads at that place being something over a mile apart. The confederate army had during the winter of 1862 erected a bridge at the ford, but upon their evacuation of Centerville they had destroyed by fire and powder all of the three bridges which crossed Bull Run between Centerville and Manassas.

We dined that day with the Holdens, and after dinner in company with Stephen, we tried to cross Bull Run to the famed battleground of the first big battle of the war. The stream was still so high that we were compelled to abandon the project. We had during the day seen large quantities of all kinds of army supplies which the confederate army had left in their flight from Centerville.

At one of the officer's quarters we saw a table set with a fine spread of dishes, roast meats, bread, cake and pie, all in the most tempting form possible. Of course no cautious person would touch food found under such circumstances. It might have been all right, or it might have contained the means of rapid death. The house in which it was found was a good sized double house, lined throughout with tenting canvas, a good floor and a fireplace, beds, tables and chairs. No doubt the quarters of officers in high rank. But the quarters of all the army were good and comfortable, I presume better than either side had during any other winter of the war.

During our tramp this day we passed a large field entirely covered with the carcasses of horses. Their number must have been many hundreds. What was singular was that none of them had sufficiently decomposed to emit any odor. We entered several of the rebel forts. No civilians had yet appeared upon these deserted army grounds except our party, and the five personal friends of President Lincoln before named, who had come upon a pass obtained directly from him. They staid over night at the same house and took their breakfast at the same table with us at Dr. Alexander's. They left Washington the next day after we did and had driven directly through in one day to Centerville. We did not see them again after we left Centerville for Bull Run. Their drive was unobstructed by the Union army as it had, all except the Harris cavalry, reached for Alexandria in advance of their arrival.

After leaving Holdens and Bull Run we returned through public roads, army roads and across battle fields to the Red Mills and the Orange & Alexandria railroad track back to Fairfax station, as tired a lot of men as one would wish to be or see. On our way we wished to enquire the route to a certain military road which had been constructed for our army, and I entered a house for such purpose. A person was covered in bed, head and all, pretending to be sick. In answer to my inquiry a man trying to assume a woman's voice directed me to the next house for the information desired. I was amused at the incident for a man's voice had bade me "come in" when I knocked at the door.

At the next house a woman stood in the door as we approached it. I made the inquiry and received the desired direction, as the road was then within our sight. Seeing no one around I said to her "You are not living here alone, are you?" Her answer was "All are off to the war. There is not a man in the neighborhood."

At that moment I saw a man going from the house to the barn at the next farm not thirty rods away. When some eight or ten rods from the house we had just left, I happened to look back and a man was standing beside the woman in the door looking us over as we were walking cross-lots towards the military road.

On arriving at the road I found an Irishman living in a log house at its side. I commenced talking with him and found him communicative. He assured us that we were running a risk as the people were all rebel, and advised to get within the army lines as soon as possible.

Soon after leaving him we heard two rifle reports in the woods only a short distance from us. The next day we learned that two Union soldiers had been shot. A short distance below we came to where the trees, some of large size, had been cut off by rifle balls. By whom the firing had been done and for what purpose we could not learn. As we stood in the road the range appeared to be towards a rise across a ravine some thirty rods distant. A large amount of lead must have been passed at the same range as one of the maple trees thus severed was fully eighteen inches in diameter. The line of the firing force was about twenty rods long.

About dark we arrived at the Orange & Alexandria railroad line, and then followed towards Fairfax station. We soon came to the soldiers who were repairing the road, and then for the first time since leaving Centerville in the morning were we within our army lines. I suppose we had run a great risk, but so far as I was concerned, I had spent the day without fear.

On arriving at the station about nine in the evening, I sought the quartermaster in command and commenced saying to him that we were civilians from the north and wished to stop with him over night, but before I had finished the sentence he broke in with "If you are civilians here in Virginia the quicker you cross the Potomac the better for you." I replied "We are on our way," and at the same time I handed him our pass. It worked like magic. His tone of voice and manner changed instantly. He was ready to do all in his power for our comfort. He soon had provided for us a supper of bread, meat and coffee, all of which was of fine quality. He at once proceeded to inquire from where we came, our route from Centerville, what we had seen, etc., to all of which queries I gave him correct answers, even to mentioning the rifle reports in the woods on the military road.

Supper being over, he called up about a dozen or more contrabands and had them give us a specimen of genuine old Virginia negro dances. It was as good as a circus and lasted for nearly an hour. He then gave us each a bed of hay with army blankets, which in addition to our own made us a good provision for a night's rest.

During the night he had found that two soldiers from the working corps had been killed in the woods the afternoon before, no doubt by the guns of which we heard the reports. Two regiments of cavalry were quartered, one of which we saw called to their saddles and start off on a raid during the night. It to us was a novel sight.

In the morning we were again furnished with the best breakfast within our host's power to supply, and when I made an effort to compensate him for our fare and his trouble he refused all with the assurance that he was obeying orders in showing every favor possible. When the train was about to leave for Alexandria I heard him giving the commanding officer orders to see that we were safely landed upon the government steamer for Washington, where we in due time safely arrived.

This digression is wholly outside of the subject I am pursuing, but the name of King brought the four days' trip so vividly to mind that I could not well resist the temptation to name a few of its incidents. If not of other interest they form a change of subject.

To see an army the size of the one then under the command of General McClellan is a sight few civilians are permitted to behold. No money would tempt me to have the memory of that trip effaced from my mind. But no words at my command can convey even an idea of the impression it produced.

While in Centerville Mr. Dibble and myself were anxious to obtain each a confederate shinplaster of small denomination. The two daughters of Dr. Alexander had a number of them but they would not sell them for silver or gold. Determined not to be disappointed in obtaining them, we started next morning for the largest farm house within sight feeling confident we could find some there. On arriving no person was found except an old negro wench well advanced in years.

She assured us that she was the only person left on the plantation and that her mistress had gone south and her master with the rebel army and that all the slaves except herself had left the plantation.

Mr. Dibble inquired of her, "Well, Aunt Dinah, what do you think of the war anyway?" Her prompt answer was "I don't care whether Lincom be president or Jeff Davis be president, old Dinah hab to work for a living anyhow."

Upon inquiring for shinplasters she brought forth two half-dollar ones, both old and worn, which she was willing to exchange for bright silver of like denominational value. I still have mine, no doubt he has his if still living. But I am inclined to believe that I am the only one of our party this side the river, whose names are written upon that memorable pass, which was to us of so much service and which I still prize so highly. It now fills a niche in our family album, and I hope and trust will long be preserved as a valuable memento.

We would willingly have given Mr. King $500 for it, and at Mr. Dibble's request I made him such an offer, but he utterly refused any compensation whatever, at the same time saying to us, "When you return come to the office and tell me of the time you have had, and I shall then be doubly paid for all my trouble. What are friends good for if they can render one no service?"

At that time a pass to enter the army lines would have brought fabulous prices if they could have been purchased, as there were hundreds of men in Washington anxious to enter the lines and visit the army. I wrote a full and correct description of our trip which was published in the Otsego Republican in two numbers in April, 1862.

DECEMBER 29, 1892

MORE ABOUT VARIOUS NEWSPAPER VENTURES IN THE VALLEY CITY (PART 1)

The "New Era" was the name of temperance paper which was started in Oneonta in 1877. Its first copy under the date of September 13th of that year, with G. D. Scramling as its "manager." It was a four-page six-column paper, and was neither well edited nor well executed mechanically.

Mr. Scramling was a native of this county and was reared on a farm near the mouth of Mill creek in Otego. After publishing the Era one year in Oneonta it was removed to Cooperstown. The first issue of its second volume was from that office under date of Jan. 3d, 1879.

Its publication was continued in Cooperstown until July, 1880, when it was removed to the village of Milford, Otsego county, with G. A. Ingalls named as its editor and proprietor. In the latter part of December the name of the New Era was discontinued and that of the Milford News substituted. Thus ended the New Era.

The Granger Alliance was started in Oneonta in 1891. It was in size 24 by 36 inches, a seven-column four-page sheet. Its first number was issued under the date of May 14th, 1891. J. D. Van Dycke was its managing editor. It was a well edited and executed paper and was devoted to the subjects of agriculture and horticulture. After the brief existence of a few months its publication was discontinued for want of sustaining patronage.

The young Men's Christian association of Oneonta has for many years been issuing a paper quarterly. It was started in 1879. It appears under various headings but its aim is ever the same—the improvement of Oneonta's young men.

Oneonta's Y. M. C. A. was organized in June, 1877, and incorporated in January, 1883. It is an organization which from its start has cast a salutary influence in this village and vicinity. Their annual issues are designed not only for the immediate benefit of the organization and this vicinity but also Cooperstown, Cobleskill, Unadilla, Sidney, Norwich, Worcester and Binghamton.

It would be hard to estimate the beneficial and vice restraining influence of these young men's christian organizations. Such associations tend to mutual good. The strong sustain and influence the weak. Their rooms form a place for social improvement and mutual benefit. Long may they live and prosper.

The Oneonta Press was started by George W. Reynolds, May 12th, 1876. After publishing it for about one year he sold it to his son, S. J. W. Reynolds, now of Cooperstown. He, after a few weeks' issue, sold it to W. H. Jefferson & Co., who commenced its publication as a Democratic organ. He continued its publication until January 1st,

1884, when he sold it to Messrs. Raymond and Smith, the first issue of the new firm was under date of January 3d, 1884.

Mr. Raymond retired from the paper April 1st, 1888 and its publication was continued by J. S. Smith, who issued his first number under date of April 5th, 1888. In the July following he sold the plant to E. E. Coates and C. E. Weed. The first issue of the new firm bears date July 12th, 1888.

The Press is Democratic in politics, and no doubt in these Democratic times will meet with a continuously increasing patronage and support. Their former efforts is evidence conclusive that no pains will be spared on their part to make the Press worthy of all the patronage it may in the future receive.

The first issue of the Oneonta Spy appeared April 21, 1877. The Spy is published on a fine quality of paper 26 by 40 inches in size. It is a clean, well-edited, newsy family paper. Its mechanical execution is good and it is a sheet worthy of an extensive patronage.

The decade of 1870 was a prolific one in newspaper enterprises. Soon after C. S. Carpenter transferred the Herald to Messrs. Capron & Johnson he commenced making arrangements to start another Oneonta paper.

A paper called the Dollar Paper was the outcome of this effort. Its publication was continued for only a short time. It was issued from an office in the Reynolds block—the old Sabin Building, since destroyed by fire. Its proving unprofitable was the cause of its discontinuance.

The Oneonta Liberal was started by James K. Polk Jackson about the time of the commencement of the Greeley campaign in 1872, and was devoted to the cause of his election. After continuing its publication for some two years, he sold the plant to C. L. Burtis, formerly of Binghamton, who started a paper under the heading of Oneonta Commercial, which ceased after a year or so and the press and stock was removed by him to Binghamton.

I regret that I have not been able to obtain the exact dates of the starting and discontinuing of these three journals, but after considerable effort I have failed to do so. It is unimportant except for the fact that I am anxious to give the exact dates of such local occurrences.

JANUARY 5, 1893

MORE ABOUT VARIOUS NEWSPAPER VENTURES IN THE VALLEY CITY (PART 2)

Our daily papers are worthy of especial notice. The Oneonta Daily Local was satrted and issued from No. 12 Broad street by the Local publishing company, May 2d, 1887. The company, as far as I can learn, was a Mr. Worth, George H. Smith and J. Sherry Smith.

Its first issue was on a sheet 13x20 inches in size, four columns and a four page paper. Its opening was in part as follows: "This day marks a new event in Oneonta's history. In recognition of the demands of our business men, and the frequently expressed wish of many of our citizens for a daily paper to record the occurrences of our embryo city the Oneonta Local steps forward and makes its introductory bow to our citizens. It is the pioneer daily in Otsego county, and with hopeful diffidence the publishers launch their little newspaper bark upon the sea of public criticism, and they trust, of public favor. Though unpretentious in size, courage is inspired by the fact that all great enterprises have sprung from small beginnings. Life itself is made up of little things, and yet how they affect the destiny of individuals as well as nations.

"The Oneonta Local, as its name implies, will make a specialty of the local news transpiring daily in town, county and vicinity. It will aim to be crisp, newsy and reliable. All matters pertaining to the general welfare of our village will be accorded a hearty welcome and support in our columns, and our readers are cordially invited to help make its visits entertaining to their homes and business places by sending in items of local news. * * * Its terms will be such as to place it within reach of all. Ten cents a week delivered at your door, or two cents a copy.

"With best wishes for all, the Local tips its hat and bids all its friends a pleasant good evening."

I give these extracts from the "greetings" of Oneonta's first established daily, as it marks an era in our history worthy of remembrance. It will at some future time form an important land mark in our daily newspaper history.

From among the news items in the Local's first issue I copy, "It is expected that the (Oneonta) Normal school bill will be disposed of by the legislature at the session this evening."

The Local with its 24th issue was increased in size to 22 by 34 inches. A few months its place of issue was removed to the Westcott block. From its start the paper was well received for a new paper, but its financial receipts were not equal to the cost of its publication.

With its 230th issue there appeared in its columns the following notice: "The Local publishing company, having been dissolved, the Oneonta Daily Local will not be published after this date." The date of its last issue was February 6th, 1888.

The Oneonta Daily News was very soon thereafter introduced to the public. Its first volume and first number bear the date of February 20th, 1888. It was "published every day, Sunday excepted, at No. 12 Broad street, Oneonta, N.Y., by the News Publishing company. It was, at its first publication, a sheet 22 by 36 inches in size.

The publication of the Oneonta Daily News was discontinued with the issue of Thursday April 30th, 1891, the want of means for its continuance being the cause of its decline and death.

The Oneonta Star was started by Harry W. Lee, June 19th, 1890. It was a seven column, 24 by 36 inch four page sheet. Its publication was begun with an entirely new outfit, and it was issued from the Wilber block on the south-westerly corner of Main and Front streets in Oneonta. Its terms were 10 cents weekly—two dollars for six months—four dollars for a year. It was published all week-days—no issue on Sunday. After the Star had been published a few months it was enlarged in size to a sheet of 26 by 42 inches. It is now receiving a liberal patronage.

The Evening News was a daily started by Geo. H. Smith & Co. in September, 1891. It was seven column sheet, 24 by 36 inches in size. It was issued from No. 13 Chestnut street, the building nearly opposite Morris Brothers flour, grain, seed and feed store. The date of the first paper was September 14th, 1891. Its price, 30 cents per month, three dollars per year.

For want of means, this daily paper was doomed to meet the fate of many like enterprises. Its last issue bore the date, August 16th, 1892.

The Oneonta Spy started the publication of a daily paper during the M. E. conference in April, 1888. Later on it was published during the Central New York fair in 1889, and after an interval of a few days, it was resumed until January 13th, 1890, at which time its last issue appeared. The Daily Spy was printed on a sheet 22 by 30 inches. Its workmanship was well done both editorially and mechanically.

This ends the history of the Oneonta daily papers to this date. There were, however, a number of small sheets issued for a few days at various times for a specific purpose, but none worthy of mention.

It is hardly possible to estimate the benefit of the press to any community or people. It is alike educational and progressive. Its power is both instructive and civilizing. These early publications, although they may be small, are but the little fountains which in time are to flow onward and become a mighty flood, irresistible in its influence and power. Whoever fails to appreciate the benefits of the public press, alike fails to notice the advance and progress of our age and to keep pace with our higher civilization.

JANUARY 12, 1893
THE EARLY SCHOOL HISTORY OF TOWN AND VILLAGE (PART 1)

The correct history of Oneonta's district schools is hard to obtain. The first school house erected in what is now the town of Oneonta was erected on the Oneonta Plains while this region was still in Montgomery county. It stood on what was years ago known as the Elder Wing farm, the one adjoining on its southeast side the Elisha Shepherd farm.

Huntington Parish attended school in it in 1811. His father moved on the first farm north of the Otego creek in 1810, on what was then the Cyrus Richmond farm. Mr. Richmond married Mr. Parish's sister. The farm years since has been known as the Emmanuel Northrup farm.

It will be remembered that on the Plains and westerly of them were the first settled lands in the town and of course there was the place for the first school. Mr. Huntington Parish says the school house was quite an old building in 1811.

The old books of record fail to give the formation of the school districts. District No. 5 in Oneonta I find in our town records to have been formerly District No. 9 of Milford, while Oneonta was a part of that town.

The school records of district No.5, from its formation to the organizing of the Union school, are lost and I have been unable to obtain official data of the first school in what is now Oneonta village, but I learn that the school house I have named in former papers as having stood where the Ford block now stands, was erected in or before 1812 and a public school started in it at that date. Huntington Parish informs me that he attended school in it in 1813 and that a school had been kept in it previous to that time.

There must have been a school in the place previous to the formation of such district as we have abundance evidence of there being a number of scholars needing school advantages previous to that date. I am informed that the school house on the south side of the river in the Swart district, and also the one in the Wolf district, were both erected about the year 1800, but have no official record.

The school house which was sold when the Union school was formed was erected in 1840, Col. W. W. Snow being the contractor for its erection. My recollection is that the first school was kept in it in the summer of 1841. Schools were annually kept therein until the formation of the Oneonta Union school in 1867.

During all the years of our existence as a separate town since 1837 until the present time, Oneonta has sustained one or more select or private schools. The first one of which I have found former scholars was kept in the building recently occupied by the Daily News, by a Mrs. Rice in the year 1837. David J. Yager was one of her pupils.

Miss Herrick taught a select school in 1838 and 1839. It was kept in the upper story of the W. S. Fritts building. She boarded with the family of Samuel J. Cooke. Miss Herrick spent a year or two in Canada, during which time her school was continued by a Miss Thayer. Miss Herrick was in Canada during the time of the coronation of Queen Victoria. That memorable event occurred in 1837. Miss Herrick was a very successful teacher and continued her school until she became the wife of William Miller of North Franklin, a man of distinction and wealth. He was the father of the late Col. S. F. Miller.

During the year 1841 a select school, principally for young men, was taught by Dr. Joseph Lindsay, a noted scholar of whom I have made former mention in these columns. He was Oneonta's pioneer physician. He was the first one to teach our people that a true regard to the laws of health and sanitary care and surroundings, as preventives, was much better for any people than was the use of medicines unattended by such health preserving means. Were Dr. Lindsay's advice as generally followed as it should be much of the suffering with which humanity is afflicted would be utterly unknown.

Miss Lizzie Hill, now the wife of Dr. Meigs Case, was the teacher of a noted and very successful school during the years 1856, 1857 and 1858. Her school was kept on the second floor of a building owned by Colonel Marvin Miller, which then occupied the present site of the First National bank block.

Among the scholars of Miss Hill can be remembered many of the successful men and women of the present time. The late Monroe Westcott, the late Datus Morris, the Morris brothers, Albert and William, of this village, Eli Rose of Howe's Cave, the sons of Col. Miller and many others who have made life worth living and business a success, were among her students. A gratifying remembrance this for Miss Hill, now Mrs. Dr. Case.

Col. William H. Chase, late of Washington, D. C., for a year or two taught a select school in Oneonta.

Miss Mary Dietz also for some years was the successful teacher of a fine private school in our village. So, too, were some others not now in mind.

Our present distinguished Professor Nathaniel N. Bull has had many years of experience as teacher in Oneonta. He taught the district school in 1848 and again in 1863. He then established a select school in the same building which had formerly been occupied by Miss Hill and taught during the year 1864 and part of 1865. He then taught in Binghamton until he was again called to Oneonta in 1870.

Our citizens all remember and all appreciate the long period of teaching by Miss Delilah Sullivan. For nearly fifty years she was engaged in teaching, and most of the time within this village. She was many years in the district school as teacher, and many are the men and women of the various ages from youth to those already in middle life who will remember her with mingled feelings of pleasure and gratitude for her beneficial councils and instructions.

She commenced teaching a select school on Deitz street in 1864 and continued it until 1889. Few persons can retire from so many years of active public instruction with so many lasting evidences of continued success.

JANUARY 19, 1893

THE EARLY SCHOOL HISTORY OF TOWN AND VILLAGE (PART 2)

The people of Oneonta, feeling that a higher and more beneficial system of instruction could be obtained by the formation of a union school, resolved to adopt a new and as they believed an improved system.

A petition was presented to Mr. Silas Sullivan, who was the only trustee of district No. 5 in Oneonta, which was signed by M. N. Elwell, Meigs Case, John Cope jr., S. Brownson, Henry Mosher, Samuel Mendel, Andrew Mendel, James H. Keyes, J. Roberts, Josiah Farmer, W. W. Snow, Chas. W. Lewis, Harvey Baker, George O. Phelps, John Cutshaw, Samuel H. Case, Timothy Sabin, George Reynolds and Christian Uebel, asking for the calling of a special school meeting to determine by vote whether the public favored and desired the establishing of a free Union school in district No. 5, in Oneonta.

Such meeting was held pursuant to due notice on the 29th day of October in 1867. Sixty-seven legal voters were present and voted. It was by such vote affirmatively resolved that "district No. 5 be thereafter known as Union Free school district, No. 5 of the town of Oneonta, Otsego county, N. Y."

It was voted to elect a board of education of six members, or as trustees. The following persons were by vote elected as such board of education: Silas Sullivan and Andrew G. Shaw for one year; David M. Miller and George O. Phelps for two years; Harvey Baker and Christian Uebel for three years.

The first move of the new board was the purchase of the large lot, now comprising the Union school grounds situated on the north side of Academy street in Oneonta village. The central portion of the present building was then erected. It was built by Hiram J. Brewer, contractor, for $7,500. It was completed and ready for use in the fall of 1868.

W. F. Saxton was employed as the first principal of the school. Miss Katherine Rose was senior assistant, Julia Ferguson in the intermediate and Elizabeth Wing in the primary department. The school was a success from its start. It was well patronized and more than met the most sanguine anticipations of its most active advocates.

At the close of the second year of his service as principal, Prof. Saxton, on account of failing health, resigned his position. After a few months of rest and recuperation Mr. Saxton went to Michigan and again engaged in teaching, his favorite profession and one for which he was so well fitted. He was, after the lapse of a few months, compelled to again leave school and soon thereafter died, sincerely mourned by all who knew him.

The writer, having for many years known Professor Nathaniel N. Bull, wrote to him at Binghamton asking him to come to Oneonta and assume the charge of our school. He finally came and was employed and has to this time occupied continuously the position of principal of Oneonta Union school.

The school under his able management has known continued prosperity. It has sent forth into the world young men and young women who have been there educated and amply fitted to fill with honor and ability all and every position in active and useful business life.

Such has been the growth of the school under his supervision that three large additions have been made to the school building since he assumed its charge, and an additional building was in 1873 erected on West Broadway, below the railroad shops, which has now given place to the fine and spacious brick structure on River street, which is now being occupied for the first school term.

Seldom, indeed, is it the privilege of any school teacher or superintendent to live to witness such successful results of one's labor as has fallen to the good fortune of Professor Bull.

This new River street school building, with its site, structure and equipments, has cost the district about $14,000. The estimated value of all the real school property in district No. 5 in Oneonta village at this date is about $39,000, of the furniture and apparatus $5,000, school library $2,200.

Total paid for teachers' wages for the past school year $8,003.25, other expenses exclusive of new school buildings $265.19.

Number of scholars of school age in the district at the last census in 1892 was 1,612, number in attendance at the schools was 969, number of days' attendance 121,667.

Amount of public money received as applicable to teachers' wages was $3,586.83. Amount raised in district by tax for like purposee was $7,855.42. The sum received from the state for use in purchase of books for library, $50.11; received from Regents for library, $241.27; from loan exhibition, $30.63; from George I. Wilber and Harvey Baker $5 each; from commencement exercises, $121.25, making an aggregate amount of library money for the year of 1892 of $453.36. Received from Regents in addition to above sums $208,92, which went into the school fund.

The number of volnmes in the library at the close of the school year was 2,146, with the new purchases still to be added.

The members of the school board at this writing, September 20th, 1892, are W. A. E. Tompkins, Albert Morris, John Skinner, Charles Aussiker, William Edmunds and J. O. Rowe, with Mr. Tompkins as president of the board. Alva Seybolt is secretary, Samuel Coon collector and Silas I. Wright, treasurer.

Happening to have retained the school report of the same district for the year 1852, just forty years ago, I will give the figures of that school year, that the reader may see by contrast the change which has taken place in school district No. 5 during the lapse of years.

In 1852 the number of taxpayers' names on the tax roll of the district was 60; the amount of tax levied was $60.20; the amount of public money received was $146; the number of children of school age in the district was 220; the number attending school was 127; the number of days attendance was 6,334; cost of fuel for the year was $20; cost of repairs of school house for the year was $13.03; number of volumes in the library was 233. Harvey Baker and Andrew Parish were the trustees.

It is doubtful whether any more convincing proof of Oneonta's actual prosperity can be given than is demonstrated in the increase and success of her public schools. Since writing the above I find in the Star of September 20th, 1892, the following: "the assessed valuation of the property in the district is $1,279,730." In the Star of the 26th the number of library books is given as 3,102 in the district library.

FEBRUARY 9, 1893
THE ONEONTA NORMAL SCHOOL

This school was the outgrowth of the efforts of some of Oneonta's young men. Prominent among them were Willard E. Yager and G. W. Fairchild, then joint editors of THE ONEONTA HERALD. We old men were but few of us cognizant of the movement until we saw the notice of the bill in the public journals.

Frank B. Arnold, member of the legislature from the second district of Otsego county, introduced a bill early in the session of 1887 appropriating $45,000 towards erecting a Normal school in Oneonta. It was received with favor, and by his efforts it became a law the 18th day of May, 1887.

The needs of such an institution of learning in so large an area of the thickly populated portion of our state of which Oneonta was the central point, was no doubt a powerful factor in aiding in the favorable legislation and executive approval. It, too, was an indisputable evidence of the wisdom and foresight of its originators and early advocates.

The first meeting of the commissioners to select the site was held at Oneonta on the 30th day of June following. Several sites were shown them for their approval, but after their examination the commissioners adjourned to meet at the office of the attorney general in Albany on the 8th day of July at 10 a.m. Before adjourning they notified the citizens of Oneonta that they would not accept a parcel of land of less than ten acres in extent for the purpose of such school grounds.

At the adjourned meeting the site offered by Delos Yager was the one which the commission approved and resolutions to that effect were adopted. They then adjourned subject to the call of their chairman, Hon. A. S. Draper. On the 27th day of July the land for the site was duly conveyed by its owners to the state and the location permanently settled.

On September 7th, 1887, Hon. A. S. Draper appointed the following persons as the local board of managers of such school: Frank B. Arnold of Unadilla; James Stewart, Geo. I. Wilber, Walter L. Brown, Eugene Raymond, Willard E. Yager, Reuben Reynolds, William H. Morris of Oneonta; Charles D. Hammond, Frederick A. Head of Albany; Samuel M. Thurber of East Worcester.

September 12th, 1887, the newly appointed members of the Normal board met at the Central hotel in Oneonta and chose William H. Morris as permanent chairman of the board, Eugene Raymond as secretary and James Stewart, treasurer. After the appointing of the necessary committees the board adjourned to the 10th of October.

The board met October 10th as per adjournment and after transacting the necessary arrangements for architects' plans, etc., adjourned to meet October 26th. At this meeting Messrs. Fuller and Wheeler, architects of Albany, were selected. A committee to select a principal for such school was appointed, and a list of his necessary qualifications also adopted. The board then adjourned to meet the first Monday in December at one p.m.

The board met as per adjournment Dec. 5th, and after receiving reports from committees adjourned to Dec. 24th. At the adjourned meeting the building committee reported that the building to conform with the design would cost $95,000, if constructed by parts would cost about $18,000 more. After receiving the reports the board adjourned to January 20th, 1888. No meeting was held on the adjourned day.

A meeting of the board was called for April 19th, 1888, at which time they met. The committee on selection of principal reported the selection of Professor James M. Milne. On vote by ballot he received eight votes, being an affirmative vote of every member of the board present. A motion was carried that no selection of teachers be then made and that all applications be filed with the secretary until September 1st, 1888. Also that the salary of the principal commence September 1st, 1889. The action of the local board was approved by Superintendent Draper May 21st, 1888.

April 17th an act was passed appropriating $69,000, or so much thereof as might be necessary, for the erection of the Oneonta Normal school.

At a meeting of the board May 25th, the plans and specifications of the architects were examined and slightly changed and adopted. Sealed proposals were ordered advertised for, to be received until June 25th at noon of that day. The board then adjourned to meet the following day, June 26th.

On the 26th the bids were opened and examined. Twenty-four bids had been received. The building committee was instructed to examine fully and report at an adjourned meeting on Saturday, June 30th.

At the adjourned meeting it was found that Messrs. Ryan, Rafferty & O'Hara and Baker & McAllister of Syracuse were the lowest bidders on the mason and carpenter work and had offered satisfactory securities. The contracts were ordered executed to them. The contracts for heating were deferred for further consideration. The masons' and carpenters' bids were for $88,846. Messrs W. E. Yager, S. M. Thurber and F. B. Arnold were made the committee on the laying of the corner stone. Adjourned subject to the call of the president.

August 7th the board met pursuant to such call. The bills of the architects, surveyors, for advertising, etc., were received and ordered paid. A. J. O'Neil being the lowest bidder, the plumbing was awarded to him. Adjourned to meet at call.

Board met on call, November 27th. No important business worth mentioning except some slight additions and payment of bills was before the board. Certain grading was also ordered done. Adjourned subject to call.

The board met Dec. 15th, Dr. Milne and Architect Fuller were present. Estimates for the furnishing of the building were received from Dr. Milne, an itemized bill was submitted; its estimated cost was $23,800. Skylights were ordered in the scientific department. After other business, adjourned to meet on call.

Board met April 12th, 1889, and transacted a large amount of business Bills for extra work were ordered paid. The list for the full number of professors and teachers was approved. A resolution to celebrate the opening was passed. Many minor details of finishing were arranged. The hiring of a janitor ordered. After completing the vast amount of business the board adjourned to meet on call.

The board met May 25th with a large amount of business before them. Dr. Milne was also present. At this meeting the kind of seats, desks and all other fixtures was decided upon, also the terms and tuition named. Several special committees with power to decide and execute were appointed. Adjourned to meet on call.

July 1st the board met pursuant to call. Dr. Milne was present. Reports of the various committees and approval of their doings was the principal business. Committees for new business were appointed, among which was one on students' rooming and boarding places. Adjourned to meet on call.

The board met August 21st. The principal business was arranging the time and orator for the dedicatory services. The day was fixed at September 4th at 2 p.m., in the large hall of the Normal school building, and superintendent Draper to deliver the principal address.

The next meeting of the board was held September 3d. At this meeting the acceptance of the building from the various contractors was approved and their payment in full ordered, also payment for extra work still unpaid.

I have thus given a glance of the work performed by our members in the state legislature and by the Normal school board that my readers may be able to form a faint idea of the work so willingly and well performed in securing and completing this noble and much needed institution for the education of the youth of our county.

I have watched its progress closely from its start before the legislature until its full and final completion, not only as an interested citizen of Oneonta, but as a veritable critic of all their acts done and work performed. For the first time in my observation during my long life has a public work of this cost and importance been projected and pushed forward to completion without a jar, a mistake, an ill feeling, a charge of speculation, or of poorly planned or poorly performed work. Everyone connected with it in all its various parts emerges from the work with clean hands and a clean record, and is entitled to the lasting gratitude of the public and the state.

If an error of any kind has been made, it is that the institution, fine and large as it is, has already in popular favor even so soon outgrown its capacity for the accommodation of all who would gladly become its patrons. But this success so early in its history is no doubt mostly and deservedly attributable to it superior and able corps of professors and teachers as well as the splendid quarters in which they perform their work. If the past and the present are indicative of the future of the Oneonta Normal school we may well and safely predict for it a success seldom achieved by such institutions.

Another important feature of this school must not be overlooked, and that is the uniformly gentlemanly and ladylike deportment of its pupils and the marked success of its graduates. No doubt the principal and his efficient aides, the teachers, are entitled to a full share of credit for this marked and, I may add, remarkable feature. The pupils have, no doubt, been taught that a low or mean act degrades its actor in his or her own estimation as well as in that of others, and also that the moral standard of the American citizen has more to do towards his future influence and success than high literary attainments. In fact these latter qualifications often only tend to make one's vices the more conspicuous and degrading. When the rising generation can be made to fully understand that immorality, vice and crime in all their forms are but so many barriers against one's own usefulness and happiness, a marked improvement in society and in civil and social well-being will have been attained.

My notes of the Normal school having already exceeded my intended limits, I will not extend them. The secluded life of the writer has prevented his forming an acquaintance with many of the professors, teachers or pupils of either the Union or Normal school of Oneonta, but that does not in the least detract from his personal interest in their prosperity and welfare.

Two views of the Delaware & Hudson railroad shops, from the collection of Greater Oneonta Historical Society.

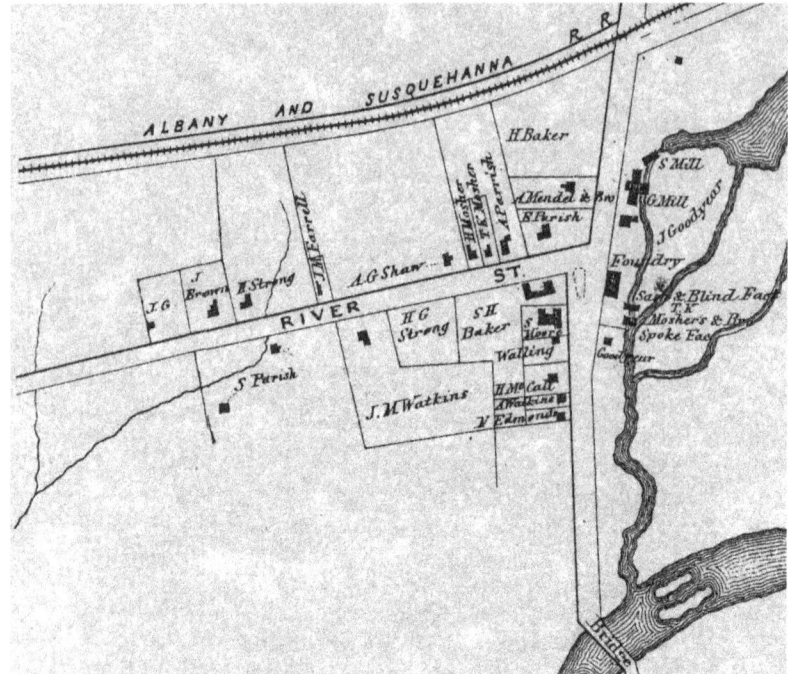

Top: Detail of Oneonta at the corner of River and Main Streets in 1868, from the Beers *Atlas of Otsego County*, 1868. Harvey Baker's property can be seen at top right. Bottom: Same area from L.R. Burleigh's map of Oneonta of 1884, showing the development of the railroad shops and roundhouse. Baker Street can be seen near the center.

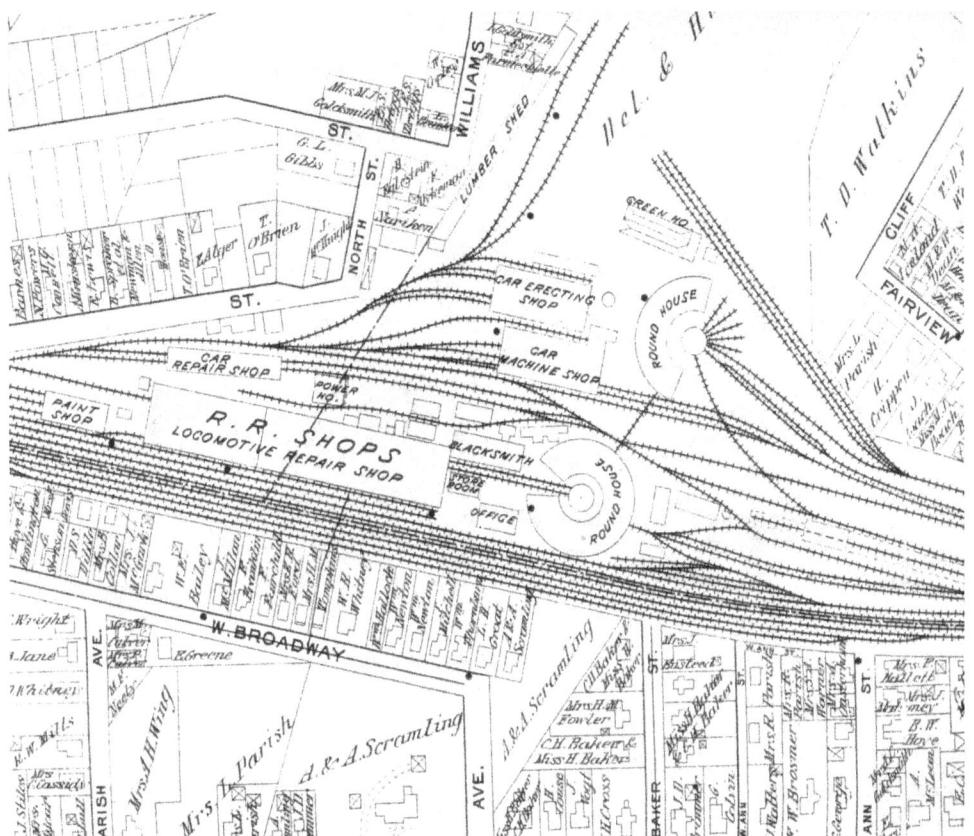

Top: Detail of Oneonta near the same location, from the *New Century Atlas of Otsego County*, 1903. Baker Street and the Baker family properties can be seen directly south of the lower roundhouse. Bottom: Detail of the D&H railroad and canal system map of 1892, the year Harvey Baker began publishing these articles.

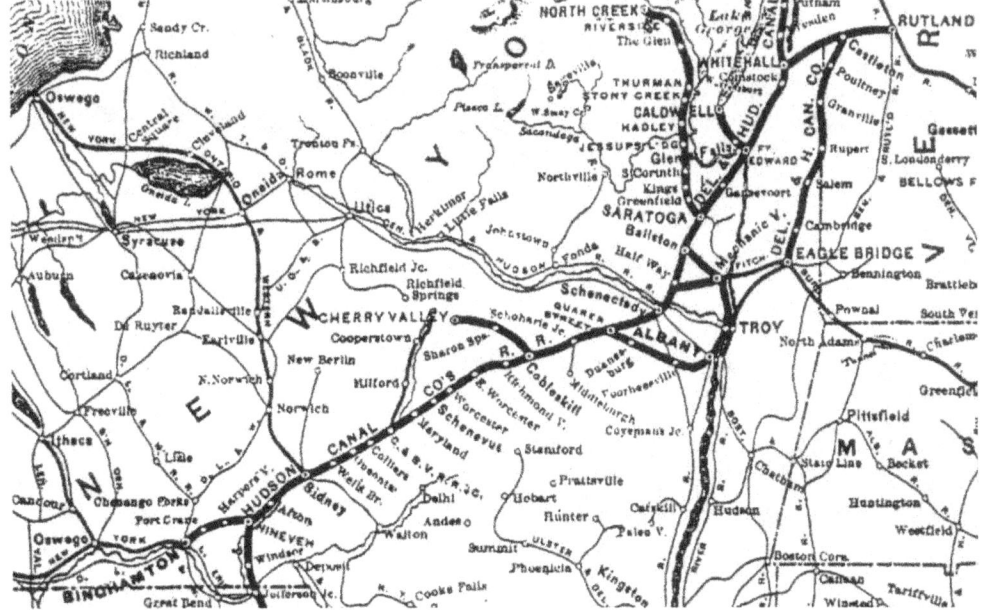

Top: The Susquehanna House, where Harvey Baker celebrated the completion of the Albany & Susquehanna railroad into Oneonta. Postcard from the private collection of John Carney.

Bottom: View of Broad Street. Postcard from the private collection of John Carney.

Main Street. Postcard from the private collection of John Carney.

Main Street. Postcard from the collection of the Greater Oneonta Historical Society.

The building and offices of the Rowe company. Postcards from the private collection of John Carney.

Top: Photograph of the Elwell Mill. From the collection of Greater Oneonta Historical Society. Bottom: The State Normal School at Oneonta. Postcard from the private collection of John Carney.

Oneonta.
Its peculiar history, and its first settlement

Oneonta is an Indian anglo american name taken from a creek within its bounds of the same name; We will in a few words give its history   (see opposite page)

In 1492 Christopher Columbus discovered the evidence of an American Continent. In 1497 Cabot, in the exclusive service sailed from Florida to Latitude 68° North along the American coast. and thus England laid claim to the whole continent. In 1534 & 5 Cartier in the service of France sailed up the river St Lawrence to what is now Montreal, and the French by the same right laid claim to that country, being the first Europeans who had thus far into the interior of North America. At this time New York state was occupied by the Iroquois Indians known as the Five Nations. In 1608 Hendrick Hudson an Englishman sailing under a dutch flag came up the North

A sample page from Harvey Baker's early manuscripts for these articles. From the private collection of Kermit and Margaret Baker Witherbee.

BITS OF ONEONTA HISTORY.

HARVEY BAKER CONTINUES HIS INTERESTING SERIES OF ARTICLES.

FEBRUARY 23, 1893
THE HISTORY OF THE PRESBYTERIAN CHURCH AND SOCIETY FROM ITS ORGANIZATION

The Presbyterian Church of Oneonta can justly claim to be the oldest church organization in town. It dates its first formation back to 1786, while this region was a part of Montgomery county. The state gazetteers name the Rev. Alex Conkey as its first pastor. Its records, like most of those of early times, are meager and unsatisfactory. As early as 1805 preparations were made to erect a house of worship and a portion of the materials got together, but the edifice was not erected until 1816. It was then built by that noted builder of early times, William Angel, one of Oneonta's early citizens whose name has so often appeared in this paper.

The house of worship antedates by some years that of the deed for the church grounds. The latter bears the date of January, 1823; it was made to the church by Frederick Brown. In January, 1823, the church was re-organized under the name of the Second Presbyterian church of Milford, with Rev. Mr. Pitcher as its first minister.

Between 1825 and 1842 the Rev. William Clark, Rev. C. Gilbert, Rev. Gains M. Blodgett and Rev. J. W. Paddock were its pastors. Early in the decade of 1840 a division arose in the church, its pastor, Rev. J. W. Paddock, quit the ministry and began the practice of law. The church bell was sold for debt and was purchased by the late Woodbury K. Cooke. A huge pile of straw was heaped up before the church upon which the bell was thrown when removed from the belfry. As the timbers used above in the belfry were being thrown down a Mr. Shellman was struck by one upon his head and instantly killed. Report said the bell was cracked in its fall and its fine musical tone thereafter ruined.

February 24, 1849, after some years of rest, the church was reorganized and Hezekiah Watkins, John Dillingham and Luman S. Osborn were chosen and ordained its elders. It again prospered and in 1868 the edifice was thoroughly repaired and greatly improved. A fine and valuable organ was at that time presented it by C. P. Huntington and others. Its fine deep tines have added much to the church services during all the intervening years from that date to this.

Early in 1887 the members and friends of the church decided to erect and in the future enjoy a new place of worship, and energetically commenced its erection. The contract was let to Parker Wilson & Co., and the first stone of the foundation of the new structure was laid the 24th of August, by the contractors.

The formalities of laying the corner stone were held on the 26th day of September with imposing and appropriate ceremonies. The pastor, Rev. C. G. Matteson, called the assembly to order; L. S. Osborn gave the address of welcome. Then followed the reading of letters from Rev. William Baldwin and Rev. George O. Phelps, former pastors. Scripture reading by Rev. A. B. Richardson of the Methodist church. Prayer by Rev. H. H. Allen, late pastor. Then followed the address by Rev. L. E. Richards of Stamford and the reading of the list of articles deposited in the stone by Dr. S. Hall of Morris. The sealing of the box and laying the stone then took place and was announced by Rev. L. E. Richards. Then followed the singing of "Praise God from whom all blessings flow" to the tune of Old Hundred, closing prayer by Rev. P. F. Sanborn of Otego and the benediction by the pastor, Rev. C. G. Matteson.

The inscription on the stone is as follows: "1887. Presbyterian Society formed 1786; First Presbyterian Church organized 1849. L. H. Blend, Architect."

This noble church edifice is alike an honor to the society constructing it, to the young city in which it is located, to its designing architect and to the contractors and mechanics doing the work of its erection.

The first sermon preached in the new church was on the 11th day of November, 1888, by its pastor, Rev J. H. Brandow. On the 20th the dedication and installation ceremonies were held. Rev. J. L. Jones served as moderator, Rev H. U. Swinnerton of Cherry Valley preaching the dedicatory sermon. Resolutions of thanks were adopted particularly naming many non-resident liberal donors to the edifice, among whom were C. P. Huntington of New York, W. V. Huntington of San Francisco, Cal., H. E. Huntington of Cincinnati, Mrs. D. W. Emmons of Huntington, W. Va., and Miss Alice Emmons of New York for their generous gifts of money, without which this beautiful temple could not have been reared on its present liberal and imposing scale.

At 7 o'clock in the evening the installation services of Rev. John H. Brandow as the pastor of the church were opened and carried out according to the form of the Presbyterian church. The sermon was preached by the Rev. Henry M. Cox of Herkimer, the charge to the pastor by Rev. J. O. Dennison of Cooperstown and to the people by the Rev. W. A. Dunning of Gilbertsville.

The church is a brick structure with iron cornices, slate roof and trimmings of stone. The main tower is 124 feet high, the smaller one 72 feet. Its greatest frontage is 103 feet; its greatest depth 74 feet; basement under the entire structure. The total cost of the structure complete was $20,684.74, and, strange as it may seem, when all paid left a balance of $80.05 in the church treasury. The first money raised towards its erection was given in 1884 by the infant sabbath school class of Mrs. Seymour Scott; the amount was eight cents. This noble, paid-for, complete edifice is the outgrowth of that small beginning.

A fine parsonage of like material has just been completed and is now being occupied by the pastor and his family. The present value of the church property at the low valuation we place upon property in Oneonta cannot be less than $35,000. The present membership of the church is about 350.

MARCH 2, 1893
THE HISTORY OF THE METHODIST EPISCOPAL AND THE FIRST BAPTIST SOCIETIES

The Methodist church was organized in 1830 as a branch of the Oneonta Plains circuit. Rev. George Haynor, who had it in charge, formed the class with David T. Evans, and David T. Clark as its leaders. Among the members of this first class were Elias Brewer, D. T. Evans and wife, Jacob Dietz and wife, D. T. Clark and wife and Caleb Potter and wife.

The first house of worship was erected by Lucius Holbrook, a builder from the town of Maryland, in 1844. It was erected on the site of the present presiding elder's parsonage at a cost of about $1,500. The same building is now the property of George Reynolds, and is occupied as a dwelling on Church street, No. 24.

In 1851 the legal organizing of the church was perfected. The papers were executed June 10th and were recorded in the county clerk's office August 19th.

The first parsonage lot was purchased of Gould P. Dietz and wife, the deed bearing the date of August 12th, 1852. This lot and house was on what is now Church street and is the same upon which the residence of A. D. Dimmick now stands, No. 17 Church street.

In November, 1866, the church finding their edifice too small for their increasing number of attendants resolved to purchase of William Hopkins the house and lands owned by the late Robert Hopkins, which purchase was soon thereafter consumated and a decision to erect thereon a new house of worship. The building committee appointed for carrying out the plans were George Reynolds, Jacob P. Van Woert and David J. Yager.

The contract for the erection of the new edifice was by them let to Messrs. James C. Cornish and Josiah L. Hasbrook of Worcester, to be completed as per specifications for $6,700. It was completed so as to be dedicated June 3d, 1861. The Rev. R. W. Peebles was the pastor. The dedication services were conducted by Rev. W. N. Cobb, who was ably assisted in such service by Rev. B. I. Ives. The steeple of the church not being satisfactory, it was replaced during the winter of 1871 and 1872 by a new one constructed by Architect Lyman H. Blend at a cost of $880.89.

Again the society having outgrown the size of the church edifice, during the ministration of Rev. A. B. Richardson in 1886, the present brick structure was erected. It is an imposing structure, standing upon the corner and facing both Chestnut and Church streets. It has a fine audience room, 72 by 84 feet in size, and of superior acoustic properties.

This beautiful church edifice was dedicated January 12th, 1887. The dedication sermon was preached by Bishop E. G. Andrews D. D. of New York City, a sermon of rare merit from John, chapter 4th, part of verse 24th, "God is a spirit." The evening sermon was preached by Dr. William H. Olin, a former resident of Oneonta. He resided in Oneonta during the latter part of the decade of 1840 and the fore part of 1850. He was a lawyer by profession, but changed and became a Methodist minister and preached his first sermon in the Methodist church at the Oneonta Plains. He continued in the ministry until his death, which occurred September 16th, 1889. Death came suddenly in Michigan, while on his way to meet at a family reunion of the Olin family in that state. At the time of his death he resided in his fine residence on Grand street and was the presiding elder of this district. Few men during their lifetime attain the eminence and distinction that did Dr. Olin.

The Methodist church in Oneonta has two fine parsonages upon their church property, one for the pastor and one for the presiding elder of the district. The report given at the conference made in March, 1892, gives a membership of 667, and 25 probationers. Rev. Dr. McAnulty is the present pastor. The church is in everyway highly prosperous. The church property is worth from $30,000 to $35,000.

First Baptist Church.

The First Baptist church of Oneonta was organized April 24th, 1833. Delegates from Milford, Otego, West Meredith, Franklin and Laurens were present at its organization. Rev. Alexander Smith of Franklin was moderator and Rev. Mr. Kingsley clerk.

The membership of the church at its formation was eighteen, of that number Nathaniel Edmunds is the only one of its charter members now living. The first deacons of the church were Jas. Slade, David Yager and Hiram McCall; the first clerk was Ira Babcock; Rev. D. B. Crane was its first pastor.

The first church edifice was erected in 1834 upon the present church site. Its builder, cost and the date of its dedication and by whom are all among the things of which I have been unable to obtain a reliable record.

In 1835, Rev. John Smith, late of Otego, was its second pastor. He commenced his service while a young man in 1835, and continued as its pastor until March, 1848.

He was succeeded in1848, June, by the Rev. Homer Clark, who served until March, 1849. The following August Rev. A. B. Earle was called as its pastor and continued his services until March, 1853. From that date until January, 1854, the church was without a pastor. At that date Rev. Erastus Westcott was employed, who served as its pastor until July 12th, 1857.

From July, 1857, to February, 1858, Rev. C. M. Pattengill was its pastor. Rev. John Smith was then recalled and continued from February 13th, 1858, until March 11th, 1865. June 11th he was succeeded by Rev. A. Reynolds, who served as its pastor until September 25th, 1870.

Nov. 1st, 1871, Rev. George R. Burnside was called as its pastor and served until April

12th, 1874. He was on April 19th following succeeded by Rev. H. Brotherton, who continued his pastorate until 1880, when he was followed by Rev. P. D. Root. In 1883 Rev. E. D. Clough became its pastor and served until 1886, when Rev. A. B. Coats assumed charge. He was followed in 1891 by Rev. C. C. Pierce, its present pastor.

In 1867, under the direction Rev. A. Reynolds, the church was thoroughly repaired and greatly improved and a new organ added the following season.

In 1884, under the direction of Rev. E. D. Clough, the old church was moved back and a new church edifice erected, the old one being repaired and retained as assembly rooms for the society.

A good parsonage and commodious private sheds have been recently built. The present membership of the church is 440. D. W. Ford, A. A. Whitcomb and James Andrews are deacons.

The valuation of the church property is about $20,000. A large sabbath school and other institutions for religious improvement are connected with the church organization.

MARCH 9, 1893
THE HISTORY OF THE EPISCOPAL, FREE BAPTIST AND UNIVERSALIST SOCIETIES

The first Episcopal services were held in Oneonta early in the decade of 1830. A building was erected, mostly by Roderick J. Emmons, for such church services. The building stood upon the Brown farm, easterly of where the Central hotel block now stands, and the property afterwards passed into the ownership of E. R. Ford.

During the latter part of the decade of 1840 the society enjoyed the ministration of Rev. Mr. Spencer, a brother of the then celebrated Joshua A. Spencer, one of the most noted lawyers in the state. When minister here, he was a man in advanced years and will be remembered by our old citizens for his extreme care of the wants of the poor within the village and vicinity. When a case of need came to his knowledge he would immediately start out and ask of each business man such donation as was necessary in the aggregate to supply the want. His calls were from ten to fifty cents each, and were seldom, if ever, refused. A barrel of flour and a fine ham or other articles of food would be thus by him procured and sent to the needy family. People became accustomed to his calls and responded to them with pleasure. They, at his approach, would often save him the trouble of a personal appeal by asking him "how much could they aid him to-day?" His reply would be, "I need a small sum to supply the immediate wants of———family," naming the sum which seldom exceeded twenty-five cents. We all felt that we had lost a noble citizen when he left us.

For a number of years thereafter the Episcopal society were without a settled rector and services were not continuously held. In April, 1871, the parish was regularly incorporated under the name of "The Rector, Church Wardens and Vestrymen of St. James' church," and was received into the diocese of Albany, January 4th, 1875.

The first rector after its incorporation was the Rev. Robert Washborn, a brother of Mrs. John Cope. His ministration continued from April, 1871 until February, 1873, when he resigned his charge. During these years the site was purchased and the massive stone edifice, situate upon the corners of Main and Elm streets, was erected. Its erection was due to the untiring efforts of the Rev. R. Washborn and the Hon. John Cope of this place.

The corner stone of the new church edifice was laid the 27th day of June, 1871, Bishop W. C. Doane of Albany conducting the ceremonies, the Rev. Robert Washborn rector.

The consecration service was held the 7th day of November, 1890, by Bishop Doane of Albany, Rev. E. A. Hartman rector.

The Episcopal society has steadily prospered from its incorporation, and is now erecting a fine parsonage upon the Elm street portion of their church lot. The present rector is the Rev. John E. Bold, who succeeded Rev. E. A. Hartmann upon that gentleman's departure for California in the autumn of 1892. The value of the church property is about $20,000.

The Free Baptist Church.

The Free Baptist church of Oneonta was organized at the Emmons school, February 25th, 1856. Its organizing counsel was composed of Rev. A. Wing, Rev. D. Green and Rev. O. T. Moulton, and Joseph Jenks and Harvey Mackey laymen. The confession of faith and church covenant of the Free Baptist denomination was adopted. Sixteen members then received the right hand of fellowship. Rev. O. T. Moulten was the first pastor.

In 1857 the present site of the church, on the westerly corner of Main and Maple streets, was purchased in Oneonta village and the first church erected. It was a good wood edifice and was dedicated January 20th, 1858. Rev. M. C. Brown preached the dedicatory sermon from the following text: "And let them make me a sanctuary that I may dwell among them."

The church having outgrown the capacity of the first edifice, in the year 1889 the present beautiful and commodious brick structure was erected. It was dedicated June 11th, 1890. The Rev. A. T. Worden preached the dedication sermon.

The church hall prospered greatly under the ministration of the present pastor, Rev. A. E. Wilson. It now numbers 330 communicants, and has a sabbath school of 400 scholars. The Y. P. S. C. E. now numbers 130 active and 25 associate members. Three of the original members of the church are still among its most active workers.

The church some years ago erected a fine parsonage on a portion of the church property as a home for its pastors. It has as a society prospered ever since its organization. The church property is now worth from $25,000 to $30,000.

The Universalist Church.

The formation of the Universalists' church is of comparatively recent date. Their church edifice was erected during the year of 1878. Its dedication ceremonies were held in it January 29th and 30th, 1879. The discourse preached on the afternoon of the 29th was by the Rev. D. Ballou of Utica, the sermon of the evening service by the Rev. L. F. Porter.

On the 30th the forenoon sermon was preached by Dr. A. B. Hervey, the present president of the St. Lawrence university at Canton, N. Y. The afternoon dedicatory sermon by Dr. E. H. Chapin, D.D., of New York city. His death following in 1880, the church from that date was christened the "Chapin Memorial Church."

Its first pastor was the Rev. L. F. Porter, who was succeeded in 1891 by the Rev. H. K. White. The first and second days of 1880, the state Universalist association was held at the Chapin Memorial church. Delegates were present from various parts of the state. (The writer attended both the dedication and association services, and these dates are taken from the entries made at the time in his diary.)

The Rev. H. K. White was followed as pastor in 1884 and 5 by the Rev. Benjamin Brunning. Next came the Rev. E. F. Temple from 1885 to 1888. Rev. J. C. Gumbine, 1889; Rev. C. P. Hall, 1890; Rev. W. L. Stowe, 1891, and the Rev. E. F. Temple, recalled in 1892, is still its pastor.

The parish contains about ninety families, and the church membership numbers seventy. The church has a fine sabbath school with professor Bugbee of the Normal as its superintendent.

The church edifice occupies a central position on Ford Avenue, and the church property is valued at about $8,000.

MARCH 16, 1893
THE ROMAN CATHOLIC AND UNITED PRESBYTERIAN CHURCHES

The St. Mary's Catholic church parish was established July 29th, 1883, with the Rev. James H. Maney as its pastor. He immediately thereafter commenced making arrangements for the erection of a church edifice. Plans were prepared, a site purchased and the work so far progressed that the corner stone was laid October 5th, 1884, with imposing ceremonies witnessed by an immense crowd of interested people.

The church was formally dedicated June 24th, 1885, with distinguished ceremonies conducted by Right Reverend Bishop McNierney of Albany. Among the other Catholic priests present and participating in the exercises were Reverends Walworth, Mangan, Reilly and Haplin of Albany, Hourigan of Binghamton, Lynch of Utica, McDonald of Waterville, O'Mahoney of Lake George, O'Brien of Fonda, Hughes of Cooperstown and Curtin of Fort Schuyler. Religious ceremonies of such distinction had never before been witnessed in Oneonta. Rev. Father O'Mahoney preached an eloquent dedicatory sermon. At the close of the vesper service the bishop administered the sacrament to about sixty children.

The church edifice is an imposing brick structure, located upon a fine site on the southeast corner of Main and Grand streets. A commodious parsonage is situated just south of the church upon the church premises. This parish is one of great prosperity, its members now numbering over 500.

The parish also owns a cemetery situated just north of the fair grounds and south of Main street and within the corporate limits.

The growth and prosperity of the Catholic society has been phenomenal, and a promising future is before it. Rev. D. E. Murphy is its present pastor. The value of the church property is from $25,000 to $30,000.

The United Presbyterian Society.

The United Presbyterian is the latest in organization of any of the Oneonta religious societies. It was duly organized in May, 1889, under the direct efforts of Rev. L. E. Hawk, its present pastor.

Its church edifice is located on the easterly side of Dietz street, centrally in the village. The pastor purchased the conservatory of music building, which is occupied as the place of holding its present meetings. Arrangements are now being made for the erection of a fine church edifice which will no doubt be completed during the coming summer.

The society is prospering under the faithful ministration of Rev. L. E. Hawk; so too, are the services and Sunday school held by him weekly in the chapel building on River street each Sunday afternoon. The society has before it a promising future.

MARCH 30, 1893
AN HISTORICAL SKETCH OF THE OLD EMMONS FAMILY

Communities and nations are but the aggregation of individuals. In the settling of a new country its first citizens almost invariably leave their individual impress upon the following generations.

Hence arises the necessity of preserving, as far as possible, the individual history of early pioneers, as well as of the generations following them. Such history, where success has been achieved, ever acts as a stimulus to those to whom a record tradition of such acts may in future time come.

Every active individual in any community tends to influence for good or evil those with whom he may come in contact. The future effect of such influence is beyond possible human estimate. It may enlarge and expand with each passing generation, continually extending its circle of influence, as the passing seasons follow each other, in their continued, unceasing rounds.

Our object in the following biographical sketches, is to perpetuate the names and doings of some of Oneonta's most successful pioneers.

Asa Emmons, the eldest, was born at Sheffield, Litchfield county, Connecticut, August 3d, 1775. He first saw life at the start of that struggle of our fathers to free themselves and their country from oppression, and to plant deep in our soil the seeds of equality and liberty. He was an early settler in our town, upon the south side of the Susquehanna river. He resided upon what is now the Slade farm, in 1800.

Upon the river, just below where the old Indian village was in the past located, he had a saw-mill, a wool-carding and cloth-dressing establishment. He engaged in lumbering, farming and operating the above named establishment. If tradition can be relied upon, he was one of the most thorough, energetic business men among our pioneer citizens. He died in 1820, in the state of Maryland, while he was there for the selling of lumber.

He married for his wife, Eunice Prentice, of Harpersfield, Delaware county. He was, for a time, in business at that place before settling in the Susquehanna valley.

She died in 1839, surviving her husband nineteen years.

Four boys were born unto them. Edward J. was the eldest, Carlton was the third child of the family. He was born February 26th, 1804. The other sons, whom I never saw, except Carlton, were Roderick J. and Morton B., the latter of whom for many years lived on his farm on South Hill, near Emmons Lake. R. J. Emmons, was for many years in business in Oneonta Village.

Carlton Emmons, although only sixteen years of age at the death of his father, at once assumed the charge of his extensive business, which he prosecuted with marked success until the year 1840, besides farming and other business, manufacturing large quantities of lumber and rafting it down the river, as had his father.

While thus engaged he continually kept a number of hired men, among whom for some time was our present respected and aged townsman, Huntington Parish. He did his lumbering mostly with ox teams, as was almost the universal practice in early times.

While Parish was in his employ, he also at the same time had a young man by the name of Fairchild. Emmons had a very fine team of horses, which he highly prized. These young men having each of them a best girl, often coveted, but seldom obtained the use of the horses for rides with their sweethearts, on Sundays and holidays.

Rats were very numerous and troublesome, about the Emmons buildings. One morning Parish and Fairchild, while at the barns early, chanced to kill each a large rat. Mr. Emmons happening to see them latter killed, said to them: "Boys, you may have the horses to drive out a mile and a half for each rat you kill on my premises."

This was a tempting offer for the boys. Visions of future sleigh rides with their loved ones at once rose to view. Rats were plenty enough to secure the horses all they needed or desired, but how they were to catch them was the question. Already three miles ride was paid for, but how could they quadruple the distance?

The following morning, while Parish was in the granery getting oats for the horses, he saw a rat ran in a hole near the floor, behind the oat bin. He listened and learned by the noise that there were more of them there. He at once informed Fairchild. They resolved to catch them, but how was it to be done?

Parish said, "You take a stick and drive them out, and I will put on my buckskin mittens and catch them at the hole where I saw one enter." Parish got in position to catch the rats, and Fairchild poked away between the studs, but started none. Near by they had a hog-house in which was a kettle of hot water. Parish got a pail of the boiling water and a dipper, and suggested that he try that and see if it did not start them.

At the pouring in of the first dipper of water, out came the rats. Parish caught and killed them as fast as possible. Occasionally they came too fast and one would pass him, but he caught nearly all that came. When hot water would start no more rats, they proceeded to count the game, and as they did so they threw the dead rats into a half bushel measure. It was full and heaped up to its uttermost capacity.

Emmons just then coming out of the house, the boys called him to the granery. He came and for a full minute looked at the huge pile of rats as if completely dazed. He then exclaimed: "Oh, my poor horses will take many trips to pay the bill, but as I promised them, you shall have them until paid." Every person who ever knew Carlton Emmons knew he ever kept all his promises. Parish and Fairchild, with their chosen girls, had their rides, and Emmons' buildings were free from rats, for if not all killed, the balance left for safer quarters. I have this story from Parish's own lips.

Carlton Emmons married for his wife Maria, daughter of William Fairchild of Cooperstown. About 1840 he moved to his large farm at East Oneonta, better known as

"Emmons," and there for many years kept the most popular farmers' and travelers' hotel in all the country for many miles.

Two children were born to them, Delos W., now of Huntington, West Virginia. He married Miss Mary Stoddard, a lady of rare worth; the sister of the first wife of C. P. Huntington. He married her in Oneonta. It has proved a happy union.

The daughter, Rosa A., married the late Julius T. Alden of Little Falls, New York. He was a model husband and a man of superior business ability, making a success of all his undertakings. The children still retain the old homestead, occasionally making it for a time their summer home and place of family reunion.

Carleton Emmons was supervisor of the town for the years 1843-49, and 1852-3. He was also a justice of the peace, and for some years held the office of railroad commissioner for the town.

His name, and that of Allen Scramling and that of the writer, appears upon all the bonds issued by the town of Oneonta to aid in the construction of the A. & S. railroad, to the amount of $70,000. That of the writer is also attached to all of the coupons upon these bonds.

Mrs. Carlton Emmons died August 2d, 1872, aged 67 years.

Carlton Emmons died June 12th, 1879, aged 75 years. The remains rest on the family lot, south of and adjoining the Ford Lot in Riverside cemetery in Oneonta village.

Morton B. Emmons for many years resided, as before named, on his farm near Emmons Lake. It was situated about three miles south-easterly from Oneonta village.

Ira Emmons, the brother of Asa, next younger, was born October 11th, 1777, at the same place in Connecticut as was Asa. He came to Oneonta in 1821 and made a purchase of the farm still known as the Esq. Emmons farm, or the Emmons stone house farm, located about three and a half miles easterly of Oneonta village. The stone house was erected by him during the years 1821, '2 and '3. For many years, while the travel up and down this valley was by the wagon road, it was a land mark in the valley. The house is still standing in a good condition, and, if not otherwise destroyed except by the action of time, is good for many generations.

Ira Emmons was a noted land surveyor, having at one time and another surveyed nearly all the land the country round. He reared quite a family, of whom the late Mrs. E. R. Ford was the eldest. The others were born in the order named: Horace Clyde, Leroy, Samuel Rodney, Elanso Carson, Ira Jeffers, Salmon Lester, Charlotte, Wilton Homer and Asa Newton. Carson and Lester are residents and prominent citizens of our village. Further mention of Mrs. Ford will appear in the biography of Mr. Ford.

Ira Emmons died August 16th, 1883, aged 86 years.

Salmon Emmons, a younger brother of Asa and Ira, married Sally Walling, the daughter of Simeon Walling, the sister of Joseph Walling and aunt of our recent townsman, J. R. L. Walling. They used to reside on the farm I have before described as the William Bronson farm, which was east of and adjoining Maple street.

They had one daughter named Harriet, who married Daniel Stevens. She now resides in New York. Salmon Emmons died young and his widow married David T. Clark, who lived and died in this town. He at one time owned and lived upon the farm next east of the Dexter Brown farm on the south side of the river, the second farm west of the Slade farm.

He died June 8th, 1873, aged 67 years, 11 months, 22 days. His wife Sally died January 21st, 1875, aged 78 years and six months.

APRIL 6, 1893
AN HISTORICAL SKETCH OF THE MCDONALD FAMILY

The McDonald family were among the early settlers of the town of Oneonta. They were originally from the northern part of Ireland and were of those known as "Scotch Irish." Tradition says they are descendants of the noted McDonald chieftain of Scotland, some of whose descendants were known to plant by emigration their Scottish name among the citizens of the Emerald Isle.

Nicholas McDonald emigrated to this country and settled near Boston previous to the Revolution. He was born about 1718 and settled in Massachusetts near Boston about 1738. James McDonald was born in 1759 and was married to Miss Huldah Goff about 17-0.

The family soon thereafter, about the time of the close of the Revolution, moved to Ballston, Saratoga county. That county and Washington county settled very rapidly after the close of the war. The notoriety they received from being the active seat of the war, coupled with the success of the American arms by the surrender of that most noted British general, Burgoyne, early brought them into universal prominence.

Joseph McDonald was the first of the sons of Nicholas who came to this valley about 1792 and settled on the plains. James and his father with their families followed in 1796. It was then just in the new town of Otego. The plains, since known as Oneonta Plains, had already a tavern, a school and a store. James McDonald purchased the store and tavern and engaged in both the mercantile business and the keeping of a public house.

Joseph about that date purchased what has since been known as the McDonald farm and moved into a log house upon it which stood near where M. N. Elwell's house new stands. A grist mill had been erected some time before by one VanDerwerker some forty rods southeasterly of the site of the present mill. The McDonalds readily saw that a better water power than the one in use still remained unimproved. The Susquehanna river then came down to the point of the hill northeasterly of where the gas works now stand, and a natural ravine extended nearly all the way from where the river turned southward, where the present head and tail race are. It required but a low dam and slight excavation to turn the water into that natural channel.

No sooner had Joseph McDonald made the purchase than he commenced to make this undeveloped water power available. The natural channel of the creek now known as Silver creek followed the course of the head race to where the old saw mill stood, and thence of the tail race to the river, the portion needing opening and made deeper being the portion from the creek to the river. The flow of the creek most of the year furnished a large portion of the water needed for propelling the saw mill, that being the first mill built. It stood just its length above where the old saw mill foundation now stands. I tore the old mill down in 1843 and erected the one recently torn down.

The first saw mill was built in 1806. About that date James McDonald purchased the property of his brother Joseph and moved into a log house near where C. C. Stewart's house now stands. The Stewart well still in use was thus early dug by Mr. McDonald.

There is a conflict in tradition as to the actual date of the erection of the old grist mill now standing. Some of the family still living say it built about 1807 by Joseph McDonald, others later by James. Mrs. Parish, the daughter of James, says her father built it over in 1815, but that there was a mill there when she was seven years old, which would place its erection in 1807, the next year after that of the saw mill. Its exact date would be unimportant except for the correctness of its history.

The house recently standing northerly of the old saw mill was built about 1808. This was the house in which occurred the late Scanlin tragedy. It was occupied by Joseph McDonald first and later by Nicholas, his father. Joseph McDonald built the first river bridge about 1805. It was a low trestle structure and stood on the old road some rods above the present structure. The old road used to go up the flat and rise the hill back of John Youngman's house, between it and the river. Its old road bed is plainly visible. A road intersected it at that point which extended south up the hill to the old Barton McGuire farm at the hill top. This road was discontinued only a few years ago. The McGuire farm is now owned and occupied by John Sigsbee.

The old river road used to pass the Andrew Parish farm and the Morenus farm and across the C. H. Baker farm, leaving the present road at the creek just east of Baker's house. The old site is still visible. It intersected the road which passed north of Youngman's about opposite the present Charles Youngman barn.

This bridge erected by Joseph McDonald was carried away by the flood of 1816 and another higher from the water of a like kind was erected by James McDonald upon the site of the present structure. That bridge stood until about 1835, when a Burr covered bridge was erected by that notable bridge builder, William Richardson. That stood until the present iron structure was built in the fall of 1888 and in January, 1889.

James McDonald erected the house still standing on the northerly corner of Main and River streets in 1810 and opened it as a tavern in 1811 and in 1815 repaired the grist mill. In 1817 the first post office was established in the McDonald tavern and he was the first postmaster.

Since the settlement of Joseph McDonald the place had had just the name of McDonald's Bridge, next it was called McDonald's Mills. When James McDonald was made postmaster the place was called Milfordville. It retained that name until 1832, when the name of the post office was changed to Oneonta. The mail route from Unadilla to Cooperstown was up the river road and by this tavern.

James McDonald, I have just learned, started a military company here as early as 1806 of which he was the first captain, but no record of it appears on the state papers in the adjutant general's office.

James McDonald was a fine penman and a splendid business man. He was almost continuously in town office for many of the first years of his residence in the place.

In 1829 he sold his mill property and all his land east of Main street and twenty acres west of it from the river north to E. R. Ford's purchase and thence westward to the Lawrence Swart farm to Messrs. Collier and Goodyear.

In 1828 he sold to E. R. Ford the lot lying between River street and the line above named, about two acres of land. It embraced what was then made into four lots, Mason Gilbert's being the south one and E. R. Ford's the north one, upon the latter Mr. Ford erected his store and residence.

After the purchase of the mills by Messrs Collier and Goodyear they thoroughly repaired them, made the pond above the mill and cut the ditch for a waterway which still runs down the east line of the mill lands purchased of McDonald. A flood which occurred in 1816 had changed the course of the river and a dam had been made in the river where the present river dam now stands.

Messrs. Collier and Goodyear also made an aquaduct to convey the water and gravel of the Oneonta creek over across the mill race, both for the purpose of relieving it of the varying amount of water before running into the mill race from it and also to avoid the gravel which its every rise carried into the mill race.

James McDonald was three times married. By his first wife he had eight children, two by his second wife and six by his third wife. One daughter by his first wife, Mrs. Andrew Parish, still resides in Oneonta at No. 14 River street, now aged 92 years, and another daughter, Mrs. Stephen Parish (a son of Andrew Parish), who resides at No. 27 River street, a daughter by his third wife.

Few of the pioneers of Oneonta have left within it more of the imprints of a useful, active life than has James McDonald. He in anticipation foresaw what his posterity have many of them been privileged to see actually accomplished, the progress and advancement which in time was sure to come to this place.

He continued to keep the public house during his life. He died July 18th, 1834. Nicholas, his father, died at the advanced age of 100 years in 1819. After the death of his wife he spent many of his last years with the family of his son James.

At the time James McDonald moved from Oneonta Plains to his home in this place all the land from the west line of the corporation along where River street now runs, was one continuous forest of hemlock trees of large size and dense thickness. A single small clearing had been made near the river on what is now the Wilcox farm west of the grove on what was known as the Indian camping ground, and another where Main street passes north of River street. The swamp north of the railroad shops and west of it was often the home of bears and wolves and the shrill voice of the panther was familiar to all the pioneers.

The river was then the home of innumerable trout, herring and shad, each spring added hosts more of the fish by their annual spring migration to these waters.

The waters of the river and creeks were then abundant and uniform in their flow compared with their present diminutive size. Game was plenty. The Susquehanna valley had from time immemorial been noted for its hunting and fishing grounds.

Indians, too, were plenty. All the tribes for many leagues were accustomed to roam up and down this valley. For years after they had fully surrendered all claims of possession to it they used to pay it frequent visits and its white inhabitants were ever familiar with these wandering Indians.

APRIL 13, 1893

A BRIEF HISTORICAL SKETCH OF THE WELL-KNOWN BROWN FAMILY

Frederick Brown was a pioneer in Oneonta. He has left indelible imprints for its good upon his adopted town and village.

He was born on Bowman's creek, Schoharie county, August 30th, 1773. He married for his wife Catherine Houck, January 17th, 1798. Immediately after their marriage he moved to this place. He had previously purchased the farm since known as the E. R. Ford farm but formerly known as the Van Derwerker farm, and moved upon it. Where their first residence was located I have been unable to learn. But in 1812 the family resided in a frame house standing at or near where D. F. Wilber's residence now stands.

It will be seen that the lands purchased by Mr. Brown comprised those upon which quite an important part of Oneonta village now stands. Our place is now and will for all future time enjoy many privileges vouchsafed to it by the liberality of Frederick Brown. The lands occupied by the Presbyterian church yard and parsonage, together with the burying ground adjoining, were a gift from Mr. Brown to that society.

Previous to the erection of the church building, which was built by Mr. William Angel in 1816, the house of Mr. Brown during the cold part of the season was ever open for religious worship. During the warm part of the season his commodious barn was utilized for such purpose.

It was upon this Brown farm that the land force of General Clinton's army spent their second night after leaving Otsego lake, while on their way to join the army of General Sullivan at Tioga in 1779. The force upon the 250 boats which carried their supplies bivouaced the same night upon what is now the Williams farm upon the opposite side of the river.

The site for the first school house erected for and in school district No. 9 of Milford, now No. 5 of Oneonta, was furnished by Mr. Brown. It stood on the lands now occupied by the Ford block and was erected in 1812; it was used for a school house until 1839 or '40, when it was removed, after the purchase of the Brown farm by E. R. Ford. Mr. Frederick Brown died October 30th, 1843.

As the Brown family was at that time a prominent one I will name the date of birth and marriage of their children in the order in which they occurred, Lany Brown June 15th, 1799, and was married to Eli Derby, August 17th, 1815. They resided many years in a house which stood near where the late John Pardoe house now stands. They reared four children, Louisa, Frederick, Lucy and Ira. They will be remembered by our older citizens.

Cornelius Brown was born May 21st, 1801. He married Miss Laura Jones February

17th, 1826. They reared four children, only one of whom is now living. She is the wife of Rev. George Hearn, now residing in Stamford, Delaware County.

Adam Brown was born September 4th, 1804. He married Rachel Houghtaling June 29th, 1828. He was for a number of years in trade with S. J. Cook in this place. The firm was Cook & Brown. It was from the second story of their store that the first newspaper ever published in Oneonta was printed.

Mr. Brown was the first town clerk of Oneonta for the first three years after the formation of the town, and for a number of years an acting justice of the peace in this town.

They had five children, Adaline, Mark, Emeline, Mary and Agnes. Adaline married William Williams and now resides at Middlesex, Yates county, and is very prosperous. Mark, at Galena, Ill., was one of the first to enlist in the first regiment raised by General Grant and was made its quartermaster. He served with distinction through the war. He has since died. Agnes, the youngest, is the wife of Charles Cook of Galena, Ill. She is prominently connected with the World's Fair in the woman's department at Chicago.

Adam Brown and family were my nearest neighbors during the latter part of the decade of 1840, and every memory of them is pleasant. His wife died in Illinois October 6th, 1847, and he the 8th of August, 1857.

Catharine Brown was born April 6, 1806. She married Zachariah Van Leuvan. They were ancestors of those of the name now living in this town. She died June 7th, 1851.

Ann Brown was born May 9th 1808. She married Wright Stoddard; I do not know the date. Two daughters were born to them. One resides in Albany and the other in Hancock, Delaware county. Ann died July 17th, 1845.

Eliza Brown was born June 13th, 1810. She married Erastus Grannis and had two children. They moved in early life to Michigan. Eliza died June 25th, 1837.

Susan Brown was born February 3d, 1814. She married Orrin Parker a noted musician and teacher of music, and moved to Franklin, Delaware county. They had one daughter. She is the wife of Dr. Bassett of Downsville, Delaware county, N. Y. Susan died May 21st, 1849.

Jacob Brown, the youngest of the family, was born August 17th, 1816. He was married to Miss Anna Potter the only child of Caleb and Triphena Potter, June 21st, 1839. The marriage occurred in the building still standing on Chestnut street, where the Oneonta Evening News was recently published.

They have ever resided in Oneonta. Two daughters were born to them, one of who died in childhood, the other, Emma, is the wife of Byron Rose. Jacob Brown died February 1st, 1892, aged 76 years, having lived many more years than did any of his father's family. His wife, daughter Emma and a granddaughter Anna, still survive him.

APRIL 20, 1893

A BRIEF HISTORICAL SKETCH OF THE WELL-KNOWN PARISH FAMILY

Among the pioneer citizens of Oneonta whose names demand especial mention is that of Andrew Parish. He called from Massachusetts to this town in 1808. He first settled on the first farm as we cross Otego creek in going from Oneonta Plains northerly, which has for years been known as the Esq. Northrup farm.

The first business in which he engaged was that of manufacturing brick. He was the pioneer brick maker of the town. The brick used in the James McDonald, Elisha Brown, Frances Brewer and other early erected houses, were of his manufacture. From the Northrup farm he moved to the farm now known as the John Fritts farm, where he lived about two years. Not being able to obtain a satisfactory title for it, he then purchased a farm on the hill to the south, in Delaware county, where he resided for a few years. He then purchased the farm now occupied by Mr. Brown, known recently as the Stephen Parish farm, and the late John Amsden farm on the south side of the Susquehanna river, where he resided until about 1839, when he sold the farm to his son Ephraim and purchased of E. R. Ford the farm now known as the Scramling and Huntington Parish farms. While living on the south side of the river he was for many years an active justice of the peace for Delaware county.

When I first came to this place he was living on the Scramling and Parish farms above named. During the decade of 1840, he sold the farm to his son Ephraim, and purchased the one next west, and for some years resided in the building now known as the chapel, it then being his farm residence.

While owning that place he purchased the old Ford residence on Main street and resided in it for about one year. He then sold it to N. S. Goodrich and moved again to his farm below. In the early part of the decade of 1860 he purchased of me the stone house now No. 14 River street, the house in which he died, August 16th, 1867, at the advanced age of 84 years. His widow still lives in the same house, and has there resided since his death.

Esq. Parish was a pioneer lumberman in this place. Next to Asa Emmons, no man pursued the business with more perseverance or energy.

A large portion of all this region was at that time heavily wooded with large pine trees of a superior quality. The best of these trees were sawed into lumber and transported down the river for sale; Its value when in market barely paid the cost of the labor expenced in its manufacture and marketing, yet still it gave work, which was far better than idleness. In fact for years most of the money circulating among the people came from that source.

So low in price was the best of pine lumber, that even as late as the decade 1840, it would bring but from five to seven dollars per thousand feet, while hemlock of the best quality would bring but four. I have myself manufactured and sold hundreds of thousands of feet at from four to five dollars per thousand feet for hemlock, and from five to eight for pine, since my residence in this place.

Esq. Parish was the finest of neighbors and citizens. I made his acquaintance immediately after coming to town, and every memory of him is pleasant to call to mind.

He was three times married. By his first wife he had six sons, three of whom still reside in town, and three, the youngest, have passsed the river to its other side.

His second wife was a sister of his first wife, his brother's widow, who still lived but a few months after their marriage; his third one, the daughter of James McDonald, who as before named still survives him.

It is pleasant to call up the memory of the old citizens who have left so many imprints of private worth and of worthy examples behind them. They fulfilled their mission in life, they finished their work and left the world every way better for their having lived in it. Their precepts and examples will live in the generations succeeding them for their good.

APRIL 27, 1893
A TRIBUTE TO ELIAKIM R. FORD, LONG ONEONTA'S MOST DISTINGUISHED CITIZEN
(PART 1)

Eliakim R. Ford was for many years the most prominent citizen of Oneonta. He was a native of Albany county. He was born upon a farm in Westerlo in that county, November 9th, 1797. He was the first born of a family of fourteen children, seven sons and seven daughters.

He remained at home on the farm until he was twelve years old when he went to reside with his uncle, Abijah Reed, a merchant residing in Greenville, Greene county. He remained in the employ of his uncle until twenty-four years old and during these twelve years of business training under so good a tutor were developed those sterling business qualities which were to become so useful during his future active life.

In 1822 he came to Oneonta and in a small building near where the Free Baptist church now stands, he commenced the career on a small scale which was in the future, under his superior business talents and industry, to develop the man and his ability as inferior to no other in all the country round.

Soon after coming to Oneonta he made the acquaintance of Miss Harriet Emmons, daughter of Ira Emmons, which acquaintance soon led to a stronger attachment and on the 24th day of July, 1823, they were married. The bride was a young woman of great attractiveness, and of rare worth and accomplishments for those early times. All the years of her future life were but a living proof of the wisdom of his choice for a companion for life.

After his marriage he moved his store to a building standing on the southwest corner of Main and Chestnut streets, where he continued business until the spring of 1829, when he moved into his newly erected store on the south corner of Main and River streets.

At that time the travel on the river road, the mills, the wool-carding and clothdressing business and the apparent business center of the village was at that point.

Immediately after the change, he was appointed postmaster of the place, and the post office was removed from the James McDonald tavern to his store. The name of the village and post office was then Milfordville.

In 1828 Eliakim R. Ford had been made a military captain, and at that date was in actual command of the first military company of infantry organized in this vicinity. The next year he was also appointed as justice of the peace. Thus it will be seen that within the eight years of his residence in what was then the town of Milford and the village of

Milfordville, he had married a wife, been elected military captain, appointed postmaster and a justice of the peace, and besides had established the largest business and erected the finest dwelling and the best store building in the town. Such are some of the evidences of the superior ability of Mr. Ford and of the public confidence he had so soon won.

In 1830 the town of Oneonta was formed, and in 1832 the name of the village and post office was changed from Milfordville to Oneonta, and Mr. Ford was reappointed postmaster of the newly named office. He was also one of the first magistrates of the newly formed town. His business prospered and his wealth increased. He purchased what are now the Scramling and Parish farms and added farming to his mercantile business.

In the meantime the Dietz and Angel interests had increased, and by 1835 the Charlotte turnpike had been built and the stage and mail routes changed to the upper part of the village, the Angel tavern built and the business prospects of that part of the town were gaining the ascendancy.

Mr. Ford was far from failing to note the tendency of things. The first the public knew Mr. Ford had purchased the Frederick Brown farm, and was making arrangements to change both his residence and place of business. With him ever, after plans were made, was to act with life and promptness. His gains had now made him by far the wealthiest man in town.

About 1838, by some mishap, Mr. Ford lamed one of his legs so that for some time he was confined to the house. Dr. Case used to say that while thus nursing his lame leg he conceived and matured the plan of purchasing the Brown farm and erecting upon it the buildings which he soon thereafter built. Dr. Case used to tell Mr. Ford, in his jocose, laughing way, that that accident was the most lucky one in his business life.

In 1839, 1840 and 1841 he erected and completed his fine stone mansion, which still stands as a living evidence of his foresight, and his stone store, which for nearly fifty years formed the center of business on the streets of our village. It stood where the Ford block now stands.

The rows of Maple trees still standing across his old farm on River street and those standing on the westerly side of Maple street and most of those on Main street are evidences of his love for trees, and of his personal industry in obtaining and setting out and caring for them. No other man in our village has left so many like evidences of care for the future.

Mr. Ford was elected and ably served the town as its supervisor for the years of 1844, 1845 and 1846. If he would have consented he could have held the office during the following active years of his life, so great was the confidence of his townsmen in his integrity and ability to serve them.

When the village of Oneonta was incorporated Mr. Ford was unanimously elected a trustee and the president of the board for the years of 1848, 1849, 1850 and 1851, thus serving as the first officer of the village for the first four years of its corporate existence.

Mr. Ford was a man of wonderful business ability. His executive powers are rarely surpassed. Physically and mentally strong, he gave his personal attention to all his undertakings. No idlers or dead heads were allowed about him. His judgment of men and property was of a superior order. He had strong will power, and also perfect self command. If he got out of humor, he seldom made any outward manifestation of it.

He was a remarkable salesman of goods, or any kind of property. Few men were in these matters his equal.

In all matters tending to the advancement of our village interests he ever took a prominent part. When the charter for the Schenectady & Binghamton railroad was obtained in 1846 he was named in it, as one of its directors, but when the Albany & Susquehanna company was formed under the general law, by some means S. B. Beach was named as our Oneonta director. At an early date, however, Mr. Ford was elected in his place.

No railroad could or need have a more efficient director or friend than did our road in Mr. Ford. He would under no circumstances consent to anything which in his judgment would delay, or embarrass the enterprise. His entire energies were ever readily and willingly given in all ways which would tend to its just advancement.

I think I never knew a man whose name abroad carried more influence with it in matters of finance than did that of Mr. Ford. His upright, prompt business reputation was widely extended. During my long acquaintance with him I had many opportunities to observe this.

To persevere until he won was another characteristic of his. He knew no such word as fail. That principle was fully demonstrated in the Susquehanna railroad construction. He was always ready after the work was started on its construction to aid it with his credit even to a risky amount.

Another characteristic was his confidence in his friends and those whom he tried and tested in business transactions. He was always averse to putting off a certainty for an uncertainty, in his personal confidence. If he had tried a man and found him competent and reliable, he stuck to him.

His patriotism was of the highest order. With an unbounded love for his family yet his love for his country was so strong that he consented that two of his sons, Raymond and Clinton, should enlist and go to the front and take all the chances incident to a soldier's life for his country's sake. But with even that great personal sacrifice, he was unwilling that I should join the army in any way.

When Richard Franchot was mustering a regiment and I had enlisted he personally interposed and had my name stricken from the role. He said other men could fill my place in the army, but that I could not be spared from the railroad work.

MAY 4, 1893
A TRIBUTE TO ELIAKIM R. FORD, LONG ONEONTA'S MOST DISTINGUISHED CITIZEN (PART 2)

Early in March in 1862 Dr. S. H. Case, E. R. Ford, Cornelius Miller, David Dibble and myself went to Washington to see the army, our children and friends and to learn what we could of the great rebellion and the future outlook. We arrived in the city the first day after the Monitor so signally triumphed over the famous iron clad Merrimac. In fact we had not reached Pennsylvania avenue before we saw one of the men off the Monitor, still black with the powder and smoke of the fray, and from him learned the first particulars of its success.

At that time all northerners were forbidden to pass the Potomac without an army pass, and such a piece of pasteboard was hard to obtain. McClellan's army had just advanced upon the rebel army in their stronghold in Centerville and Manassas, and there were at that time hundreds of men in the city of Washington who would gladly have given hundreds of dollars each for a pass into the lines of the Union army.

After two days' delay in the city I succeeded, through a friend, in obtaining a pass for our party directly from General McClellan's headquarters and unlimited in its privileges.

After spending four days in Virginia with our army and behind it part of the time, on our return to the capitol city, we still had another day before our start for home, which we all decided to spend as we best could for our own information and benefit.

In the afternoon Mr. Ford and myself decided to visit the government navy yard at the mouth of the Charles river, and entered a bus for that destination. Seated beside me was a former law partner of Secretary Stanton. Mr. Ford was seated directly opposite us. The conversation naturally turned upon the success of the Monitor and its possible future use in the war. From that it drifted to other naval ships. I described to him somewhat in detail the form of a steam ram which I thought would stave in the hull of any wooden ship them afloat. I also described how the same ram could be made to overturn any ordinary sized ship.

He said to me "I want you to go with me this evening to Secretary Stanton, and say to him just what you have said to me." Mr. Ford immediately said to him with much decision "that would be impossible, for we start for home this evening." The bus had just then arrived at the navy yard and we parted and I did not see my friend again.

It had been understood that we were to take the next morning train instead of the evening train and I did not know as the arrangement had been changed. Being busy looking over the government works I made no inquiry why our time of departure had been changed. After leaving the ship yard we returned by way of the capitol to bid good bye to kin and other friends after getting our suppers and settling the bill we took the evening train for New York.

An hour or so after we had started Mr. Ford came to my seat and asked Mr. Dibble, who was with me, to change for a while to his, which he did. Mr. Ford then said to me, "I came to explain to you the reason of our leaving Washington to-night instead of to morrow morning. I listened to all you said to———and if you had gone with him to Secretary Stanton and repeated what you said to him, you would have been retained to superintend the immediate construction of the ram, and then what would have become of our poor railroad?"

I will tell one more story of personal interest and then leave that subject. I tell them simply to show the unyielding interest Mr. Ford took in the A. & S. railroad and of his unwavering determination not unharness any man whom he thought necessary for its completion.

Immediately after the passage of the internal revenue law of 1862, Richard Franchot, member of congress, sent the papers for my appointment as collector for this district. He at the same time wrote me a letter saying that all the endorsement necessary for me, was that Mr. Ford approve of and recommend my appointment. He at the same time said he had sent on to John Cook esq. of Worcester to accept the appointment of assessor.

Not asking, expecting or wanting office of any kind, I took a part of two days to think of the offer before making a decision in the matter. My services were not then particularly needed for the furthering of the railroad, and after looking the matter well over I saw no reason why I could not accept the office and enter at once upon its duties.

The next forenoon I took the letter and papers up to Mr. Ford's store. I handed them to him and requested him to read the letter of Mr. Franchot. He read and re-read the letter and waited some time before saying a word. When he did speak it was as follows: "Why, Mr. Baker, you must not accept the office. I cannot consent to it at all. If we spare you our cause is lost. I shall not live long enough to ever see our railroad reach Oneonta. Our people have more at stake in the road than in the collecting of government taxes. You must return the papers and decline to accept the office."

I did so and another, Mr. Wilcox of Otego, received the appointment. Mr. Cook was a director of the railroad, and he too was not appointed. I presume Mr. Ford advised him not to accept the office. While engaged in the construction of the trestles in Richmondville two years later, when a call was made for soldiers by draft, I received a letter from which I make the following extract: "I am aware of the magnitude of the work you have commenced, but I think you will accomplish it if it can be done. I should despair if it was in any other hands. I am glad you are out of the draft. We will keep up good courage. I do not know how to say fail. Let me hear from you."

I had but just commenced the work, but so great was his anxiety that if he did not hear from or see me every week he was quite sure to write me. I sometimes thought he was overrating my services and ability in pushing forward the railroad work, but his confidence remained unchanged to the end. He never disapproved of any measure I recommended for its advancement or success, but on the contrary entered into it with all his might. When I state that Mr. Ford and Mr. Goodyear were a host in the forwarding of that work to success, the word, even if in capitals, would fail to express what it really should.

Otsego county, or Oneonta town and village never had a more true or untiring friend for their prosperity and advancement than they had in Mr. Ford. Successful in his own affairs, he never ceased to desire the success of others.

In all matters for the public good he was ever ready to bear more than his full share of its cost. He was equally so in church matters. To such men is society in all its various phases indebted for its advancement. Such are the men who build up and support communities and nations.

Mr. Ford was peculiarly happy in his family relations. His wife was a helpmeet indeed. Their latch string was ever out. They entertained more friends and strangers than any family in town. Enjoying his acquaintance and friendship so long and spending so much time with him in various ways both at home and abroad I feel competent to judge correctly of his real worth as a friend, as a neighbor, as a parent and husband and as a citizen.

It seems almost a mistake that such people should be mortal. But the real truth is if they were not, society would never really appreciate them. They while living are supposed to be guided and inspired wholly by selfish motives, and it requires a lapse of time after one's departure, before a true and correct judgment of one's aims and ends can be fully understood and appreciated.

The Fords were the pioneers in many things in social life in Oneonta. It is told by those who know that they had in their house the first yarn carpet, the first cook stove, the first piano, the first friction matches and the first stone walk in their yard of any family in Oneonta.

But notwithstanding their success, it was true of them as it was of most all others who make their mark in life, that they started at the foot of the hill and climbed it step by step, unaided except by their own persevering efforts, until the goal aimed at was reached. Industry, application and economy when rightly directed are always sure to win.

It is ever a source of pleasure to contemplate the acts of those whose lives have bettered the world in which they have lived. Such examples are a rich legacy to leave behind them when one departs.

Mr. Ford died July 22d, 1873. Two more days would have completed fifty years of married life. Mrs. Ford survived him many years. She died December 1st, 1890. They now rest in Riverside cemetery in Oneonta village.

MAY 11, 1893
THE SCRAMLING FAMILY AND EARLY INDIAN REMINISCENCES

Some time during the decade of 1760 there lived in the valley of the Mohawk, near Fort Plain, a family by the name of Scramling. It consisted of father, mother, three sons and one daughter. The elder of these sons was named Henry, the second David and the third George.

Henry having made the acquaintance of Sir William Johnson, and having also having heard much of the far-famed valley of the Susquehanna, early in the decade of 1770 made a bargain with Sir William Johnson for 1,000 acres of his Susquehanna dreamland tract, situate at the Indian village of Wauteghe, at the mouth of the Otego creek.

Previous to the commencement of the Revolutionary hostilities he came to the valley, selected his land and began his frontier life. Other settler were also in the valley. At Unadilla were mills and many inhabitants. Others were scattered up and down the Susquehanna valley, Sir William Johnson having secured the indian title to most of the lands within the valley both sides of the river.

Henry Scramling had not resided in his new home two years before the death of Sir William Johnson and the commencement of hostilities and the fleeing of Sir Grey Johnson, Sir William's successor, to Canada, compelled Mr. Scramling and Mr. Stoughton Alger and other loyal Americans to return to their former Mohawk homes.

One can imagine but never realize Henry's feelings on his return to his old home to find that his father had been tommakawked, killed and scalped by the British Indian allies, and his two brothers, David and George, taken prisoners and carried captive to Canada. His old neighbors and friends had been scattered, many of them captured, some murdered, while Indian and Tory raids rendered life and person insecure in all the Mohawk valley and surrounding country.

At the raid in which the elder Scramling was killed and his two son made prisoners, there was also many female captives taken, among whom was Miss Susanna Young, who afterwards became the wife of David Scramling.

Miss Young, when captured, was only ten years old. She manifested fear at the approach of her captors toward her; an old Indian brave, with a large number of scalps, some of which were from the heads of her own relatives and still reeking with their life blood, noticing her timidity, approached her and shaking the bleeding scalps over her shrinking, childish form, sprinkled her face, hands and clothing red with the blood of her own loved but murdered kinsmen.

These Indians, finding their female captives unable to keep up their march, the second day left them in the forest to find their way back to their former homes as best they could. There was no bounty offered for female scalps or prisoners, which, no doubt, accounted for their abandonment. They, during the following day found their way back to their former but now desolate homes.

David Scramling was born in 1759 and when captured was sixteen years old, and George was two years his junior. They were kept in Canada as prisoners for nearly two years before they were allowed to return to their old Mohawk valley home.

Immediately after the close of the war, Henry, accompanied by his two brothers, David and George, and their wives and their two brothers-in-law, David and John Young, returned to their former possessions at the mouth of the Otego creek, in the Susquehanna valley. David had in the mean time married Susanna Young, the child captive above named.

David settled on the farm since known as the John Van Woert farm; George settles on the one east of it, since known as the Peter Van Woert, and later still as the Jenks and Tyler farm. Still further up the river were the farms occupied by John and David Young, the David Young farm being the one now owned by Ephraim Parish, and before him by Stoughton Alger. Upon a knoll on this farm, about halfway between the river road and the river, is located the family burying ground, where sleep the remains of these early pioneer families.

The location of these five farms was known as the "Indian Orchards," there being an Indian clearing and apple trees planted on them all. The old title deeds also name these lands as being a part of the dreamland, or Sir William Johnson tract, or both.

These Scramling brothers, from their long tarry with the Indians became familiar with the Indian dialect which knowledge was of much service to them in their new home. The Otego creek region was for many years after the Revolution often visited by parties of Indians who would erect their wigwams upon the site of their former Indian village and often remain for months at a time.

Many were the traditions retained among the old inhabitants of these Indian visits, of their customs and doings. The farm next east of the George Scramling farm was at that early date settled by one Adrian Quackenbush, the progenitor of most of the Quackenbush families of this town. I name this because I have heard these old men relate a like story to the one recently told me by Mr. Allen Scramling of our village.

David and Susanna Young Scramling were the grand parents of Allen and Albert Scramling and their sisters, most of whom are citizens of our village. The other families of the name are the descendants of one or the other of his brothers, as no Scramlings are known in this region of country who do not owe their origin to one of these three Scramling pioneer brothers.

During the residence of David upon this old farm a party of Indians erected quarters on the bank of the river not far from his home. They were artisans, and engaged in the manufacture of silver knee and shoe buckles. Such, it will be remembered, were almost universally worn near the close of the past century. David used often to visit them and see them at their work. Understanding as he did their native tongue, these visits were thus made of much more interest than they otherwise would have been. One day while with them their supply of silver became exhausted. They dispatched one of their number across the river, upon the south side, and after an absence of about two hours he returned with an abundant supply and they proceeded with their work.

Such in substance is the story told me only a few days ago by Allen Scramling, as being often told by his father, Geo. Scramling, who had heard it from his father, David, many times repeated. I had a number of years ago heard a like story told by Nicholas Quackenbush, who at the time resided in the present George Swart farm, the former Wolf farm, situated on the south side of the river, less than a mile above where the work was done. Conrad Wolf has also told me that the same tradition was firmly believed by his father. It will be borne in mind that the father of Nicholas Quackenbush, Mr. Wolf's father and Allen Scramling's grandfather all resided within a mile of where the work was done at the time it was doing.

What was most strange among all of these old men, they seemed to believe that silver in a pure state was found by these Indians in that hill on the south side of the river. So firm was Mr. Conrad Wolf in his belief that be had a self-styled minerologist with his mineral rods for two days upon the hill, making examinations only a few years ago. He invited me to accompany him, but my faith was insufficient to inspire me to the effort.

Perhaps I ought to state that all these lands have, by different individuals, been entered as mineral lands in the secretary of state's office within a few years past. And also that much time and considerable money has been spent in endeavoring to find the paying silver ore upon the lands named; but thus far with but limited success. It is my opinion that no pure silver, and not enough in any form worth mining, exists in this region of the country. I surely place no mineral value upon the lands owned by me upon any of the traditional silver mines, although I have 150 or more acres of such traditional silver producing lands. My opinions or my lack of faith, however, will not change the fact. If silver in paying quantities exists no doubt its locality will at some future time be found.

I have before mentioned in my papers that a part of the present Scramling farm is still held by the old David Scramling title. It is the 100 acres south of the Susquehanna river, adjoining the Otego line and extending from the river to the Delaware county line.

Susanna, wife of David Scramling, was born in 1765. She died December 31st, 1820. David Scramling was born in 1759 and died in 1821.

George Scramling, son of Susanna and David, and father of Allen Scramling and his brothers and sisters, was born in 1796 and died December 1st, 4851.

George Scramling jr., the late Judge George Scramling, was born in 1840 and died Jan. 30th, 1887. With his demise our county lost one of its most able and promising men, and our community the best of citizens.

MAY 18, 1893

JACOB DIETZ AND HIS EARLY INTEREST IN THE SUSQUEHANNA RAILROAD

The name of Jacob Dietz so often appears in connection with the early history of Oneonta that my papers would be very incomplete without a somewhat extended notice of that remarkable man.

He was born in Berne, Albany county, April 7th, 1790. His wife's maiden name was Hannah Price; she was born in Albany county, March 4th, 1795. They were united in marriage September 1st, 1811, and immediately moved to Colliersville, John Dietz of that place being his brother.

The spring of 1812 they purchased the farm so long known as the Dietz farm, which lay between the old Meigs and Brown farms, almost directly in the center of our village. He, at that early date, purchased it of Michael Sherman, for the sum of $1,200. He then erected a store, which stood where the Mrs. Bundy brick store now stands, also an ashery, off the bank toward the swamp, and the house still standing and lately the residence of Mrs. L. L. Bundy, now deceased.

He was a man of liberal education for those times, and has left behind him more recorded evidences of his ability than have any of his associates of those early days.

He immediately engaged in the mercantile, ashery and lumber business, rafting his lumber down the Susquehanna river. To this, also was added that of framing. It was more due to his efforts than to these of any other man, that the present bounds of the town were established, and to him is awarded the honor of naming it Oneonta.

The first recorded office he held in the town was that of highway supervisor in 1816, which office he held for several successive years. He was for several years an acting justice of the peace. He held the office of commissioner of schools for the years 1819, '22, '23 and '24. During the years of 1825 and '26 he was supervisor of the town. It must be borne in mind that this town was then mostly in Milford. The name of Milfordville was given to this village by James McDonald in 1817, when its first post office was established, with him as postmaster. It had before this been called McDonald's Mills. Jacob Dietz was its third postmaster, receiving his appointment under date of February 1st, 1830.

Mr. Dietz early conceived the idea of a railroad through this valley, and Sherman Page of Unadilla, at their own expense, surveyed a line from Unadilla to Colliersville. He was a prominent moving spirit in all of Oneonta's early improvements, being the most liberal contributor to the erection of the Presbyterian church when built. He was also a practical surveyor, and many records of his surveys are to be found in both the town and county records.

The Charlotte turnpike was chartered April 16th, 1830 and Jacob Dietz was in it named as its first director. He was one of its most prominent originators. So, too, with the charter for the Oneonta and Franklin turnpike, which was chartered by the legislature of New York, April 22d, 1831.

To demonstrate in part his foresight into the future of canals and railroads as a developing power in our state and country, I copy a portion of an article from his pen, published in the Cooperstown Freeman's Journal of December 22d, 1828. It was one issue or a series penned by him, as I notice the preceding and succeeding numbers of the paper contain articles from his pen upon the same subject.

They were evidently written to enlighten the public in the future of canals and railroads—but particularly to raise an interest in the slack water scheme of navigating the two branches of the Susquehanna river from the Chemung to Cooperstown, rather to the head of Otsego lake.

The state made a survey and the report of the same was made to the legislature, but no definite action was ever taken in the matter that appears upon the state records of the same. The law authorizing and demanding such survey was passed March, 6th, 1830.

In the communication of Mr. Dietz, from which I copy, he gives a full and clear description of the canals then built and in process of construction or projected in our whole country, and also of the Welland canal in the Canadas; and also of the railroads then built or contemplated. He says:

"The discussion of the railway system at present time engages the attention and the talents of our most distinguished citizens in public and private life; but until that diffusion of information is effected among the great mass of people, which, happily, form the base of every public enterprise, it cannot be expected, whatever be its merits and however confident its advocates, that great enterprise will be undertaken."

"It was from this connection that I was induced to prepare for the press the following pages, which are mostly extracted from the books and reports published upon the subject. It appears that other nations have accomplished much by it. Can it be doubted that American enterprise will accomplish the same results? In England at this time between two and three thousand miles of railroads in successful operation, constructed on different plans, composed of different materials. Some entirely of wood, others of part wood and part iron.

"The United States system of railroads has been but lately introduced. The Quincy railroad was constructed about three years since and is found to operate very well in winter, though with parallel lines for four wheel carriages. Its object was to carry to the tide waters large masses of rock to build the Washington monument of Bunker Hill. It is constructed of bars of wrought iron about two inches wide and elevated about eighteen inches on timbers lengthwise. Its foundation is from the least valuable of the stone from its own quarry. For the transportation of heavy loads it is an excellent work and worthy of its object, as that object was to introduce it into the country of Washington one of the greatest means of opening its resources.

"The Mauchunk railroad in Pennsylvania is built by imbedding timbers firmly in the ground about three feet apart, upon which are placed lengthwise timbers, or string pieces secured by wooden pins. Upon these are bars of wrought iron secured in their places by nails or spikes. This constitutes their railroad, which was constructed about two years ago and cost from $2,500 to $3,000 per mile.

"The Delaware & Hudson railway now being constructed from the head of their canal at Dyberry, to the coal mines 16½ miles was estimated to cost including the stationary and traction engines $180,000 or $10,909.10 per mile.

"Its foundation is formed by excavating pits about two and one-half feet deep and two feet square. These pits are filled with small broken stone, similar to those used in construction of McAdam roads, not exceeding two inches in diameter. They are placed in layers in the pits and each successive layer is rammed with great care until the entire mass forms a firm basis. When within about three inches of the surface of the ground flat stones of sufficient size for the sills to rest upon are placed and carried up to a height not exceeding two feet. When the required height is more the rails or string pieces are supported by tressle, resting upon the transverse sills which are sustained by the stone foundation.

"Upon this foundation are lengthwise four parallel lines of string pieces firmly secured in their places by pins. Upon their top is fixed bars of rolled iron 2¼ inches wide and half an inch thick, secured thereon by four-inch wood screws with heads countersunk."

I make these long extracts to show how Mr. Dietz had made himself acquainted with what was then its infancy, railroad building. He also fully understood the canal system both constructed and projected at an early date. In speaking of a slack-water project called the Onondaga slack-water canal from Syracuse to Binghamton, he says, "It is however the most favorable situation for a railroad to form a connection between Binghamton and Onondaga salt works, the distance being 94 miles less than by the way of Utica and along the valley of the Chenango."

In this paragraph is demonstrated his prophetic foresight of the superiority of railroads over canals—which it has taken our people more than sixty years to prove by actual trial of both, and, too, in which a short-sighted class of our people are still determined to perpetuate until it virtually ruins the farmers of our state, by taxing them to keep that old Erie ditch in operation as a political source of pap. The Chenango canal however has long since succumbed to Mr. Dietz's proposed railroad. It will be a happy day for our state when all others come to a like end.

From the same Freeman's Journal I copy the following notice, which explains itself:

Notice.

An application will be made to the legislature of this state at its next session for the incorporation of a new company with a capital of $1,500,000 for the purpose of improving by means of locks, dams and canals where necessary that part of the Susquehanna river within this state from Otsego lake to the Pennsylvania line at Tioga Point, thence up the Tioga river to Chimney Narrows, in the county of Steuben, and connecting the two rivers by a canal, and for constructing a railroad from Otsego lake to the Erie canal, at or near Fort Plain, with a bank to be located in New York or Albany for the furtherence of said improvements. Dated, November 12th, 1828.

Sherman Page, Jacob Deitz, Erastus Crafts, William Campbell, S. Starkweather, Robert Campbell, T. R. Austin, Schuyler Crippen.

N. B. The editors of the Fort Plain Watch Tower, Broome Republican, Norwich Journal, Owego Gazette, Bath Advocate, New York Spectator, Delaware Gazette and Albany Argus are respectfully requested to publish the above notice six weeks and forward the certificates and bills to the Albany Argus by the first of January next, at whose office the same will be paid.

A bold project, which fortunately for its projectors was never carried into operation. I publish these extracts from that old journal to demonstrate two important points in our early history, the one is Otsego county's early interest in international improvements and that Jacob Dietz of Oneonta, then Milfordville was the moving spirit of this gigantic anticipated enterprise. Could he now return and see the railroads which he proposed in operation and his early plans so perfectly completed he would no doubt be surprised at his own foresight. The real fact is he was one of the pioneers of our present and future development.

Could he have been spared to the common age of man, no doubt he would have added much to the progress of those schemes which his early death left for his successors to finish. He died in September, 1831 and his remains repose in the Riverside cemetery in the town and village to which he gave a name.

MAY 25, 1893

BRIEF SKETCHES OF THE HOUGHTALING AND ALGER FAMILIES (PART 1)

To obtain reliable information of the first settlers of any locality, is the hardest task of the correct historian. The pioneers of a new country are seldom the ones who leave behind them historical records of their lives or of interesting events. Regret such truth as we may, it still remains the fact.

Were it not that some stranger or some passing traveler recorded what he observed, we would, after the lapse of the memory of the old inhabitants, be without any possible clew to pioneer history. The pioneers of any place, no matter how obscure and uninfluential they may be, become an important factor for its future development. For that reason, if for no other, a passing notice of them and their doings becomes essential to the history of its future inhabitents. For such reason we are ever anxious to learn what we can of those who first braved the hardships and privations, ever in former times attendant on pioneer life.

It will be my aim in this paper to snatch from obscurity the names of some of Oneonta's pioneers which in the past have been overlooked, and whose memories and doings are worthy of record and remembrance.

One of Oneonta's pioneers was one Abraham Houghtaling. In stating that Oneonta creek was early known in the Milford town records as Houghtaling creek, in a former chapter I made the mistake of locating him on the Houghtaling farm up the creek, just above the corporation. Such was not his residence. His house stood just west of the Oneonta creek on the south side of Main street on the creek bank, as it formerly ran. His farm included the lands west of the old John I. Couse farm and east of the Frederick Brown, or later, E. R. Ford farm. At that early date his title was probably simply a possession, as the land was not then surveyed for market or sale. His wife's maiden name was Sally Price. He must have settled here immediately after the Revolutionary war, or near is close.

His son, Abraham Houghtaling jr., the father of Mrs. David Orr, South Side, was the first child born in the corporate limits of Oneonta of whom we have proof of the time of his birth. He was born October 3d, 1782, and died February 3d, 1867, aged 84 years and 4 months.

His father, Abraham senior, died in Cortland county, but the exact date of his death I am unable to give. His wife, the grandmother of Mrs. Orr, died in the old log house in which Abraham jr. was born. Mrs. Orr. well remembers her, and was with her much during her last days and was present at her death, but she does not remember ever seeing her grandfather.

Abraham Houghtaling jr. lived on the farm up the Oneonta creek, just out of the corporation, when I came to town. I knew him well. He was an admirer of fine horses. In 1843 Nicholas Alger lived on the present John Miller farm. He and Abraham had each of them an extra-large and fine horse of like color and size. They often bantered each other for a change see as to bring the two fine ones together in the same team.

Alger's horse was of such remarkable strength that he used to haul heavy logs on the saw mill logway with him alone, he thus being better than a double team because he could be more easily and quickly handled. He had, one day in the fall, been down to the mill to haul on logs for a bill of lumber I was having sawed for him. On his return, near Bronson lane (now Maple street), he met Mr. Houghtaling with his best horse, upon which he was riding. Alger was also riding his.

Of course "Nick" and "Uncle Abe," as they were familiarly called, could not pass without each bragging up his own horse. Finally a small bet was made as to which was the heaviest, each claiming his the most weighty. The following morning at 10 a.m. was finally agreed that they would meet at the hay scales and by actual weight decide the bet.

Mr. Alger was an excellent judge of a horse, and he had doubts as to which was the heavier, they being so near of a size. On his way home he pondered in his mind the various ways by which he could get a few extra pounds into his horse the following morning. His ready genius, however, came to his aid. Water would add to his weight, if inside of his hide. He would try the water. On arriving home, his horse being hungry from hard work, he fed him liberally but gave him no drink, but added as much salt to his feed as he thought the horse would eat. In the morning food and salt were again fed him. Just before time for weighing he let him have all the spring water he would drink and immediately led him to the village.

"Uncle Abe" was already on hand with his horse. He was carefully weighed and his weight registered. "Nick" then led his horse on the scales and tipped the beam at an excess of ten pounds, and thus won the bet.

Mr. Alger then came down to the mill to haul away his lumber. He was in fine spirits. He had beaten Uncle Abe in a bet on the weight of his horse. "But," said he in a low voice, and with a peculiar wink of his eye, "Harvey, the water did it. If all was equal they would not vary two pounds in weight." Mr. Alger is still living, and no doubt yet enjoys the story of his bet with "Uncle Abe."

Ninety years ago there stood a log house on the north side of Main street just a little west of where William Bissell's residence now stands. In it lived John Hilsinger, the first blacksmith who lived in what is now Oneonta village. He at different times resided in other places in the village and town. His son William was born some seventy years ago, just east of Oneonta creek.

In 1841 Mr. Hillsinger lived in Colliersville, and there remained until his death. He was an excellent workman and retained his skill until extreme old age. Some time in the year 1851, while on my way to Schenevus in a very icy time, I called at his shop to have my horses shoes sharpened. He was then an old man, and my horses were both large and young, and one of them very ugly to shoe.

In answer to my inquiry whether he could shoe them, he replied, "If they are kind I will try as I want the pay." My answer was, "Take off only one shoe and sharpen and set it, and then another and by so doing you can stop if they don't prove kind at any time, and you may take all the time you want to do the work."

He commenced, took off a fore shoe of the mildest one and sharpened and set it, then another and another until both horses were well and nicely shod. The horses seemed to know he was old, and for the first time in their lives were perfectly kind and mild, never moving only as directed. The job was soon done. When completed he said, "I never shod a kinder team in my life."

When told that the off one was never shod before without a fight, and a twist on his nose, he would not believe it could be possible. The result of an old man's mildness was, that I never after had any trouble with the team while being shod. The old man's kindness and mildness had convinced them that a regular fight was not a necessary part of the job. I kept them for twelve years thereafter and they were always kind to shoe. I paid the old gentleman more than he asked me for shoeing them at the time, feeling confident that he had justly earned such increase of pay. The future fully proved the correctness of my conclusion.

JUNE 1, 1893
BRIEF SKETCHES OF THE HOUGHTALING AND ALGER FAMILIES—CONCLUDED
(PART 2)

I have before named Stoughton Alger as one of Oneonta's pioneer settlers. He came from the vicinity of Boston to this town before the war of the Revolution. He was by trade a blacksmith and the first one ever known in this vicinity. When he came here the only house within what is now the present corporation was the old log house before mentioned, where the Baird block now stands, the one in which the late David Morrell was born.

Mr. Alger at the outbreak of the war moved to the Mohawk valley and remained there and carried on his trade during the war, returning again to this place immediately after the close of the Revolution. What is now known as the Murdock, formerly the Gowey, and still prior the Deacon Beach farm was the original Stoughton Alger farm. The Ward farm so often named in the Otego and Milford records was sold to Mr. Ward by Mr. Alger. It is now owned by Mr. Pierce of Binghamton and others. When I came to town it was known as the Noxen farm. I presume these early time sales were merely sales of possession, as but few lands were in shape for market thus early in our history.

Stoughton Alger's name appears early in the records of the town of Otego. He was a citizen of the town while still in Tryon county, then Montgomery county, and finally in Otsego county. He had lived in the town of Otsego and in Unadilla before the town of Otego was formed, although all the time on the same farm. The family has lived to see all the changes of the locality from primeval forest to its present condition. But it has required three succeeding long-lived generations to reach the present time.

General Alger, the distinguished statesman of Michigan, is a descendant of the Stoughton Alger family, being a son of Josiah Alger, the brother of Stoughton Alger jr. He is a cousin of our townswoman Mrs. Ephraim Parish.

Fifty years ago Stoughton Alger jr. owned and lived upon the former Youngs farm, now the Ephraim Parish farm on the Oneonta Plains. I well remember him as one of Oneonta's most successful farmers at the time. Dr. Parish of the town of Maryland is a grandson of his.

Another brother of Stoughton Alger jr. was David Alger. He was also a blacksmith by trade, and in fact it may be said that since the first settlement of the Alger family in this vicinity the place has never been without one or more of his descendants who were by occupation blacksmiths.

Among the early settlers in Oneonta on the south side of the river we must not fail to name Anthony Crispell. He was the first settler on what is now the Charles H. Baker farm. A willow tree is still standing near the spring brook a few rods south of the public highway, which was grown from a walking stick brought up the river by a raftsman more than a hundred years ago, while the form was owned by Mr. Crispell, and stuck into the ground. It has now grown to large dimensions.

One of the peculiar remembrances of Mr. Crispell was that he owned two black slaves, the only ones I have yet learned of being owned in this vicinity, in fact I believe the only ones ever owned in the town. They consisted of a man called Som, probably a short name for Solomon, and his wife called Sayre, probably meaning Sarah.

Som, years after, was hired to Mr. Emmons to assist in running lumber down the river, and never returned. Some said he had died, and others that he was stolen and enslaved south. His wife was sold to David Brewer, who formerly owned the old Erastus Blanchard farm, now owned by John Sigsbee. She was afterward sold to a resident of Schoharie.

Som and Sayre had but one child, which died when young. When it was a babe Esquire Parish lived on the John Fritts farm. His son Huntington was a small boy and his mother took him up to Som's to see the baby. Getting but a glimpse of it in its infantile wrappings, he thought it to be a puppy. When leaving he was no sooner in the road than he desired his mother when Sayre had another puppy to get it for him.

At that early day Henry Couse lived on the David Orr farm, which was afterward known as the Simeon Mickle farm. Our townsman, Anthony Couse, was a son of Henry. The wife of Hontice J. Couse, named in a former chapter, was also his daughter. Mrs. John Hackett on the Hontice J. Couse farm, and Mrs. Hiram Fritts on the Fritts farm were John Couse's daughters.

Anthony Couse informs that the Orr farm had been a former possession, and that his father's family were its second occupants.

Henry Couse was born in 1763 and died September 13th, 1855, aged 92 years and four months.

Simeon Walling I have before mentioned as one of Oneonta's pioneers. He, too, was one of its earliest tavern keepers. He settled in 1785, as we have before recorded, on the farm recently owned and occupied by his grandson, J. R. L. Walling. The farm he so early settled upon is one of the few in the town which still remains in the ownership of the descendants of the original purchaser without change of owners. No other like case exists in the village limits. In fact few farms can be found in this locality which for one hundred seven years have remained in ownership and continued occupancy in the same family as has that of Mr. Walling.

Simeon Walling's first house was of logs, as was that of all pioneers. As soon as saw mills existed he built a frame house, which was painted red and was for many years a landmark in this valley. He lived in that house until his death.

In 1854 Joseph Walling erected the brick house in which his son, J. R. L. Walling, resided until his death. This was the first brick house erected in this village. The old red tavern house was then sold and removed east above the toll gate, recovered and is still doing service as a good dwelling.

If industry, economy, honesty, integrity, reliability, good habits and good examples make good citizens and the world better for living in it, then truly have Simeon Walling and his posterity filled their mission and accomplished the ends of true citizenship.

JUNE 15, 1893
THE WOLF FAMILY AND SOME GENERAL HISTORICAL NOTES

The Wolf family were among the pioneers in this town. Jacob Wolf settled on what is now the George Swart farm, on the south side of the river, soon after the close of the Revolution, in which war he was a soldier. He made his home in this then forest region about 1785. His wife's maiden name was Leopard. They reared a large family of children, among whom was the very prolific wife of James Blanchard, whom I have named in a former paper. The mother of our townsman, Jacob Farrington, was also a daughter of Jacob Wolf.

Among his sons I do not remember knowing but two of them. Isaac Wolf, a son, resided on the old Wolf farm when I came to town, and a number of his descendants can now be numbered among the citizens of this vicinity. Conrad Wolf was also one of his sons. He was born in, and for a long lifetime resided in this town, and during all the years of his married life, in this corporation, the westerly line of his farm being the corporate limits.

Conrad Wolf was born June 11th, 1802. He used jocosely to say that "the union of a Wolf and Leopard brought forth a Coon." He married Miss Catherine Van Woert, daughter of John Van Woert, in 1828. They immediately took up their residence upon the farm where they continued to reside during their entire married life.

Mr. Wolf was an honest, industrious and worthy man and a good neighbor and citizen. He was a very good carpenter, but the main business of his life was that of farming. In politics, until the question of extending slavery into the territories came up, he was a Democrat; but with all free-soilers he joined the Republican party and was an ardent Republican until his death. In religious faith and belief he was a Methodist. His wife was also a member of the same church.

Mr. Wolf lived to see and enjoy the changes and progress of our country and locality until December 7th, 1891, when he passed over the river, having retained his physical and mental vigor to a remarkable degree to the close of his long life.

I should signally fail in these papers if I gave no early geographical picture of Oneonta village. If by my pen I could convey a correct representation of its original state, and make a true contrast with the present, I should be content.

At its first visit by a white man it must have presented a very unique appearance. Its forests were densely wooded with every variety of trees indigenous to its soil, climate and locality. Upon its high lands and clay bottoms, pine of immense proportions were abundant. The sandy loam soils were covered with hemlocks, tall, thick and of large size. The gravely ridges were heavily wooded with maple, beech, birch, basswood, cherry, ironwood and an intermixture of other less common kinds.

The swamp lands, which were ever abundant in all uncleared forest regions, abounded in swamp pine, black ash, yellow birch, water beech, black maple and other kinds ever in our state to be found within our swamp lands.

Our present corporate limits abounded in all these varieties, as its lands embrace the varieties of soil, and the elevations and depressions admirably adapted to the growth of them all. Of course, one coming here fifty-two years ago, could not see these native forests in all, or even any of their primitive glory, but enough of them and their remains were left, so that and observing person could readily discover what had been their former condition.

The lands directly west of Main street where Luther street now is, was covered with a heavy growth of sugar maple intermixed with large butternut trees. All the table of lands, now on River street, extending to the corporate limits, was heavily wooded with hemlock, with occasionally a sprinkling of maple and pines of very large growth. The hilly portion of the corporate limits was wooded with pine, chestnut, white, black and red oak, intermixed with a few maple and beech.

The gravely portion lying up Oneonta creek had more hard wood with some pine and hemlock intermixed. If pine stumps, roots and old logs are indicative of such former growth, the swampy portion of our lands still give conclusive proof of its original forest products.

Our corporate limits contain also every possible degree and variety of elevations, from the river bed to hills of 450 feet elevation above it. It, too, has in its combination a great variety of our earth's geological formations—from the softest muck to the hardest rock.

The first white visitors to this place, of whom I have the names and dates so recorded as to be beyond cavil or dispute, were Messrs. Hawley, Woodbridge and their party, who passed through where Main street is now located, on the first day of June, 1753. A Mr. Winedecker with a portion of their party, and others, the same day passed down the river. Messrs. Hawley and Woodbridge were religious teachers from Massachusetts, on their was as missionaries among the Indians at Oquagua, accompanied by Mrs. Ashley a white woman, their interpreter, her Indian husband and several other Indians and "three or four blacks."

This Mr. Winedecker was an Indian trader who came down the river in his boat on the 31st of May, with whom the missionaries arranged to carry a part of their party. The fact of the presence of these white traders is proof positive of former visits to the valley by white men prior to the date above mentioned. And, as they say the land party traveled with horses by the Indian trail, they of course came down the main street of our village.

They came from Schoharie, by way the Schenevus creek, and Mr. Winedecker fortunately happened to be coming down the river and met them at what is now Colliersville, at the mouth of the Schenevus creek.

All the public roads within the bounds of Oneonta village fifty years ago, were the ones now known as River Street, Main Street, Chestnut street, West, Milk and Maple streets.

River street at the west boundaries of the corporation, and at its intersection with Main street at its east end, is nearly upon its old site, but all the rest of its distance within the corporation was formerly nearer the river.

The location of Main street remains near its former site. It has been changed a few rods in places on what is called lower Main street, to straighten and improve it since 1841. Chestnut street is mostly upon its former and original site. A street which intersects Chestnut, called then as now, West street, passed from Chestnut street through the north line of the corporation towards Laurens. Milk street was the east end of Academy street.

Maple street has been changed some at its passage up the creek and closed northerly in part by the Normal school structures crossing its former site. The street up the Oneonta creek in the early days was upon the east side of the creek. Its old site is still in many places plainly visible.

JUNE 22, 1893

MORE ABOUT THE EARLY APPEARANCE OF THE VILLAGE OF ONEONTA (PART 1)

The swamp lands formerly within the corporate limits demand special notice, as most successful cities have been to considerable extent constructed upon drained swamps. Witness Rochester, Syracuse and Buffalo in our own state, and Chicago, the queen city of the west.

The largest swamp within our village bounds still to quite an extent remains a swamp. It is, however, much less than its former size. It used to extend from the former point of the bluff east of the railroad shops westward for a mile and a half to near the plains. It formerly consisted of about 100 acres of land, about two thirds of which was within the corporate bounds. So much of it has been wholly or partially drained that its former dimensions are now greatly diminished, but still quite a swamp remains.

There was formerly a swamp of a few acres on the farm easterly of and adjoining the Conrad Wolfe farm between the river road and the river. It has now, however, been reclaimed. Jacob Farrington, the father of our townsman of that name, was formerly the owner of the farm upon which it was situated.

A strip of swamp lands commenced at what was fifty years ago known as Swart's eddy. It was situated just at the south ends of London and Wilcox avenues. The swamp starting at the river at that place followed the low or depressed lands across that farm northward and the old James McDonald farm up to the high bluff now north of the railroad and around to the old saw mill house recently made memorable by the Scanlin murder committed in it. This swamp was crossed by Main street nearly southeast of the present railroad crossing by a corduroy or log road, and the portion east of the street partially drained and filled so as to be used as a saw mill yard.

When I came here in 1841 the old logs of the corduroy road were still visible. Main street in 1842 was moved its width west to straighten and improve it. This swamp long impassable is now drained, improved and built upon. London avenue, Burnside avenue, Ann street, Meckley avenue, Parish street, Mosher avenue and Florence avenue are all or in part upon lands which were formerly a portion of this long strip of swamp. The railroad is also for some thirty rods from Main street westerly across this swamp. One horse and one cow were mired in lands new covered by the railroad since I came to this place. Two springs, in addition to the storm waters flowing thereon, formed its water supply. It for all former time until the railroad was built, formed the home for hosts of bull and peeping frogs, many of the former kind rivaling in size the ones described in Æsop's fables.

Another swamp, separated from the one last described only by a narrow strip or land which connected Barn hill with the high lands west of Main street and north or the railroad, started where the railroad culvert now is just southeast of the Shellman carriage shop lot and extended around the foot of the bluff upon which Main street is constructed to the high lands east of Silver creek at the Presbyterian church lot and then around the foot of the Riverside cemetery lot to the river and then westward past where the gas works now stand, thence widening southerly and narrowing westerly to the grist mill then back easterly, northerly and westerly around Barn hill to the place of beginning.

This piece of low land, which was quite a portion of it impassable for man or beast except upon its logs, roots and bogs, had a dugway road around the foot of the bank on its easterly side, which crossed the swamp at a narrow point, where is now the east line of the depot grounds, upon a corduroy road. This road was made more than a hundred years ago, if tradition gives us true history, both for the use of the farm lands between the swamp and the river and also for the purpose of hauling their native timber growth upon them.

This swamp, which was nearly in the heart of the village lands, formerly had flowing through it the stream now known as Silver creek which stream came into it at its northeast corner and flowed through it in a southeasterly direction, passing around the east end and south side of Barn hill to where the mills now stand and thence down the line of the present tail race to the river. The waters from the head race or mill pond for the mills ebbed and flowed into and out of the lower or western portion of this swamp at their daily rise and fall when the pond was full, or left it when the waters of the pond were lowered.

This condition continued until the embankment of the railroad was constructed across its southerly side. At the suggestion of the writer, that the culvert under the railroad be made at its west end instead at the old creek channel, its first location was so changed, and also at another time when he with Mr. Ford and Mr. Goodyear were together the arrangement for the change of the channel of Silver creek was made, which took its waters into the head race east of the depot instead of its passing through the lands in its former course, was consummated.

These changes made easy the drainage of this central swamp, containing from twenty to thirty acres of land susceptible of being drained and used for building purposes. The railroad embankment cut off the flow of water from the mill pond. The change of the creek took its waters around the easterly end. The culvert at its southwest corner and drain at the tail race of the saw mill took off the spring and storm waters, but the westerly portion was still a water covered swamp.

The writer thus early saw that these changes would eventually by a liberal outlay of labor render these lands both useful and valuable. He owned a small portion of them, Mr. Goodyear owned the southern and western part, Mr. I. H. Peters owned a narrow strip west of the writer's, the heirs of James T. Wild owned north and east of Baker's and Goodyear's to the E. R. Ford farm, and he owned the balance, his being the larger and higher portion of them. East of a corner of Mr. Ford's land and of the depot grounds Mr. Goodyear owned still another piece of both swamp and bank lands.

JULY 6, 1893

MORE ABOUT THE EARLY APPEARANCE OF THE VILLAGE OF ONEONTA (PART 2)

Early in 1866 the writer suggested to Mr. Goodyear that they together purchase all these lands except Mr. Ford's and drain and improve them. His reply was "You purchase them, and I will either join you in improving them or sell you what I own of them."

I at the same time made him an offer to purchase the swamp and adjoining lands lying west of Main street and south of the railroad, which he accepted. I immediately commenced their improvement. They are now virtually covered with buildings, having on them fine residences sufficient for some twenty families. These lands were a part of the swamp that raised the large frogs before named.

I then proceeded to purchase the lands of the James P. Wild estate and what I could of I. H. Peters and obtained from him a release for a street across those he still retained. After perfecting all these arrangements, Mr. Goodyear made me an offer to sell me that part of his which lay south of the old line and east of the depot, instead of joining in their improvement. I accepted his offer and took a deed.

All these lands west of the Ford farm were covered with stumps, logs, brush and water, excepting the Wild's portion, which was partly swamp grass and bogs, he having spent much labor in trying to reclaim it. I at once laid out what is now called Mechanic street, (a name given it by E. R. Ford), four rods in width, and commenced improving these lands and making the street. Mr. Ford had already made Broad street, and he opened Mechanic street the short distance across his premises to that street. Much more of the history of this improvement and the way it was met by the acts of the corporation and its final results is already recorded, and, therefore, I will omit it here.

This swamp now has upon it the line of the D. & H. railroad, its fine and commodious brick passenger and freight depot buildings; the brick electric light works plant; Moody & Gould's extensive works; Buckely's shirt manufactory; Doyle & Smith's elegantly-equipped four-story brick cigar manufactory; Dauley & Wright's extensive marble works; Lewis & Wilson's saw, grist and planing mills; and all kinds of building and wooding manufactory; W. H. Woodin's sash, door, blind and building establishment; Mayne's foundry, where all kinds of castings and machinery for agricultural, mechanical and building purposes are made; Stilson's machine shops; D. Whipple & Son's and Mills & Stone's wholesale and retail coal yards; Butts & Son, wholesale and retail dealers in agricultural tools and builders' supplies; J. O. & G. N. Rowe, wholesale grocers; Morris Brothers' fine large elevator and storehouse for the wholesale and retail flour, grain, feed and seed business; Lewis & Wilson's spacious and elegant new brick hotel, in fact dwellings, smithshops flour and feed stores, laundries, groceries, fruit dealers, hotels, etc., etc., are now successfully established upon this once impassable swamp, and more new and extensive buildings are being annually added.

The public streets now opened upon this former swamp are Goodyear street, Goldsmith street, Benton street, South Chestnut street, Broad street, Prospect street, Hamilton avenue, Front street, and Brookside avenue, besides the street leading to the gas works and farm lands south of the mill race. Already between one and two millions of dollars in value have been placed upon this once valueless land; and all of it since the spring of 1865—the spring previous to the advent of the railroad in the early fall following.

So late as 1880 one of our oldest and most distinguished citizens in a suit pending in relation to the value of a portion of these reclaimed lands stands recorded as testifying that "I don't consider it worth anything." Speaking of the part belonging to Mr. Ford, he said it was "worth one hundred dollars an acre." The demonstrated fact shows that even wise men can easily err in jugdment.

A swamp of some "two or three acres," according to Dr. S. H. Case's estimate, formerly commenced at the Sabin (now W. L. Brown) place and extended in a northeasterly direction up across Chestnut street and on up to Deitz street above where the opera house now is. Mr. David Morrel, who was born near it, described it as "a regular swamp hole." Since my residence in town, quite a portion east of Chestnut street was "a regular swamp hole" and winter skating pond. It has since been drained and filled and valuable store blocks, the Windsor hotel and its barns, the opera building, and even the Brown and Tobey & Gurney block, and the Central hotel and connecting blocks are upon its southern portion. I have myself seen the water in the spring thaws cover the ground now occupied by all the buildings named and where Dr. Meigs Case's dwelling and dispensary and the post office block now stands. The value of the buildings now standing upon the former site of that swamp, all of which have been erected since my acquaintance with it, would foot up to hundreds of thousands of dollars.

Another swamp was located in the hollow extending southeasterly from the residence of M. L. Keyes (the old Colonel Snow place) across High street, Franklin street, Ash street and Green street, which formerly contained several acres of land. It was early drained across Chestnut street at its junction with West street on its westerly end, and easterly into Silver creek years ago, while the lands around it were all farm lands. Now all is covered with fine dwellings.

Another piece of swamp land extended across the Ford farm north of where Centre street is now located, which was reclaimed by Mr. Ford shortly after the land came into his ownership. Even after it was laid into village lots and the streets worked and many buildings erected, the accumulating waters were at times very annoying before sewers and sub-drainage were provided for their escape. Part of the old drain made by Mr. ford is still visible.

JULY 13, 1893
LAST WORDS ABOUT THE EARLY APPEARANCE OF THE VILLAGE OF ONEONTA
(PART 3)

Another small swamp was just east of Oneonta creek, opposite the ice house. It extended for some distance easterly. The railroad was built through it, which virtually disposed of it as but a mere vestige of it still remains. All these swamps were fed by durable springs of water as well as by storm accumulations, and of course their waters never became stagnant.

The best part of our swamp-land history is soon told. They are all of them virtually drained and reclaimed, except the larger one named, and all of that is susceptible of being made valuable village lands. It has a solid clay sub-soil near the surface, and the time is not far distant when even this one will exist only in memory.

I know of no village or city better situated for perfect sewerage or drainage than is Oneonta. In the decade of 1870 or early in 1880 the place was visited by the late Dr. Harris of the state board of health. While riding over the site of the village, noting its surface formation, he remarked: "You have here a village so situated and located that its drainage and sewerage is susceptible of the best and most perfect sanitary regulation of any I now remember." His remark is strictly true, and if any failure in that respect ever occurs, it will be the result of bad engineering or imperfect and improper work, and not for lack of good sites and opportunities.

Before closing this paper I must say something of our high lands, now that I have partially described its low ones. The entire formation of our village site is by nature favorable to a continuous change of air, no matter what direction the wind. Nature has so formed our surroundings that no dead or stagnant air can remain unmoved. The make of its hills and its valleys is such that continual circulation is a natural sequence.

Even should the winds become chained and immovable, the changes in temperature will always give us a free circulation. I look upon this natural undulating formation of our city site as a thousand-fold preferable to an extended plain, no matter how great its elevation or how pleasant its outside surroundings. If Oneonta should ever become an unhealthy place, it will be the fault of its occupants, but never of its natural formation or its environment.

It is impossible to convey by words an idea of unseen things which will give their true appearance. But I can so describe our village location that the facts named in the last paragraph can easily be imagined. On its south bounds glides along, from east to west, in its crooked, meandering way, the Susquehanna river. At the mill dam, which is about 60 rods easterly of the depot, the river is near the line of the A. & S. R. R. From there it bears southward and then westward so that at the west bounds of the corporation its course is nearly half a mile from the line of the railroad, and the flats from the road to the river have several feet slope toward the river through the entire distance.

The Oneonta creek empties its waters into the river at the mill dam. The valley of the creek extends for miles in a north-easterly direction with quite a fall and with gradually elevating slopes to the top of the hills on both its sides. These hillsides are fertile farming lands, and the summits of the ridges, which extend about a mile north of the river, are from 200 to 300 feet in elevation. From the east, south and west there is a steady current of fresh air. The water supply for the embryo city comes from the springs forming the source of this creek, the upper reservoir being about four miles up the valley and at an elevation of about 300 feet.

Silver creek, a small stream I have often spoken of, comes down like a valley from the north and empties its waters into the mill race at the southeast corner of the depot grounds. This is also a creek fed by springs and has hillside slopes and farm lands not unlike the topography of the Oneonta creek valley.

Near the west bounds of the corporation the Susquehanna valley widens to a width of some three or four miles to the valley of the Otego creek, forming the tablelands called Oneonta Plains.

Between Silver creek and these plains is a wooded elevation of about four hundred feet in height called Rock Hill. It forms a splendid view for observation of the village, the Susquehanna valley both the east and west, the Otego creek valley, and the Charlotte valley at the south-east. In addition to this advantage as a look-out or place of observation this hill breaks from the village the severity of the north and north-westerly winds, while at the same time it changes the course of their surface currents and carries them up through the valleys of the Susquehanna and Charlotte rivers, thus supplying, as I have before said, an ever-changing and constant current of fresh air.

South of the Susquehanna river the flat lands are narrower, but the slope is gradual and continuous so that at a distance of about one and one-half miles from the river the top of this range of hills is about 650 feet above the river bed. This slope of land is not only excellent farming land, but at its different points of elevation views of the valley west, east and north are lovely and even enchanting to the lovers of beautiful natural scenery.

The time will come in the near future when these elevations which surround our village will become the dwelling places of city residents who desire to locate their summer homes in a valley and locality alike famous for its historical reminiscences and of unequaled health-preserving and life-giving properties. All these hillsides even to their very top elevations abound in springs of pure soft water uncontaminated by those deleterious combinations which destroy so often the desirability of many otherwise pleasant locations. Pure spring water, cool and soft, is a boon of inestimable value in the location of a summer home as well as for all-year residences.

The corporate limits of Oneonta contains every conceivable variety of surface and form. Every taste and fancy can be accommodated in locating homes. Nature in her wisdom has left no choice. We have no natural pest-producing localities. We have no places where long lives of good health have not been enjoyed by their occupants. The high and the low grounds have alike stood the test for generations.

The make of the surrounding hills and valleys gives desirable air changes so that no damp and malarial localities exist, as uniform good health and long lives have been spent on our lowest and highest lands, and such cases may still every day be found. Nature has done perfectly her part to render our village a natural sanitarium.

INDEX

This index is intended to be a tool for both general and local historical information. Information specific to Oneonta as a locale, town, or village is listed under the main entry of "Oneonta," otherwise general subjects are listed as their own main entries. (See "asheries.") When necessary, general subjects are further categorized by sub-entries specific to Oneonta.

The surnames of individual persons are listed as a main entry, with all those individuals of that surname listed as sub-entries, regardless of whether there is a family relationship or not. (See "Alexander.") In cases where only the surname and no first name have been provided, the individuals are further identified by some descriptive information or title. (See "Amsden.") Individuals with the same name are further identified by family relationship or other distinguishing information. (See "Alger, Stoughton.") Unabbreviated civic titles are retained since, at times, they are the only identifying information beyond the surname. (See "Alexander.")

Following Baker's style of the day, wives are identified by "Mrs." and the husband's name. In cases where their maiden surnames are known, they are cross-referenced to their birth family in parentheses. (See "Alden, Julius T.") Multiple marriages are identified by numbers in brackets. (See "Angel, Mrs. William.") In some cases where both husband and wife are mentioned together, they may bear only one entry. (See "Ashley.")

abolitionism, 129, 134. *See also* African-Americans; slaves
Adams: Ezra, 114; Orrin, 107
African-Americans, 33, 108, 140, 203, 206. *See also* abolitionism; slaves
Alagatinga (Chief of Oneontas), 5. *See also* Native Americans, Oneonta tribe
Alden, Julius T. & Mrs. (Emmons), 176
Alexander: Doctor (of Virgnia), 136, 138; Thomas D., 114
Alger: David, 202; General Russell A., 202; Josiah, 202; Nicholas, 90, 200; Stoughton, Jr., 5, 21, 22, 37, 38, 202; Stoughton, Sr., 21, 32, 37, 111, 112, 114, 192, 193, 202
Allen: Reverend H. H., 165; Samuel, 32
American Revolution. *See* Revolutionary War
Ames, Oakes, 81
Amsden: blacksmith shop, 97; John & Mrs., 11, 22, 90, 184
Andrews: Bishop E. G., 167; James, 168
Andrus, George, 109
Ange, Jack, 65
Angel: William, 34, 39, 40, 88, 97, 98, 103, 105, 109, 115, 136, 164, 182, 187; Mrs. William [2] (McDonald, Gates [1]), 98
Angell, James R., 121
Anti-Rent War, 103
Arnold, Frank B., 151, 152
asheries, 94, 195
Ashley, Mrs. & Mr., 7, 206
Aussiker, Charles, 149
Austin, T. R., 198

Averill (farm), 22
Avery, A. S., 130
Babcock: Ira, 167; W., 102
Badger, John, 114
Bailey, James, 76, 77
Baird, George B., 41, 108
Baker: Albert, 135; Alexander, xii; Charles H., 90, 179, 203; Mrs. Charles H. (Birdsall), xii; Clarence, xii; Clark W., 117; Enos, xii; Fred, xii; Harry, xii; Mrs. Harvey (Rose), xii, xiii; Helen, xii; Louis, xii; Merton, xii; Thomas & Mrs., xii
Baker, Harvey. *See also frontispiece and illustrations.*
   business career: as millwright and mechanic, 12, 87, 88, 106, 179; as land owner, 32, 83, 85, 86, 89, 91, 95, 96, 105, 106, 122, 179, 184, 209, 211; as lumberman, 55, 59, 83, 185, 200; Howe's Cave Lime and Cement Company, 55, 83
   civic career: as board of education member, 148-150; as town railroad commissioner, 51, 53; as town supervisor, 115; as income tax collector, 190; as village street commissioner, 122; as village trustee, 121-123, 125; as chairman of Otsego County jail committee, 83
   commentaries and opinions: Fire Island crisis, 120; frontier and modern life compared, 29; great men, 79-81, 191; liquor, 65, 68; military organizations, 119, 120; Native American culture, 12, 16; Oneonta's geographical advantages, 213-215; Oneonta's residential advantages, 126; Oneonta's population decline, 39; political advice, 41; public press, 145; railroads and canals compared, 110; schooling methods and systems, 30; State Normal School, 153, 154
   personal life: biography, xii, xiii; family of, xii, 41, 94, 112; early life, 28, 37, 88; arrival in Oneonta, 41, 87, 97, 110, 185, 208; illnesses suffered, 83, 97; military enlistment avoided, 188, 190; residences of, 41, 89, 95, 101, 105, 107, 183; travels during Civil War, 134-141, 189, 190; vacation travels, 82; writer and historian, ix, 80, 81
   railroad career: early involvement, 41-43; as lobbyist, 47-52, 54, 71; as investor and stockholder, xii, 176; as general contractor, 50, 54-70, 82-84; as land agent, 54, 56, 58, 67, 83, 84, 209; as freight agent, 56; promotion of Oneonta location, 84, 85; retirement from, 84, 86; career praised by others, 86, 188, 190, 191
Baldwin, Reverend William, 165
Ballard: Nelson, 53; S. M., 123, 125
Ballou, Reverend D., 170
banks: First National Bank, 103, 147; Oneonta Savings Bank, 13
barbers, 108
Barnes: Ansel, 94; Harvey, 121
Barton, Ezra, 32
Bassett, Doctor, 183
Beach: Deacon, 202; Samuel B., 43, 102, 108, 109, 188
Beatty, Lieutenant Erkuries, 10, 11, 111
Beauregard, General P. G. T., 135, 137
Becker, Harmon, 48
Benedict, Czar, 32
Benjamin (house), 107
Bennett: Caleb, 106, 109; Err W., 122, 123; Lena, 105; Nathan, 94, 96

Benson, John, 47
Bently (neighbor of Bakers), 37
Betts, Samuel, Jr., 115
Bevins, Jon, 112
Bidwell, Samuel, 113
Bingham (farm), 21, 37, 114
Birdsall: Emma (Mrs. Charles H. Baker), xii; Harvey & Mrs. Jane, xii;
Bissell, William, 200
Bixby: Edward, 109; George, 105, 109;
Blackall, R. C., 65
blacksmiths, 37, 91, 97, 103, 106, 109, 200-202
Blanchard: Erastus, 92, 93, 203; Mrs. Erastus (Brewer), 92; James & Mrs. (Wolf), 92, 205
Blend: Abram, 117; Esek, 41, 108; Lyman H., 166
Blodgett, Reverend Gains M., 164
Bold, Reverend John E., 170
Bornt, Frederick, 117
Brandow, Reverend J. H., 165
Brant, Joseph, 10
Brewer: Aaron, 92, 93; Asa, 91; Chauncey M., 117; Darius, 109; David, 203; Elias, 91, 92, 106, 166; Francis, 91, 184; Hiram J., 148; Isaac, 95; Jonathan, 90, 115
Brink, Aaron, 112-114
Brockway (house), 102
Bronson, William, 21, 107, 121-123, 125, 176
Brotherton, Reverend H., 168
Brown: Adaline (Mrs. William Williams), 183; Adam, 105, 108, 115, 183; Mrs. Adam (Houghtaling), 183; Agnes (Mrs. Charles Cook), 183; Ann (Mrs. Wright Stoddard), 183; Catharine (Mrs. Zacariah Van Leuvan), 183; Cornelius & Mrs. (Jones), 182; Dexter, 177; Elihu, 98, 99, 109, 128; Elisha, 184; Eliza (Mrs. Erastus Grannius), 183; Emeline, 183; Emma (Mrs. Byron Rose), 183; Enos S., 100, 115; Frederick, 11, 100, 108, 164, 169, 182, 187, 195, 199; Mrs. Frederick (Houck), 182; Jacob, 41, 109, 183; Mrs. Jacob (Potter), 109; Brown, Lany (Mrs. Eli Derby), 182; Reverend M. C., 170; Mark, 183; Mary, 183; Susan (Mrs. Orrin Parker), 183; Walter L., 96, 115, 151, 212
Brownson, S., 148
Brunning, Reverend Benjamin, 171
Buckely (shirt manufactory), 211
Bugbee, Professor, 171
Bull: Professor Henry & Mrs. (Dietz), 88, 115; Professor Nathaniel N., 147-149
Bundy: Harlow E., 34; L. L., 33, 53, 54, 100; Mrs. L. L., 33, 100, 195
Burnside: General S. S., 48, 49, 105; Reverend George R., 167
Burrus (farm), 23
Burtis, C. L., 143
Burton: Potter C., 105, 108, 109, 128; Burton, Mrs. Potter C., 108
Butler, Colonel William, 12, 23, 111, 112
Butts: house, 107; Jacob, 32;
Cagger, Peter, 53
Calkins (farm), 5, 22
Campbell: Dudley M., 97; Gilbert, 103; Loomis J., 18, 97; Robert, 198; William, 198
canals, 39, 110, 196, 197; Chenango canal, 197; Erie canal, 197, 198; Onondaga slack-water canal, 197; Susquehanna slack-water canal, 40, 196, 198; Welland canal, 196
Capron (newspaper publisher), 131, 132, 143
Carfts, Alfred, 117
Carpenter: C. S., 131, 132, 143; Harvey,

117; L. P., 131; Samuel, 115
carpenters, joiners and mechanics, 12, 32, 33, 35-37, 59-62, 97, 98, 101, 105, 107, 108, 109, 152, 205. *See also* contractors and builders; factories
Carson, Christopher "Kit", 72
Carter, J. H., 62
Caryl, Leonard, 40, 43, 129
Case: Doctor Meigs, 41, 135, 147, 148, 212; Mrs. Meigs (Hill), 147; Doctor Samuel H., 41, 53, 54, 83, 86, 100, 109, 115, 121, 122, 134, 135, 148, 187, 189, 212
cemeteries, 22, 172, 176, 182, 191, 193, 198, 209
Chamberlain, Bedford, 103
Champlain, Samuel, 3
Chapin, Doctor E. H., 170
Chase, Colonel William H., 134, 147; George W., 43; Seth, 43
Chatfield, Levi S., 129
churches: clergymen, 109, 164-173, 183, 206; First Baptist, 101, 109, 167; Free Baptist, 100, 170, 186; Roman Catholic, 102, 172; Episcopalian, 100, 169, 170; Methodist, 108, 165, 166; Presbyterian, 80, 94, 97, 98, 102, 164, 165, 182, 195, 209; Second Presbyterian, 164; United Presbyterian, 100, 172, 173; Universalist, 170, 171
Civil War, 134-141, 189, 190; local soldiers in, 98, 118, 134-136, 183, 188, 190
Clark: David T. [2], & Mrs. (Walling, Emmons [1]), 166, 177; George, 40; Reverend Homer, 167; Reverend William, 164
Clinton: Governor Dewitt, 112; General George, 9-11, 21-23, 91, 106, 111, 112, 182
Clough, Reverend E. D., 168

Clyde (& Cook), 100
coalyards: D. Whipple & Son's, 211; Mills & Stone's, 211
Coates, E. E., 143
Coats, Reverend A. B., 168
Cobb, Reverend W. N., 166
Cockburn, William, 19
Cole, Nelson, 22
Collier: Isaac, 11, 14, 22, 112; Major Peter, 11, 14, 18, 23, 40, 88, 94, 106, 114
commodity prices, 128
Conkey, Reverend Alex, 164
contractors and builders, 35-37, 89, 93, 98, 99, 105, 107-109, 146, 148, 152, 164, 166, 167, 179, 182, 195. *See also* carpenters, joiners and mechanics
Cook: Amos, 115; Charles & Mrs. (Brown), 183; Judge Erastus & Mrs. (Gates), 98; John, 190; Robert, 114, 115; Samuel J., 32, 34, 100, 105, 108, 121, 122, 147, 183
Cooke, Woodbury K., 105, 130, 164
Coon, Samuel, 94, 149
coopers: 101, 109
Cope, John & Mrs. (Washborn), 34, 85, 115, 148, 169
Copley, Enoch, 105
cornerstone layings, 118, 152, 164, 165, 169, 172
Corning, Erastus, Jr., 43, 48
Cornish, James C., 166
Coryell, Colonel, 84
Courter, Charles, 43, 46, 58
Couse: Anthony, 203; Henry, 203; Hontice J. & Mrs., 93, 203; John I., 85, 125, 199
Cox, Reverend Henry M., 165
Craft, Griffin, 32
Crafts, Erastus, 198
Crandall, Joseph, 89

Crane, Reverend D. B., 167
Crippen, Schuyler, 198
Crispell, Anthony, 203
Crocker: Charles, 76; E. B., 76
Cronkite, John, 109
Cross, Chester G., 108, 109, 128
Cully: David, 113; Matthew, 117
Culver: foundry, 99; Joseph, 112
Curley, Thomas, 61
Curtin, Reverend, 172
Cushing, Charles, 105
Custer, General George A., 118
Cutshaw, John, 41, 105, 117, 121, 122, 148
Dauley (& Wright), 211
Dean, James F., 115
Decker, William, 59
DeGraff (railroad contractor), 68
Delevan, Edward C., 43
Dennison, Reverend J. O., 165
Derby: Eli & Mrs. (Brown), 108, 182; Frederick, 182; Ira, 182; Louisa, 182; Lucy, 182
Devereaux (railroad contractor), 57, 58
Dibble, Daniel/David, 134, 135, 140, 141, 189, 190
Dicks, Peter, 115
Dickson (railroad official), 85
Dietz (also Deitz): Gould P. & Mrs., 166; Henry, 88; Jacob C., 33, 39, 40, 53, 100, 114, 166, 187, 195, 196, 198; Mrs. Jacob C. (Price), 195; Dietz, John, 11, 114, 195; Mary, 147; William, 88
Dillingham, John, 115, 164
Dimmick, A. D., 166
Dinah (slave in Virginia), 140. *See also* African-Americans; slaves
disasters: fire of 1881, 103; fire of 1891, 105; flood of 1816, 179; flood of 1842, 88, 103
diseases, 106. *See also* doctors and physicians
distilleries, 102, 103, 109
Dix: blacksmith shop, 106; John A., 117
Doane, Bishop W. C., 169
doctors and physicians, 83, 96, 97, 100, 106, 109, 129, 147
Dodge, G. A., 131
Doolittle, Samuel, 113
Dorsey: Bill, 68; Mike, 68, 69, 82
Douglas, Senator Stephen, 75
Doyle (--- & Smith), 211
Draper: A. S., 151, 153; Willis, 32
Drew, Daniel, 67, 69
Dunham: Henry, 95; Pem., 90
Dunning, Reverend W. A., 165
Dutton, Tommy, 61, 62
Dye (farm), 89
Earle, Reverend A. B., 167
Edgerton, John, 71
Edmunds: Nathaniel, 167; William, 149
Eldred, Charles, 32
Elwell, M. N., 94-96, 106, 148, 178
Emmons: Alice, 165; Asa, 174, 184, 203; Mrs. Asa (Prentice), 174; Asa Newton, 176; Carlton, 51, 98, 115, 127, 174-176; Mrs. Carlton (Fairchild), 127, 175, 176; Charlotte, 176; Delos W., 176; Mrs. Delos W. (Stoddard), 165, 176; Edward J., 174; Elanso Carson, 176; Emmons, Harriet (Mrs. Daniel Stevens), 176; Emmons, Harriet (Mrs. Eliakim R. Ford), 186; Horace Clyde, 176; Emmons, Ira, 109, 176, 186; Emmons, Ira Jeffers, 176; Emmons, Leroy, 176; Emmons, Morton B., 174, 176; Roderick J., 90, 99, 100, 103, 109, 128, 169, 174; Rosa A. (Mrs. Julius T. Alden), 176; Salmon, 176, 177; Mrs. Salmon [1] (Walling, Clark[2]), 166, 176, 177; Salmon Lester, 176; Samuel Rodney, 176; Wilton Homer, 176

Ensworth, D. A. A., 34

Evans: Doctor David T., 101, 102, 109, 122, 166; Mrs. David T., 166;

factories: bricks, 184; cabinets, 108, 128; chairs, 100, 109, 128; cigars, 211; harness and shoe blacking, 102, 109; harnesses, 107, 109; hoes, 106; sash, door, blind and wood products, 211; shaving and toilet soap, 102, 109; shirts, 211; shoes, 100, 109; trunks, 107; wrought nails, 91

Fairchild: G. W., 132, 151; Maria (Mrs. Carlton Emmons), 175; William, 95, 175

Farmer: store clerk, 91; Josiah, 148

farriers, 109, 201

Farrington: Jacob, Sr., 94, 205, 208; Mrs. Jacob, Sr. (Wolf), 205; Jacob, Jr., 94, 205, 208

Felton, John Jr., 113

Ferguson, Julia, 148

Fern: James, 117; Joseph, 117

Fisk, James, 84

Flower, Governor Roswell P., 120

folk stories and local legends:

Doctor Lindsay's overcoat, 96; the heaviest horse in town, 200; the ice-walking cow, 96; Keech the builder, 35-37; the lost silver mines, 37, 38, 194; the missing Blanchard child; the rat-killing contest, 175; Som and Sayre's puppy, 203; the walking cane willow tree, 90, 203

Follett, Ezekiel, 98

Fonda, H. A., 94

Ford: Aaron & Mrs., 117, 127; Amanda (Mrs. Hansen Gould), 128; Clinton, 135, 188; D. W., 41, 123, 168; DeWitt, 121; Ford, Eliakim R., 11, 33, 40, 41, 43, 44, 57, 69, 84, 86, 88-90, 94, 96, 99, 100, 102, 105, 107-109, 114, 115, 117, 121-123, 128, 129, 134-136, 138, 139, 169, 176, 180, 182, 184, 186-191, 199, 209-212; Mrs. Eliakim R. (Emmons), 176, 186, 191; Ford, Isaac S., 134; Ford, Newton I. & Mrs. (Shepherd), 41, 108; Raymond, 135, 188; Sylvester, 96

foundries and iron works, 33; Culver foundry, 99; R. J. Emmons foundry, 99, 103 109; Mayne foundry, 211; Joseph Tabor foundry, 99

Franchot, Richard, 47, 56, 188, 190

Fremont, John C., 72

French & Indian War, 4, 17

French, Daniel, 113

Fritts: John, 28, 90, 115, 184, 203; Hiram & Mrs. (Couse), 203; William S., 34, 99, 103, 108, 109, 121, 128, 147

frontier life: typical life of frontier settler described, 24, 25; accidental deaths, 91, 164; apple paring bees, 27; barn raising, 26, 35, 36; building construction techniques, 34, 100; compared with Baker's contemporary society, 29; corn husking bees, 26; courtship traditions, 27, 175; fishing, 88; games, 27; holiday celebrations, 26; lightning strikes, 89; maple sugaring, 91; military training, 26, 92; quilting bees, 26; rat problems, 175; schools, 29, 30; social gatherings, 26; spinning bees, 27; taxes, 28, 29; timber logging bees, 26; transportation methods, 27, 28, 39, 87, 88; wealth and clothing, 28; witchcraft and superstitions, 35, 37; wolf bounties, 32; wood chopping bees, 26; wood hauling bees, 26

Gallup (farm), 22

Gates, General Theodore B., 98, 136

Gifford: farm, 114; Daniel & Mrs. (Houghtaling), 107; Obediah, 115

Gilbert: Butler, 32; Reverend C., 164; Mason, 88, 102, 106, 128, 180
Goff, Huldah (Mrs. James McDonald), 178
Goldsmith: house, 109; store, 105
Goodrich, N. S., 184
Goodyear, Jared, 40, 42, 43, 45, 48, 53, 56, 58, 71, 84, 88, 94, 106, 191, 209-211
Gould: Moody & ---, 211; Hansen & Mrs. (Ford), 128; Jason "Jay", 84
Gowey, 202
Grannius, Erastus & Mrs. (Brown), 183
Grant, Richard J., 46
Graves: Edward & Mrs., 127; Nathan, 100
Greeley, Horace, 143
Green, Reverend D., 170
Gregory, Samuel, 32
Griswold: farm, 68, public house, 98
Gumbine, Reverend J. C., 171
Gwin, Senator William M., 75
Hackett: John, Jr., 91, 95, 203; Mrs. John, Jr. (Couse), 203; John, Sr., 11, 91, 92; Leroy, 108; William & Mrs. (Brewer), 92
Hadley, William J., 46
Hall, Rev. C. P., 171
Hamilton: Hamilton, Doctor, 102, 106; Hosea A., 115, 121, 122
Hamlin, David, 113
Hammond, Charles D., 151
Haplin, Reverend, 172
Hard (& Peck), 52
Harding, H. G., 121
harness makers, 107, 109
Harper, Mrs. Nancy M., 127
Harrington, Aaron, 32
Harris, Doctor, 213
Harrison, Truman, 32
Hartman, Reverend E. A., 169, 170

Hasbrook, Josiah L., 166
hat makers, 88, 106, 128
Hawk, Reverend L. E., 172, 173
Hawkins, Anson, 91
Hawley, Reverend Gideon, 5, 7, 206
Haynor, Reverend George, 166
Head, Frederick A., 151
Hearn, Reverend George, 183
Hecox, D. L., 107
Hemstreet, Nathan, 118
Hendrick (Chief of Mohawks), 18, 19
Herrick (school teacher), 109, 147
Hervey, Doctor A. B., 170
Hill, Lizzie (Mrs. Meigs Case), 147
Hillsinger: Jacob, 117; John, 91, 200, 201; William, 200
Hobbs, 57, 58
Hodge, Ephraim C., 121, 122
Holbrook, Lucius, 166
Holden, Stephen, 138, 139
Holt, General Walter, 118
Hopkins: Mark, 73, 76, 77; Robert W., 41, 101, 108, 109, 128, 166; William, 166
hops, 82, 128
Hotchkiss, Gideon, 43
hotels. *See* public houses
Houck, Catherine (Mrs. Frederick Brown), 182
Houghtaling: Abraham, Jr., 199, 200; Abraham, Sr., 107, 114, 199; Mrs. Abraham, Sr. (Price), 199; Rachel (Mrs. Adam Brown), 183
Hourigan, Reverend, 172
Howe's Cave Lime and Cement Company, xiii, 55, 83, 86
Hudson, Sarel, 91
Hughes, Reverend, 172
Huntington: Collis P., 72, 73, 75-81, 121, 122, 164, 165, 176; H. E., 165; Solon, 41, 72, 103, 108, 109, 122, 123; W. V., 165; William, 80

Hyde: Festus, 129; James, 121
Ingalls, G. A., 142
inns. *See* public houses
Ives, Rev. B. I., 166
Jackson, James K. Polk, 143
jails: Oneonta village, 123; Otsego County, 83
Jefferson, William H., 131, 142
Jenkins (house), 108
Jenks: Joseph, 170; Leroy, 32; Willard, 22, 23, 193
jewelers and silver smiths, 109, 127, 128
Johnson: A. G., 43; E. M., 131, 132 143; Sir Guy (Grey), 10, 192; Henry, 43; Sir John, 8, 10; Jonathan, 32; Nelson, 87; Sir William, 4-8, 17-21, 23, 192, 193
Jones: Laura (Mrs. Cornelius Brown), 182; Reverend J. L., 165
Judah, Theodore D., 75-77
Juliand, Richard W., 43
Keech (builder), 35-37, 101
Kelly, Kelsey R., 22
Keyes: James H., 108, 148; M. L., 212
King: John B., 134; Smith D., 134; William S., 134, 141
Kingsley, Reverend, 167
Knapp: Knapp, Doctor, 102, 109; William, 127; Mrs. William (McDonald), 109, 127; William J., 109, 127, 130
Lacey (house), 96
Lake, Caleb, 108
Lamb: Anthony, 117; Thomas, 65
land grant patents: Charlotte patent, 5; Johnson tract, 18, 20; Lindsay patent, 111; Otego patent, 18, 19, 111, 125; Otsego patent, 5; Royal grant, 18, 19; Wallace patent, 18, 93. *See also* Johnson, Sir William
land surveyors, 19, 109, 176, 195
Lane (railroad contractor), 68, 82

Lathrop: Doctor, 100; Horace, 121
Lawyer: Demosthenes, 42; General, 48
lawyers, 18, 57, 58, 103, 105, 122, 128, 164, 167, 169
Lee, Harry W., 145
Lewis: --- & Wilson, 211; Charles W., 148
libraries, 80, 97, 149, 150
Lincoln, Abraham, 136, 138
Lindsay: Jacob, 96; John, 96; Doctor Joseph, 18, 96, 97, 102, 109, 147; Mrs. Joseph, 96; Sally Ann, 96
lumbermen, 55, 59, 61, 83, 174, 175, 184, 185, 195, 200, 203, 209. *See also* Baker, Harvey, business career; mills
Luther (store), 103
Lyman, Ella, 11
Lynch, Reverend, 172
Mackey, Harvey, 170
Manchester, Doctor & Mrs., 94
Maney, Reverend James H., 172
Mangan, Reverend, 172
Many, William V., 43
Marcy, Governor William L., 117
Mariom sisters, 106
Marvin: Ansel, 115; David, 117
masons, 62, 99, 109, 152; Dauley & Wright marble works, 211
Matteson, Reverend C. G., 164, 165
Maynard, Almiron L., 89
Mayne (foundry), 211
McAnulty, Reverend Doctor, 167
McCall: Hiram, 167; Horace, 103, 128; Mrs. Horace (Yager), 128; Turner, 53, 54, 103
McClellan, General George C., 134, 135, 140, 189
McCrany: John, 106, 121-123, 125; Samuel, 106, 109
McCrum, William, 28, 41, 101, 108, 121, 122, 127
McDonald: James, 32, 33, 88, 94, 95, 98,

118, 127, 178-180, 184-186, 195, 208; Mrs. James [1] (Goff), 178, 180; Mrs. James [2/3], 95, 180; John, 117, 118; Joseph, 106, 178, 179; Leander, 117; Nicholas, 178, 179; Oliver, 117; Reverend, 172

McGuire, Barton, 179

McNierney, Bishop, 172

McWhorter, Doctor, 12

Meigs (farm), 195

Mendel: Andrew, 148; Samuel, 103, 148

Mickle, Simeon, 89, 203

Miles (house), 108

military organizations, 26, 92, 179, 186; National Guard units, 118, 119; state armory building, 110, 118, 119; state militia units, 117, 118

Miller: Cornelius, 134, 135, 189; David M., 148; E. H., 73; Jedediah, 43, 48; John, 200; Colonel Marvin, 147; Colonel S. F., 109, 147; William & Mrs. (Herrick), 109, 147

mills, xii, 87, 95, 186, 192
    fulling and wool-carding mills, 33. *See also* wool-carding and cloth-dressing
    distillery mills, 103. *See also* distilleries
    grist mills, xii, 12, 23, 33, 109, 111, 209; Collier & Goodyear, xii, 122, 180; Elwell, 106, *see also illustrations*; Lewis & Wilson 211; McDonald, 179, 180; Van Derwerker, 22, 178
    saw mills, xii, 23, 33, 67, 106, 111, 122, 178, 179, 200, 208, 209; Collier & Goodyear, xii, 88, 122, 180; Wilber, 103; Emmons, 174; Lewis & Wilson, 211; McDonald, 106, 179; Snyder, 109. *See also* lumbermen

Mills (--- & Stone), 211

Milne, Professor James M., 152

Montgomery, General Richard, 31

Moody (--- & Gould), 211

Moore: James, 112, 113; John, 112, 114

Morehouse, Deborah (Mrs. Nathan Rose), xii

Morenus: Jeremy P., 90, 91, 179; Martin, 90, 179; Thomas & Mrs., 90, 91

Morgan, Governor Edwin D., 53, 54

Morrell: farm, 11; house, 108; David, 22, 202, 212; Jacob, 117

Morris: --- & Place, 69, Albert, 147, 149; Datus, 147; William H., 115, 118, 147, 151

Mosher, Henry, 68, 106, 148

Moulton, Reverend O. T., 170

Mumford: Alonzo, 59, 63; Joseph, 117

Munson, Lois (Mrs. Thomas Baker), xii

Murdock (farm), 37, 202

Murphy, Reverend D. E., 172

Native Americans: Baker's opinion on contemporary culture, 12, 16; white captives, 7, 192, 206. *See also* French & Indian War; Johnson, Sir William; New York State colonial era; Revolutionary War
    Iroquois confederacy: Five Nations, 3, 4; Six Nations, 4, 8-10, 13, 17, 23; Cayugas, 3; Genesee village, 9; Mohawks, 3-10, 12, 17, 18, 102; Oneidas, 3, 8; Onondagas, 3; Senecas, 3, 4, 9; Tuscaroras, 3, 4
    Oneonta tribe: 5, 7, 181; mining traditions, 14, 16, 193, 194; village and orchards, 6, 174, 180, 193; salt manufacturing, 14
    Oneonta area tribes: Chenangoes, 8; Colliers village, 5, 7; Oquagas, 5, 7, 8, 206; Otego village, 7; Schoharies, 5, 7, 13; Unadillas, 5, 7; Wauteghe village, 5, 6, 17, 23, 192
    other tribes and nations: Adirondacks, 3, 4; Cherokees, 4, 12

Nelson, Judge H. D., 34

New York State colonial era: Native American tribes and nations during, 3-7; French exploration, 3; Dutch exploration and settlement, 4; English claims to land, 4, 10; German Palantine settlers, 13, first whites to Oneonta area, 5. *See also* French & Indan War; land grant patents; Johnson, Sir William; Native Americans; Revolutionary War

Newkirk, Jacob, 117

newspapers.

    Oneonta newspapers: lack of, 130; Commercial, 143; Daily Local, 144, 145; Daily News, 109, 145, 146; Daily Spy, 145; Daily Star, 13; Dollar Paper, 143; Evening News, 97, 145, 183; Granger Alliance, 142; Herald (first), 127; Herald (second), 9, 49, 54, 90, 100, 131-133, 143, 151; Herald and Democrat, 131, 132; Liberal, 143; New Era, 142; Press, 103, 142; Spy, 143, 145; Star, 145, 150; Susquehanna Independent, 131; Weekly Journal, 105, 109, 127, 130; Y. M. C. A. quarterly, 142

    other newspapers: Albany Argus, 198; American Banner, 134; Bath Advocate, 198; Broome Republican, 198; Chenango Telegraph, 132; Freeman's Journal, 131, 196; Delaware Gazette, 198; Fort Plain Watch Tower, 198; Franklin Visitor, 134; Home and Abroad, 131; Milford News, 142; New York Spectator, 198; Norwich Journal, 198; Otsego Democrat, 131; Otsego Farmer, xiii; Otsego Herald, 127; Otsego Republican, 141; Owego Gazette, 198

Noble: Charles, 102, 109; George H., 43; Sylvenus, 102, 109

Northrup: railroad director, 67; Emanuel, 115, 146, 184; Jonah, 115

Nott, Joel B., 43

Nowlen, Addison J., 54

Noxen (Farm), 202

O'Neil: A. J., 152; Mrs. (property owner), 107

O'Brien, Reverend, 172

O'Mahoney, Reverend, 172

Ogden (farm), 11

Olin, William H., 121, 122, 167

Oneonta: African-American residents, 108, 203; eligible voters, 32; former names, 5, 33, 179, 186, 195, 198; impact of railroad, 110; Native American residents, 10, 12, 14, 15, 90, 193; population and census statistics, 32, 33, 39, 111, 149, 150; real estate values, 33, 94, 95, 110, 212; representatives in government, 39, 40, 42, 56, 106, 129, 151; social issues, 29; taxes, 29, 30, 32, 114, 122, 123, 125, 126, 149

first things: blacksmiths, 37, 200, 202; bridge over Susquehanna, 179; board of education, 148; child born in the corporate limits, 199; church organization, 164; farm settled, 92; grist mill, 22; house (brick), 21, 101, 203; house (oldest), 106; household luxury items, 191; newspaper, 127, 183; newspaper (daily), 144; postmaster in town, 33; prison, 123; saw mill, 178; school house, 146; tavern, 22; white visitors to area, 206

geographical features: pre-settlement, 205, 206, 208-210, 213; Barn hill, 209; Beam's island, 5; Beams' hill,

18; Emmons lake, 176; high lands, 209, 213; Morrell flats, 22; Oneonta plains, 18, 38, 146, 166, 167, 178, 180, 184, 202, 214; rock hill, 38; swamp lands, 95, 96, 208-213; Swart's eddy, 208

public works, services and utilities: electric light works plant, 211; fire protection, 72, 122-124; gas works plant, 178, 209, 212; postal services, 33, 34, 95, 98, 103, 104, 110, 128, 129, 179, 186, 187, 195; sewer systems, 124, 212, 213; street building and locations, 95, 207-209, 211, 212; water supply systems, 105, 123, 208

structural landmarks: aquaduct, 180; Baird block, 98, 106, 128, 202; Baker Row, xii; Brown block, 212; Burr covered bridge, 179; First National bank block, 103, 147; Florence block, 95; Ford block, 103, 146, 182, 187; McCrum & Saunders block, 103, 132; Parish bridge, 93; Reynolds & Wilcox block, 102; Reynolds block, 143; river bridge, 179; Sabin building, 143; stone architecture, 99; Tobey & Gurney block, 212; Tobey & Brown block, 100; Westcott block, 102, 144; Wilber block, 145

town: as part of other towns and counties, 31, 32, 93, 111-115, 146, 164, 202; formation of town, 33, 114, 115, 187; first elected officials, 114, 115; records lost, 115; railroad commissioners, 51

village, incorporation of, 121, 122, 125, 187; by-laws, 124, 130; charter revisions, 93, 125; codes and laws, 124; corporate limits, 93, 125; first elected officials, 121-123, 125

opera house, 212

Orr, David & Mrs. (Houghtaling), 89, 93, 199, 203

Osborn, Luman S., 90, 115, 164, 165

Ottman (railroad conductor), 68

Paddock: Dominic, 96, 103; Reverend J. W., 94, 109, 164;

Page, Sherman, 195, 198

painters, 109

Palmatier (wagon maker), 68

Pardoe, John, 108, 182

Parish: Andrew, 22, 28, 32, 90, 94, 98, 125, 146, 150, 179, 180, 184, 203; Mrs. Andrew (McDonald), 98, 179, 180, 184, 185; Doctor, 202; Ephraim, 5, 18, 21, 22, 37, 38, 41, 90, 95, 184, 193, 202; Mrs. Ephraim (Alger), 18, 21, 37, 38, 202; George, 41, 89; Huntington, 11, 41, 89, 90, 146, 175, 184, 187, 203; Stephen, 41, 51, 53, 115, 180, 184; Mrs. Stephen (McDonald), 180

Parker, Orrin & Mrs. (Brown), 183

Parr, Major, 10

Pattengill, Reverend C. M., 167

Peck (Hard & ---), 53

Peebles, Reverend R. W., 166

Pendleton, James, 103, 109

Pepper, Cary B., 34

Pete (Oneonta Indian), 14, 15

Peters, Isaac H., 93, 96, 209, 211

Petrie: Ben & Aunt Dinah, 108. *See also* African-Americans; slaves

Phelps: George O., 148, 165; W. L. M., 55, 56

Phinney, Elihu, 127

Pierce: farm, 21, 202; Reverend C. C., 168

Pitcher, Reverend, 164

Place (Morris & ---), 69

Platt, Andrew H., 53

Porter: John K., 46; Reverend L. F., 170

Potter: Anna (Mrs. Jacob Brown), 183; Caleb & Mrs., 109, 166, 183; Stafford, 106

Pratt: Colonel George W., 98, 136; Colonel Zadock, 136

Prentice: E. P., 45, 56-58; Eunice (Mrs. Asa Emmons), 174

Price: Hannah (Mrs. Jacob C. Dietz), 195; Sally (Mrs. Abraham Houghtaling, Sr.), 199

printers, 109, 130, 144, 145. *See also* newspapers

Pruyn, Robert H., 43

public houses: American Hotel, 48, 98; Brewer family tavern, 92; Isaac Brewer tavern, 95; Central Hotel, 100, 151, 169, 212; Andrew Dunham hotel, 52; Henry Dunham tavern, 95; Carlton Emmons hotel, 176; William Fairchild inn, 95; Hallsville hotel, 71; Kniskern tavern, 82; Lewis & Wilson hotel, 211; James McDonald tavern, 33, 94, 95, 98, 178-180, 186; Merchants Hotel (Albany), 118; Oneonta House (William Angel), 88, 97, 98, 105, 109, 128 187; Otsego House (Elihu Brown), 98, 99, 108, 109, 128; James Ray tavern, 95; Scott's (Nineveh), 84; George Scramling tavern, 22; David Sullivan tavern, 88, 94, 95, 109; Susquehanna House (Morris & Place), 69, see also *illustrations*; Van Tuyl tavern, 42; Simeon Walling tavern, 101, 203, 204; John M. Watkins hotel, 53, 95, 98, 99, 121; Windsor Hotel, 123, 212; John Young tavern, 22;

Quackenbush: Adrian, 22, 193; Isaac, 135; John T., 115; Nicholas, 194; Orlando, 83

railroads: compared with canals, 110, 197; impact of Western railroad migration on Oneonta, 39; New York State Senate committee on, 47, 51; Schuyler fraud, 44

Albany & Susquehanna railroad, 43-86, 110, 119, 130, 131, 176, 188, 190; bridge construction, 65, 82, 83; completed to Afton, 55; completed to Central Bridge, 56; completed to Cobleskill, 56; completed to Harpursville, 84; completed to Oneonta, 69; completed to Richmondville, 67; completed to Sidney, 83; completed to Unadilla, 82; contractors, 44, 45, 55, 57, 65, 83, 84, 86; Delevan engine, 68; funding, 44, 45, 50, 52-54, 56, 67, 69, 71, 83, 176; leased to Delaware & Hudson company, 56, 84; opposition to, 44-48, 51, 52, 69, 71; shops and engine houses, 65, 84, 85; takeover attempt by Erie railroad, 56, 84; track laying, 65-68, 82; trestle construction, 58, 59, 61-65; worker wages, 50, 57-59, 68, 69, 82, 83

paper railroads near Oneonta, 40; Cherry Valley & Susquehanna Valley railroad, 40; Cooperstown to Colliers railroad, 40; Otsego & Schoharie railroad, 40; Otsego Lake to Erie Canal, 198; Schenectady & Susquehanna railroad, 42, 188; Schoharie to Susquehanna valley railroad, 40; Unadilla to Colliersville, 195; Utica & Susquehanna Valley railroad, 40

other railroads: construction of various, 197; Albany Northern railroad, 47; Central Pacific, 75; Delaware & Hudson company, xii, 56, 84, 85, 86, 197, 211, *see also illustrations*; Erie railroad, 40, 41, 56, 84, 110; Mauch Chunk railroad, 197; New York Central railroad, 41; Orange & Alexandria railroad, 134, 139; Quincy railroad, 196; transcontinental railroad, 72, 75-79; Union Pacific, 76

Ramsey, Joseph H., 47, 48, 52, 53, 55-58, 84

Ray: Gideon, 94; James, 94, 95

Raymond: newspaper publisher, 143; Eugene, 151; William F., 107, 109

Reed: Abijah, 186; Charles, 18

Reilly, Reverend, 172

Revolutionary War: local soldiers in, 21, 90, 179, 205; local Tory presence, 8, 12, 112, 192; Native American and British alliance, 9, 17, 192; Cherry Valley & Wyoming massacres, 16; Sullivan-Clinton Campaign, 8-12, 21-23, 91, 106, 111, 112, 182; Sidney, NY (Albout), 7, 11, 23, 111; Unadilla, NY (Wattle's Ferry), 7, 11, 12, 23, 111. *See also* Butler, Colonel William; Clinton, General George; Johnson, Sir William; Sullivan, General John; Washington, General George; Native Americans; New York State colonial era; French & Indian War

Reynolds: building, 104; Reverend A., 167, 168; Charles, 41; George W., 34, 107, 131, 134, 142, 148, 166; John, 107, 109; Mrs. John, 102, 107; Reuben, 151; S. J. W., 142

Rice (school teacher), 146

Richards: Joseph, 59; Reverend L. E., 165

Richardson: Reverend. A. B., 165, 166; William, 41, 115, 179

Richmond, Cyrus & Mrs. (Parish), 146

Riddle, Robert, 100

Roberts, J., 148

Root, Reverend P. D., 168

Rose: Anna, 183; Betsey (Mrs. Harvey Baker), xii; Byron & Mrs. (Brown), 183; Eli, 147; Jesse, 40; Katherine, 148; Rose, Nathan & Mrs. (Morehouse), xii

Rowe, J. O., 149

Ruland, Richard, 106

Sabin, Timothy, 34, 41, 96, 104, 108, 109, 115, 128, 129, 148, 212

Sanborn, Reverend P. F., 165

Sawyer (land), 56

Saxton: A. B.,132; Professor W. F., 148

Sayre (slave of Crispell), 203. *See also* African-Americans; slaves

Scanlin murder, 179, 208

Schofield, William H., 101, 109, 121

schools: Academy Street, 109; Baker's views on schooling methods, 30; budgets and taxes, 30, 149, 150; first school in district, 146; teachers, 96, 97, 102, 109, 138, 146, 147, 149, 152

  private and select schools: Nathaniel N. Bull select school, 147; William Chase select school, 147; Miss Dietz select school, 147; Emmons school house, 170; Ford block school house, 105; Franklin Institute, 138; Miss Herrick select school, 147; Miss Hill select school, 147; Dr. Joseph Lindsay select school, 96, 102, 147; Joseph McDonald school house; 178; Miss Sullivan select school, 147; George Swart school house, 91, 146; Wing school house, 146; Wolf school house, 146

  public schools, 146, 148-150; board of education, 148, 149; Oneonta Union school, 146, 148, 149

Scott: Henry, 112, 113; Mrs. Seymour, 165; Walter, 119

Scramling: Albert, 22, 193; Allen, 22, 90, 94, 125, 176, 184, 187, 193, 194; David, 21, 22, 192-194; Mrs. David (Young), 192-194; George, (brother of David), 21, 22, 192; George, Jr., (grandson of David), 142, 194; George, Sr., (son of David), 21, 32, 115, 193, 194; Henry, 21, 22, 111, 112, 192, 193; John, 89

Sergeants, Lemuel, 113

Sessions, Frank, 91, 92

Seybolt, Alva, 149

Seymour, Governor Horatio, 54

Shafer, Jacob & Mrs., 68

Shaw: Andrew G. & Mrs. (McDonald), 34, 53, 94, 103, 118, 121, 123, 148;

Shelland, Charles F., 34

Shellman: carriage maker, 95, 209; accidentally killed man, 164

Shepherd: --- & Osborn, 90; Elisha, 108, 121, 146; Hiram, 115; Isaac, 115

Sheridan, General Philip, 118

Sherman, Michael, 195

shoe makers and cobblers, 100, 109

shops: Henry Dietz shop, 88; machine shops, 107; plow shops, 106; Shellman carriage shop, 95, 209; Stilson machine shops, 211

Shove, E. B., 123

Sigsbee, John, 179, 203

Simerson, Mrs. (Brewer), 91

Skinner, John, 149

Slade: farm, 5, 21, 174, 177; James, 167

slaves, 33, 108, 140, 203. *See also* abolitionism; African-Americans

Sleeper, Samuel, 32

Slingerland (house), 100

Smith: Doyle & ---, 211; Reverend Alexander, 167; George H., 144, 145; George W., 115; Henry, 117; J. Sherry, 143, 144; Reverend John, 95, 101, 109, 128, 167; Sylvenus, 102, 117; William, 117; William J., 90, 93

Snow, Colonel William W., 42, 86, 89, 96, 103, 106, 109, 115, 128, 146, 148, 212

Snyder, David, 106, 109

Som (slave of Crispell), 203. *See also* African-Americans; slaves

Spencer: Joshua A., 169; Nathaniel, 32; Reverend, 169

Spoor, Charles, 94

stage coaches, 39, 108, 110, 187

Stanford, Leland, 76, 77

Stanton, Henry, 189, 190

Stark, Christopher Lovis, 32

Starkweather, S., 198

State Normal School, 107, 110, 144, 151-153. *See also illustrations.*

Steele, John B., 103, 128

Steere (& Windsor), 69, 71

Stevens, Daniel, 176

Stewart: C. C., 106, 179; James, 151

Stilson (machine shop), 211

Stoddard: Joel, 112; Mary (Mrs. Delos W. Emmons), 176; Wright & Mrs. (Brown), 183

Stone (Mills & ---), 211

stores: lists of stores, 109, 211; Bennett & Smith store, 128; Mrs. L. L. Bundy store, 100, 195; Butts & Son farm tools, 211; Clyde & Cook store, 100, 109, 128, 129; Cook & Brown store, 105, 109, 127-129, 183; Cornell Brothers, 41, 99; Devereaux grocers, 57; Jacob Dietz store, 100, 195; R. J. Emmons cabinet ware, 90, 99, 100, 109, 128; E. R. Ford stores, 88, 99, 103, 105, 107, 186, 187; Goldsmith store, 105; Hard & Peck store, 52; Hopkins & Miller, 73; R. W. Hopkins cabinet ware, 109; Huntington & Hopkins, 73; Huntington brothers, 72,

99, 103; Luther cabinet ware, 103; James McDonald store, 178; Mendel Brothers store, 72, 103; Morris Brothers flour, grain, seed and feed, 108, 145, 211; J. O. & G. N. Rowe grocers, 211, see also *illustrations*; Timothy Sabin store, 99, 104; Sabin & Carpenter store, 128; Shepherd & Osborne store, 90; Smith & Carpenter store, 109; Snow & Van Woert, 103, 128; T. Willahan store, 131;

Stowe, Reverend W. L., 171

Strait, Job, 32

Sullivan: Daniel, 107, 117; David & Mrs., 88, 94, 95, 109, 115, 117; Delilah, 147; General John, 8, 9, 21-23, 91, 112, 182; Orlando, 121; Silas, 34, 104, 115, 148

Swart: George, 91, 92, 146, 194, 205; Lawrence, 94, 180; William, 91; William, Sr., 92

Swinnerton, Reverend H. U., 165

Tabor, Joseph, 99

tailors, 101-103, 105, 109

Tanner, John, 102, 109

Tarbox, Levi, 117

taverns. *See* public houses

temperance movement, 142

Temple, Reverend E. F., 171

Terrill, Samuel, 68

Thayer (school teacher), 147

Throop, Washington, 115

Thurber: E. R., 51, 52; Samuel M., 151, 152

Tickner, Jonathan, 32

tinsmiths, 103, 109

Toller, Reverend, 128

Tompkins: Governor Daniel D., 117; W. A. E., 149

Townsend: Franklin, 43, 118; Counselor R. M., 18

trunk and harness makers, 107

Tryon, Governor William, 31

turnpikes: Catskill turnpike, 101; Charlotte turnpike, 39, 40, 98, 187, 196; Oneonta & Franklin turnpike, 40, 90, 98, 196

Tyler (farm), 22, 193

Uebel, Christian, 148

Van Benthuysen, Charles, 43

Van Derwerker: Molly (Mrs. John Young), 22; Yokam & Mrs., 11, 22, 182;

Van Dycke, J. D., 142

Van Hovenburgh, Lieutenant, 11, 111

Van Leuvan, Zachariah & Mrs. (Brown), 183

Van Schaick, David, 82

Van Tuyl (tavern), 42

Van Valkenburgh: Everett, 22; Garrett, 22; James, 106; Joachim, 11, 22, 91, 106, 111

Van Woert: Catherine (Mrs. Conrad Wolf), 205; Jacob P., 103, 109, 166; John, 21, 22, 115, 193, 205; Peter, 5, 17, 22, 193; Stafford, 103

Vanderbilt (family), 81

veterinarians, 101

Vosburgh (house), 100, 134

wagon makers, 103, 108, 109, 128; Henry Mosher & Sons, 68; Palmatier, 68

Walling: J. R. L., 14, 18, 21, 37, 41, 101, 115, 125, 176, 203; Joseph, 101, 115, 117, 125, 176, 203; Lee, 21; Sally (Mrs. Salmon Emmons [1], Mrs. David T. Clark [2]), 176, 177; Simeon, 21, 35, 37, 101, 107, 176, 203, 204; Timothy & Mrs. Sarah, 14

Walworth, Reverend, 172

Wans, Gloud, 22

War of 1812, local soldiers in, 90

Ward (farm), 114, 202

Warren, Admiral Sir Peter, 17

Washborn, Reverend Robert, 169
Washington, General George, 9
Watkins: Abiatha H., 108; Hezekiah, 108, 109, 121-123, 164; John H., 118; John M., 53, 95, 98-100, 115, 117, 121, 123; Mrs. John M. (McDonald), 98, 99, 118; Munson R. & Mrs. (Morrell), 37, 53, 98, 108; 108; Timothy D., 108, 121
Watson, Arnold B., 43
Weed, C. E., 143
Wentz, C. William, 47, 55, 57, 58, 82, 84-86
Westcott: Reverend Erastus, 95, 167; James, 113, 114; Monroe, 147
Westover: John, 40; Judge, 62
Wetsell (freight customer), 56
Wheeler, Judge, 28
Whipple, D., 211
Whitcomb, A. A., 168
White: Anthony, 41, 108; Daniel, 108; Reverend H. K., 170, 171
Whitmarsh, Samuel, 112
Wilber: David F., 70, 103, 182; Deforest, 115; George I., 149, 151
Wilcox: tax collector from Otego, 190; Henry, 88, 94, 101, 180; Mrs. Henry (Smith), 101
Wild, James T., 122, 123, 209, 211
Willahan, T., 131
Willard, Judge, 44
Williams: T., 11, 22, 91, 182; William & Mrs. (Brown), 183
Wilson: Lewis & ---, 211; Reverend A. E., 170
Windecker, George, 7, 206
Windsor (Steere & ---), 69, 71
Wing: Reverend A., 146, 170; Elizabeth, 148
Wolcott, A. C., 106
Wolf: Conrad, 92, 94, 125, 194, 205, 208; Mrs. Conrad (Van Woert), 94, 205; Wolf, Isaac, 205; Jacob & Mrs. (Leopard), 205; Mary (Mrs. James Blanchard), 92, 205
Wood: Celey, 94; Henry G., 115, 118
Woodbridge, Timothy, 7, 206
Woodin, W. H., 211
wool-carding and cloth-dressing, 33, 106, 109, 128, 174, 186
Worden, Reverend A. T., 170
Worth (newspaper publisher), 144
Wright: Dauley & ---, 211; Justice D., 47; Silas I., 149; Judge William B., 46; Worthington, 121
Y. M. C. A., 142
Yager: David, 102, 128, 167; David J., 41, 102, 115, 117, 121, 123, 132, 146, 166; Delos, 151; Eliza (Mrs. Horace McCall), 128; Henry, 117; John D., 117; John S., 115; Peter, 117; Solomon, 117; Willard E., 151, 152
Yorkams farm. *See* Van Derwerker, Yokam
Young: David, 21, 22, 193; John & Mrs. (Van Derwerker) 21, 22, 193; Susanna (Mrs. David Scramling), 194
Youngman: Charles, 91, 179; John, 11, 179
Youngs (farm), 202

ADVERTISEMENT.

INTERESTING BOOK TITLES ABOUT

UPSTATE NEW YORK HISTORY

AVAILABLE ONLINE OR

AT BOOK DEALERS EVERYWHERE

Compiled by the
Writers and Local Historians
of Upstate New York.

SQUARE CIRCLE PRESS
WWW.SQUARECIRCLEPRESS.COM

www.ingramcontent.com/pod-product-compliance
Lightning Source LLC
Chambersburg PA
CBHW081833170426
43199CB00017B/2714